The
ALTERATIONS
LADY

An Afghan Refugee,
an American,
and the Stories
that Define Us

APOLLO
PUBLISHERS

The ALTERATIONS LADY

An Afghan Refugee, an American, and the Stories that Define Us

CINDY MILLER WITH LAILOMA SHAHWALI

APOLLO
PUBLISHERS

Visit our website at www.apollopublishers.com.

Published in compliance with California's Proposition 65.

Library of Congress Control Number: 2023951538

Print ISBN: 978-1-954641-30-3
Ebook ISBN: 978-1-954641-31-0

Printed in the United States of America.

TO COURAGEOUS,
UNSTOPPABLE
WOMEN EVERYWHERE.

CONTENTS

MAP OF AFGHANISTAN

AFGHAN RULERS

1919   Afghanistan becomes an independent nation. Amir Amanullah Khan becomes king.

1929   Facing backlash, Khan abdicates. Habibullah Ghazi becomes king and is executed the same year.

1929   Mohammad Nader Shah becomes king.

1933   Mohammad Nader Shah is executed and Mohammed Zahir Shah becomes king.

1973   Shah is overthrown by Mohammed Daoud Khan.

1978   Kahn is killed in a communist coup. Nur Mohammad Taraki becomes president.

1979   Taraki is killed in conflict by Hafizullah Amin supporters. Babrak Karmal becomes prime minister.

1986   Mohammad Najibullah is elected president.

1992   Najibullah is ousted. Burhanuddin Rabbani becomes president.

1996   The Taliban executes Najibullah.

2001	Taliban rule ends. With representatives from various Afghan groups, an international committee names Hamid Karzai leader of the interim government.
2002	A traditional Afghan assembly declares Hamid Karzai president of a transitional government.
2004	Afghanistan approves a new constitution, and Karzai is elected president.
2014	Ashraf Ghani becomes president.
2021	The Afghanistan government collapses. The Taliban takes over Kabul.

PREFACE

When I met Lailoma Shahwali, writing a book was the furthest thing from my mind. My oldest daughter was home on break from her studies, and I was on a mission to have her wedding dress altered before she left Arizona and went back to school in Missouri. However, what Lailoma revealed the day we met in her condo's bedroom-turned-sewing room was so compelling I couldn't *not* pursue more information and transcribe her story.

I am grateful to Lailoma for opening her home to me before she went to work on Saturday mornings and allowing me to learn the details of her remarkable family saga and her relentless drive to survive and succeed. We continued our conversation over the course of several years before I felt I could adequately retell her amazing journey and bring it to a nice, neat conclusion with a happy ending.

Of course, the story of the Afghan struggle for freedom has no nice, neat conclusion. Long after Lailoma arrived in the United States as a refugee in 2000 and gained her citizenship in 2007, the cycle of tyranny in her homeland renewed itself when the United States withdrew its troops in 2021, essentially ceding control of the country to the Taliban. Just as Lailoma's education was disrupted when the Taliban seized control of the country in 1996, the education of young women two decades later also has been disrupted. And while Lailoma and her son, Maiwand, are safe and thriving in the United States, many members of her family remain in Afghanistan, and she fears for their safety and well-being.

Getting to know Lailoma allowed me to walk in the shoes of someone from a country and culture far different from my own. Talking with her made me realize that so often we interact with people in our daily lives without giving a thought to their stories. Who are they? What has defined and shaped them? What motivates them? My goal became to offer a glimpse into a life I came to appreciate through my friendship with Lailoma.

CHAPTER 1

ARIZONA, 2009

Lailoma grasped the boning in the back of the slightly too-big bodice of my daughter's ivory satin wedding gown. "It's a beautiful dress," she told Lindsay, her eyes admiring the crystal buttons running down the full length of the back, the tucking on the bodice, and the simple lace band with just a touch of sparkle at the fitted waist.

"This boning will have to come out first," Lailoma said knowingly, revealing the first step in the alteration process. Lauren, my middle daughter, and I sat on the carpeted floor behind her, watching the process as the seamstress masterfully assessed how to sculpt the dress to the bride-to-be's trim body. "Then I will take the seams in a little bit and put the boning back in."

Lindsay's face revealed the question she didn't have to voice. *What's boning?*

"The bones are these stiff pieces that give the bodice its structure," Lailoma explained, recognizing that Lindsay didn't understand. "It's OK. I can make this fit you perfectly."

The four of us were gathered on the hot midsummer morning in the upstairs bedroom-turned-sewing room of Lailoma's condo in Scottsdale, Arizona. Lindsay faced the full-length floor mirror as Lailoma inserted a few straight pins to mark how much to take in on each side. Then the seamstress got down on her knees with her ruler and methodically circled the mounds of ivory, pinning the skirt and train to the perfect length.

"Now walk forward," she instructed Lindsay. "You want the front to be long enough, but you don't want to catch the toe of your shoe in the hem."

1

Recognizing her deftness—and confidence—I asked, "How long have you been doing alterations?"

"Nine years here, and before that in my country," Lailoma responded.

I had met Lailoma when I purchased an evening gown that required tailoring at a local boutique. When I returned to pick up the gown, it was altered so perfectly that I asked if she did freelance work, not knowing at the time that her employment at the boutique was a moonlighting activity. She gave me her card, which I tucked away for future reference. I remembered it the day we learned the bridal shop where we purchased Lindsay's gown didn't do alterations.

When I first met Lailoma, I hadn't detected an accent that would have suggested she wasn't originally from the United States. If I had listened more carefully, I would have. Her accent was slight, but it was there.

"Where are you from?" I asked now.

"Afghanistan," she answered. "I wanted to be a doctor."

"She's a doctor," I said proudly, pointing to Lindsay. Later I would wish that I had bitten my tongue.

"I passed my test to study medicine at the university, but then things changed and I didn't get to attend," Lailoma said. Her words hung heavily, shifting the atmosphere of the room, as if sucking out the air.

Lailoma never took her eyes from the hem she was pinning as she continued. "The Taliban came into our home, yanked my husband outside, and hanged him from a tree while I watched with my son from our bedroom window. He was five. Then they shot my husband in the head. I had to leave."

These words began a conversation that would cause tears to roll down Lindsay's face and prompt Lauren to reach for a tissue for her own misty eyes. As a journalist, I couldn't get enough of the story and probed for information. Both of my daughters drilled me with their eyes, silently willing me to stop talking, stop asking questions, but I simply couldn't.

As we left Lailoma's condo that morning, I asked if her remarkable story had ever been written. "No," she answered, "I don't write that well in English."

"I would love to talk with you more about this," I replied. "Are you willing to share more details with me?"

"Yes," she answered.

Throughout the previous hour or so we were together, she'd revealed no emotion. Nor did she now. But she clearly was interested and willing to share her story.

After the wedding, I called Lailoma and made plans to return to her condo on a Saturday morning in mid-January 2010. During that first morning session, I tape-recorded our conversation. Then I left the recorder and an assignment for her to continue capturing her recollections whenever she thought of something additional. The recordings made me realize how little I knew of life in Afghanistan. And actually, the realization made me personally uncomfortable, even embarrassed, that I hadn't really considered what it might be like, especially for a woman, to live in a country so culturally different from my own.

After only a couple of sessions, our Saturday-morning conversations moved from her living room sofa to the dining room table. I left the tape recorder at home and arrived instead with a laptop, realizing this story was far more extensive than what could be captured quickly on tape. I also realized I wasn't dealing with a several-page article. It became clear that to tell Lailoma's story, I would be endeavoring to write a book. Each Saturday, Lailoma served warm tea with cardamom and graciously offered frozen walnuts and mulberries in a pretty glass serving dish. Sometimes she served fresh fruit she had cut and arranged on a plate. Both of us nibbled and sipped, and I asked questions and typed as she recalled with remarkable detail her family saga and the story of her bold escape with her son, Maiwand (pronounced My-wand), to America. Sometimes Maiwand, who was in high school when we started our conversations, stopped by to chat for a few moments. Sometimes Lailoma's mother, Qurisha (pronounced Kur-eesha), came to say hello and shake my hand.

Our collaboration continued for several years, and each time we met I learned more details of her family and culture. In some ways, her family's path from its farming roots in a small village to the large city of Kabul didn't seem so different from the saga of many families, even my own. My mother grew up in a large family that clothed and fed themselves by working the land, and as in Lailoma's family, the division of labor between the sons and daughters was traditional. Like Lailoma's family, my mother's family was close and the siblings gave each other emotional support throughout their lives. "What's so different?" I was tempted to ask. As I learned, almost everything.

Lailoma's story here is based on her firsthand recollection of events. In situations where she was not present, she has reconstructed conversations as she was told they unfolded. Until this written account, the family history has been an oral one, verbally shared from one generation to the next.

The names of Lailoma's immediate family and acquaintances have been changed for the safety of those who remain in Afghanistan as well as the privacy of those who live in the United States. In some cases, she did not know the names of older relatives, particularly of her great-grandparents and their spouses. To her, they were *baba* and *ana* (grandfather and grandmother). Where this is the case, she has suggested names that would have been appropriate for the time.

The accuracy of dates for occurrences in Afghanistan was difficult to establish, partly because of a lack of recordkeeping, as is explained later, and partly because Afghanistan uses the Islamic calendar, which bears little resemblance to the Gregorian calendar, the world's most common date-keeping system. The sequence of events is not at issue, but except where noted or a matter of public record, the date may be an estimate.

My chance connection with Lailoma led me to realize how often we interact with people in our communities—some on a frequent basis—without really seeing them, without considering what they may have gone through. That first summer morning in Lailoma's condo, I knew I wanted to see the person behind the warm brown eyes and kind smile. I wanted an understanding, however incomplete, of what it might be like to walk in her shoes. Her story inspires me, and I hope it will inspire you too.

KABUL, 1996

Whooo. The ugly sound of bombers overhead began each morning after prayers, around 8 a.m. People filled the streets, frantically running for cover. Relative quiet returned during noon prayers, and then the chilling sound started anew.

If people had access to a basement, that was the best place to take shelter. But even basements didn't assure survival. On any given day, bodies—some whole, some fractured, nearly all covered with blood—were scattered everywhere.

How will we go on? Lailoma wondered.

The stench of blood pervaded the air. Sometimes she found a body part, but who it belonged to was often hard to tell. The traditional Muslim belief that a body must return to Allah as a whole, unaltered by man, had to be suspended. If she saw a piece of clothing on someone that matched what was on a severed arm or leg, she could place it with the rest of the body.

Sometimes she found a pair of children's shoes. Or children's clothes. Outside, parents frantically searched for their children or other family members. Sometimes they were successful. Often they were not.

Alongside the stench of blood, the combined smell of burning chemicals and human flesh would never leave the memories of those who survived. Everyone lived on edge, waiting for the sound of the planes. If there was no time—or no basement—they might dive to take shelter under a table or bed. But a table or bed offered no defense against a bomb. When Lailoma saw the injured, her heart broke. There was no way to take them to the hospital. No cars. No drivers if you had a car.

Having executed Mohammed Najibullah, Afghanistan's former president, and driven out the most recent president, Burhanuddin Rabbani, the Taliban rocketed and shelled Kabul. All Lailoma could do was put her agile hands to work, helping where she could. She had bandages and a few medical supplies in her apartment and with these she helped take care of flesh wounds.

5

One day a young neighbor girl got hit with shattered glass flying from a window destroyed by a rocket. The rest of the family had run to the basement, but the youngest daughter, Amina, didn't make it in time. A neighbor brought her to Lailoma. "Please help her," she pleaded.

But the glass had disappeared into Amina's chest.

"I can't do anything," Lailoma told the neighbor in despair. Lailoma, her neighbors, and the child's family watched Amina draw her last breath.

Always on edge, people were exhausted. Some tried to sleep during morning prayer time. But this time was brief, and when the bombing resumed, more houses were hit. At night, if they sat down to eat dinner with their children and an attack came, the food—what little there was—remained on the *dastarkhan*, the oilcloth they had spread out on the floor, untouched. The US State Department has estimated that in 1996 about 325 civilians in Kabul lost their lives during the Taliban's random barrage of bombs.

ARIZONA, 2013

Mindful of her surroundings, Lailoma didn't act on her urge. She didn't press her hands to the sides of her head and squeeze her eyes tightly shut. She didn't scream.

How am I here? was the track that played in her head. Some days, no matter how she distracted herself, she couldn't stop the bloody images, the screaming of rockets, or the desperate wailing.

Some days, the silence was worse.

Lailoma and the rest of the local Neiman Marcus employees were gathered at the tony Hotel Valley Ho for the annual Neiman Marcus "Best" awards, the luxury retailer's most prestigious recognitions. The employees of the Scottsdale store assembled prior to the holidays for breakfast and the much-anticipated year-end awards. In addition to the employees and the store's general manager, the president of the company had flown in from Dallas for the occasion.

How am I alive? I don't know how I raised my son, and I don't know how I can live now, how I can keep going. Stay busy, she reminded herself daily. *Keep working; don't close your eyes. Watch TV, listen to music. Then maybe the voices will stop. Then maybe I can stop the child from screaming in my head.*

"Lailoma, it's you!" Coworkers on either side of her urged her forward. "Stand up." Their voices yanked her from the violent images and sounds in her head, pulling her back into her present surroundings.

For the awards breakfast, the employees were attired in their work uniforms—well-tailored suits for retail salespersons, pants and shirts for security people, skirts and pretty blouses that could be covered with smocks or white jackets for those in the makeup and beauty department, an attractive dress for the woman who served in the café. Lailoma wore a black camisole with her black pants and blazer. When the celebratory breakfast concluded, they would get into their cars and drive the few blocks to the store to begin their workday.

The mood was convivial, festive. The aroma of scrambled eggs and the hotel's trademark short-rib hash mingled with that of the freshly brewed coffee (a smell Lailoma still hadn't learned to appreciate), adding to the warmth of the gathering.

As the plates were cleared and cups refilled, the store's general manager clinked his spoon on his water glass, quieting the conversation. "First," he said, "we appreciate the people who are celebrating anniversaries with the company today." The year marked Lailoma's tenth with the company, and she beamed when he handed her and two others silver pens to commemorate their anniversaries.

Then he singled her out for another reason. Coming as a total surprise, he presented her with a silver nameplate, a special designation bestowed only on outstanding employees. Some employees work years before being given this honor; some never achieve it, continuing to wear the standard-issue white name tag they received when they were first employed.

Had it really been ten years since she had been offered and accepted the job in the alterations department? How had she convinced them to hire her—with her halting English, when, despite her skill with a needle and thread, she had been so nervous during her interviews and sewing tests?

"As you know," the general manager continued, "at the end of each year, we recognize outstanding employees with Neiman Marcus Best awards. This year, we honor three employees."

Polite applause and a few cheers went up for the first two awardees, both outstanding salespeople. Then the general manager continued.

"Customer service is what sets Neiman Marcus apart. The spine of our store is the alterations department. Each member of the alterations team is charged with treating our customers respectfully and tailoring their garments to fit perfectly. Some customers might not be as easy to work with as others," he said, prompting a few chuckles from his audience, "but going above and beyond is what it takes to earn a Neiman Marcus Best award.

"This year's third Best winner always greets customers with a smile. I'm sure some days she doesn't feel as cheerful as she looks, but everyone has difficulties in their lives. She leaves hers at home. When she's at work, she is focused on the customer. I've heard her patience with the women and men whose clothing she pins to fit. She does what it takes to make each one happy, whether it's removing shoulder pads or reshaping sleeves.

"This year's third Best award goes to Lailoma Shahwali. Lailoma exemplifies Neiman Marcus service. She goes the extra mile to make her customers happy and pleased with their purchase. Happy customers return again and again."

Lailoma's heart thundered in her chest, and she realized she was holding her breath. Did she hear correctly? Had he said her name?

"Stand up," her coworkers repeated. Yes, the general manager had said her name.

Lailoma rose to her feet and worked her way to the front of the room where the general manager stood with flowers and a crystal clock bearing a gold plate engraved with her name.

Please don't faint, she told herself.

"Thank you," she said in a voice barely louder than a whisper.

The general manager shook her hand, handed her the clock and flowers, and then put his arm around her shoulders, giving her a brief hug. Lailoma beamed.

As a seamstress, Lailoma was mostly self-taught. Though her mother had schooled her in the use of her elementary hand-crank sewing machine as she was growing up in the '70s and early '80s, the professional sewing machines she now used were frighteningly powerful—and quick, necessitating caution. A light touch of her foot on the pedal sent the needle whirring up and down at lightning speed.

Being an alterations lady to the wealthiest women in the Valley— ripping and resewing seams out of pricey designer clothing often made of delicate fabric and embellished with trim—requires more than knowing how to control a powerful machine. Sometimes a garment has to be almost totally deconstructed and reassembled and still maintain the integrity of the original design, with a bespoke fit as the ultimate goal.

The job requires patience with even the most difficult customers. Reaching this pinnacle moment had demanded she stay calm and occasionally bite her tongue.

Like those of the physician she might have become, Lailoma's skillful hands are steady and sure. Though her educational achievements had pointed to an entirely different career, the life she planned had unraveled thread by thread. In response, she picked up those threads, embraced reality, and adjusted by seizing whatever opportunities she could find—or create.

Most of the unexpected events in her life had dealt crushing blows to herself and her family. But on this day, she felt a warm satisfaction.

I've surprised people, she thought. *I think I must have done OK, for a girl.*

By 10 a.m., when the store opened and Lailoma started her shift, she was already exhausted, as she almost always was, but after the excitement of hearing her name called at the awards ceremony, she was able to forget how tired she was for the rest of the afternoon.

When closing time came, she placed her crystal clock and flowers carefully on the front passenger seat of her six-year-old dark blue Corolla, eased into the driver's seat, and wondered what her mother would prepare for dinner. Would the smell of lamb greet her when she opened the condo door? Qurisha loved to serve lamb and rice with a dollop of the yogurt she made fresh daily. Lailoma enjoyed the traditional food of her homeland, and no doubt that was one of her mother's favorite meals, but if her mother hadn't planned anything, maybe this would be a pizza night. Her son would like that. She smiled to herself, remembering how she had shuddered at the thought of eating pizza just a few years earlier.

But first she had to make a stop. It was payday, and so she pulled into the convenience store where she had learned to wire money via Western Union. Until about two years ago, she had been sending a check to an import/export man in California and he would then send the money to her older brother. At the convenience store, she had seen posters for Western Union, but she didn't know what the service was, let alone how to use it.

"What is Western Union?" she finally asked the cashier one day.

"You can wire money to someone," he explained. "You don't have to mail a check. If you wire the money, the transfer can be made very quickly.

"Here's a form to fill out," he told her. "You can do it online if you want."

That's all? Lailoma thought.

When she had arrived home that evening, she sat at the computer she shared with her son, typed in westernunion.com, and clicked on "Get Started."

"Where would you like to send money?" the automated prompt asked.

She scrolled through the pull-down menu until she reached Pakistan and then clicked on it.

"Amount?"

"$600," she typed.

"Recipient?"

"Ahmadwali Shahwali." Lailoma entered her brother's name and cell phone number. Where the form asked for the recipient's city, she again typed

"Pakistan." No reason to give away his exact location. She also listed a nine-digit number for her brother to reference.

Each month when Lailoma sent money, she called her brother to let him know a check was waiting. At first, she sent one hundred dollars a month. Then two hundred dollars. By 2013, she was sending six hundred dollars monthly. It was a stretch for her paycheck to meet her needs and send the money as well, but she made it happen every single month. Her entire family counted on her.

QURISHA

Lailoma was the fourth of nine children born to her mother, Qurisha, and her father, Shahwali. Her oldest sibling was her sister Shaima. A second child, Gulwali—a son who died at two of what was presumed to be jaundice—was rarely spoken of. In many ways, Lailoma was closest to her older brother Ahmadwali, the third born. Then there was Lailoma and after Lailoma came another brother, Naim, and then four more sisters—Laila, Sonita, Sitara, and Susan.

Qurisha and Shahwali had been raised in a small village in Wardak, a province 119 kilometers driving distance—about seventy-three miles—southwest of Kabul, the capital city of Afghanistan and Kabul Province. Both Wardak and Kabul are located in the eastern part of the country, with Kabul being around 472 kilometers—about a three-hundred-mile drive—from the Pakistani border.

Qurisha and Shahwali grew up in very conservative Sunni households, and while they eventually raised their family in the more modern Kabul, the values and traditions of the past greatly influenced the way they brought up their children. The girls washed the clothing, prepared the meals, and cleaned the home. The boys went to school, played in the streets or on the roof, and were expected to become men who would support their families.

Those traditions were the basis of Qurisha and Shahwali's marriage in the early 1960s, and they had no reason to think things would be different for their children.

When I met Qurisha in 2013, she was about sixty-five. She appeared tall, but maybe that was because she was so slender. The olive skin of her face was soft and pliant, but her demeanor suggested a much older woman, revealing a hint of anxiety and something akin to sadness. Otherwise, her appearance was dignified, almost regal as she moved gracefully through Lailoma's three-bedroom Scottsdale townhouse, where she had lived with her daughter and grandson since 2009.

Traces of Lailoma's family's culture gave their simple condo character. Strands of alternating clear and transparent-gold acrylic beads, reminiscent of the Muslim rosary, hung from the ceiling in two places—above the transition from the living room to the dining room and above the steps leading from the living room to the home's three upstairs bedrooms. Tied back, they formed drapes to define the living space.

Traditional step pads in tan accented with burgundy softened the travertine-style beige ceramic tile of the stairs. A large burgundy area rug anchored the seating area in the living room, which consisted of a sofa and love seat upholstered in heavy, tapestry-like gold fabric. These existed harmoniously with an animal-print occasional chair that Lailoma had purchased online, the sleek modern dining table and chairs that came from a nearby furniture store, and the large, wall-mounted flat-screen TV.

On the second floor, space was a little tighter. There was the sewing room where Lailoma moonlighted, taking in extra alterations projects from people she met through her part-time job at a bridal shop. Lailoma and Qurisha shared one of the two bedrooms, with Qurisha sleeping on the single bed and Lailoma on the carpeted floor, sans mattress, beside her. Maiwand occupied the third room.

Though Qurisha spoke little more than "good morning," "hello," and "how are you?" in English, she extended her hand to greet me with a kind handshake and warm brown eyes. She wore her silvery white hair fashioned with waves to frame her face and braided. Left alone the braid would hang long down her back, but usually she twisted it into a bun at the nape of her neck. In Afghanistan, long hair was considered very beautiful, so as was the custom, Qurisha had never cut her hair. When she let her braid down, its end reached nearly to her waist. At one time, she said, her hair came down to her knees, but as she had aged, the ends had broken, causing the braid to thin at the bottom.

She wore the traditional attire of an Afghan woman: long, shapeless, printed cotton dresses in various colors over narrow white cotton pants that ended with lace trim around her ankles. She rarely wore Western clothing; she was comfortable in what she knew. In the condominium, she went barefoot.

I was struck by her graciousness and calm demeanor, but her constant trips to the outdoor patio, where she lit cigarette after cigarette, sometimes pacing rather than sitting, revealed inner turmoil. She ate very little, usually just once a day in the evening, and then, very small portions.

"She raised us to be strong," Lailoma told me. "She has always been a worrier, and she worries more now than ever, but inside she is strong too. She has had to be."

AFGHANISTAN, 1950S AND EARLY 1960S

Lailoma's journey to America really began when Qurisha left Wardak as a new bride. She had been promised to her future husband's parents for their son when she was just a toddler, and she was married at thirteen, a blossoming new teen who hadn't yet experienced her first menstrual cycle. Shahwali, her husband, was past thirty-five when they wed. While in the United States, this arrangement would be illegal, it was not atypical for Islamic families in Muslim countries. In Afghanistan, as in many countries around the world, a young woman can marry before age sixteen with the permission of her father. This is especially common in rural areas, where parents might not be able to support their female children, and since girls were not educated at the time, it was unlikely they would be able to find employment.

"I didn't even know what 'engagement' meant," Qurisha later told Lailoma and Shaima as they were growing up.

Their *ana*—Qurisha's mother—had explained life to her simply and matter-of-factly: "A woman grows up learning how to manage a home. You learn to cook and clean. You learn to wash clothes. You learn to be respectful of all men and especially your elders. You work with whatever resources you have.

"When the time comes, you will get married. Parents want their daughters to marry a prosperous man who will be able to make money to take care of the family. Your father and I chose Shahwali for you when you were just a little girl. He will be your husband. Together, you are going to make a family."

Make a family? Qurisha thought. *How? What does that mean?*

She knew she lived in a large household, but she hadn't given much thought to how they all came to be. Her sisters might speculate, but they weren't of much help in supplying real information. Her mother kept silent on the subject of sex, and it would have been impertinent for Qurisha to ask for details. She would have to learn those details from her husband, not from her mother.

In her formative years, Qurisha and her siblings enjoyed the rural life of Hamza, their somewhat isolated village, one of ninety or so walled compounds in Wardak Province. Her brothers rarely left the village, and she wasn't allowed to step outside the village walls by herself until she became a bride and left its security with her husband, bound for the capital city of Kabul.

The last king of Afghanistan, Mohammed Zahir Shah, during whose rule (1933 to 1973) Qurisha grew up, tried to improve Afghanistan, which is just slightly smaller than Texas. His vision was a modern democratic state. Though "neutral" during the Cold War, he was practical. He obtained machinery and weapons from the Soviets and financial aid from the Americans. He took on economic development projects, building irrigation systems and highways. He championed women's rights, making the burqa optional.

In Kabul, women enrolled in the university—Kabul University opened to women in 1947—and pursued careers in medicine and other professions.

Young women in Kabul didn't look much different from those you might have seen in any Western European city during that time.

Shah's programs, however, had little effect outside Kabul. In the villages of Wardak, women continued covering their heads and wearing traditional clothing.

Before her marriage to Shahwali, Qurisha worked in the home with her stepsisters and mother, who taught her to clean and cook. Learning to bake came later, when she became tall enough to reach the tandoor, a clay, wood-burning oven outside the home on the patio. On the rare occasion she left the confines of their home, she would wear a large scarf to conceal her face and hair as well as a full-length dress and long pants, which serve as underwear and are akin to leggings.

The large household consisted of eleven children, plus the two parents. Qurisha's father, Amin, had four sons and two daughters from his first marriage to his brother's widow. When she died, he married Qurisha's mother, Kobra. Together, they had Qurisha and two sons. In order, they were stepbrothers Anbar, Rahim, Ashraf, and Khalid and stepsisters Shapiry and Hawa (all of whom had been born to Amin's brother and his wife), and then Qurisha, Fazel, and Naeem. Like Amin, Kobra had children from a previous marriage: a son, Gholamghous, and a daughter, also named Hawa. These children lived with them as well. It was a happy, energetic family that blended together as one.

Each morning began with prayers, followed by breakfast—a piece of naan and a cup of warm, sweetened tea. When the men took the animals to graze in the mountains, Qurisha and her stepsisters cleaned and put away the dishes. Then they picked up the mattresses on which the family had slept and put them in the closet.

Milking the cows daily was Qurisha's mother's job. Kobra brought the fresh milk into the house and boiled it over a fire built by her daughters. Then she added a little yogurt to the boiled milk to make fresh yogurt for the next day (a practice Qurisha continued throughout her life).

Every second day, they made *doqh*—a liquid left over from making the yogurt—to drink. They separated the butter and kept it in a cool place for the annual "oil" day, when the entire village brought all the butter they had saved to put into a big pot, cooked it until it liquified, and then strained it through a coarse cloth. The resulting ghee became their cooking oil for the winter.

The next chore was to sweep the ever-present dust from the floors and take the burgundy rug made in northern Afghanistan—a source of pride, as opposed to having an Iranian-made rug—outside to beat it.

Then it was time to cook lunch. Then clean.

Kobra also had to fit in the never-ending mending and washing the family's clothing by hand in a tub she filled with water from the river. After the laundry had dried and been folded and put away, Qurisha and her stepsisters helped their mother cook and serve the evening meal.

Evening was the one time of day the females left their homes. As a group, the village women covered their heads and faces and walked to the Bande Chak, the river that flowed through Hamza. Here, they replenished their homes's supplies of water for the next day, carrying it back in jars on their shoulders.

"Did you hear Abra had another daughter?" someone might ask.

"Ha! No gifts for the *daiee!*" was a usual response, referring to the tradition of only giving midwives and nurses gifts when boys are born. "This is her third daughter. No son. Maybe Rashid will marry another wife!"

Giggles followed, though all of them were aware this was a real possibility. Even though the water was heavy, the women appreciated the brief time to socialize.

While the family of thirteen could enjoy their meals together in one room, there wasn't enough room for everyone to sleep inside. As the sons grew older, they slept outside in the *tandoorkhana*, an outdoor kitchen where the heat of the oven kept them warm in winter. In the summer, some of the male members of the family slept on the home's flat roof and some laid their mattresses outside on the patio to sleep. The females weren't allowed to sleep out in the open, but when the crowded floor became too stifling in the summer, some of the women slept in the tandoorkhana, which was cool in warm-weather months because the tandoor would be taken outside for baking.

The villagers were self-sufficient and self-reliant. The men grew the grains and produce they needed on their land outside the village. When the wheat was harvested, they took it to the mill to be turned into flour for the winter. In a good year, their pantries were bursting by the end of the summer season, filled with potatoes, flour, beans, onions, and more. To last until the next harvest, these had to be consumed judiciously.

There was no local market. If a family ran out of something vital, the men had to get up early in the morning to catch the one bus that served the village for a long, dusty ride to a market in Ghazni Province, some fifty or sixty miles south. Shopping was men's work.

By the time Qurisha was old enough to be helpful around the house, her younger brothers, Fazel and Naeem, attended the village school. They also helped their father work the family's small farm outside the village. Sometimes, but very rarely, they went to Ghazni with their father to sell some of their sheep or buy extra grain. Occasionally, if Amin had enough money, he bought them special treats from one of the vendors who had set up shop on the narrow, dusty streets. Maybe he could afford kebabs or an ear of roasted corn or some warm, freshly baked naan.

Qurisha welcomed the days when her father and brothers went on these trips. She and her stepsisters didn't get the same treats, but at least for that day, the girls and their mother could cook smaller amounts of food and wash fewer clothes.

Only when they couldn't find what they needed in Ghazni did villagers undertake the strenuous trip to Kabul. To reach the big city, they crowded into—and often on top of—a standing-room-only bus to make the more than two-hour, seventy-mile journey along the dusty, bumpy roads. Sometimes when the bus door got backed up with people paying fares, parents hoisted their children up to the roof of the bus, which was fortunately surrounded by a rail. "Hold on tight!" they urged the children.

When there was no longer standing room, people hung outside the door, clinging to the handrail. Occasionally someone lost their grip on the handrail or slipped between the bars of the roof rail and fell off.

Such a trip required food, especially in case the bus broke down on the way, and Qurisha and her mother packed snacks of naan and maybe a piece of fruit for Amin and his sons to eat along the way.

The seven sons, Anbar, Rahim, Ashraf, Khalid, Fazel, Naeem, and Gholamghous, as in any Afghan family, were the priority. Sons grew up to work and help support the extended family. Sons inherited the family's wealth. A daughter had merit as a different kind of asset. A good marriage for her would bring prestige, money, and other treasures to the family. It would also assure her continuing welfare.

By the time she was twelve years old, Qurisha must have been quite lovely: slender, well-mannered, and pretty. Innocent.

Her fiancé, Shahwali, was educated; Qurisha, of course, was not. Shahwali had finished ninth grade in the village, after which he studied with the local imam in the mosque, where he finished high school. He worked with his father on the Wardak farm before moving to Kabul in his mid- to late-twenties, where he finished auto-mechanic school and found an executive position with the government in the office of the state trucking company.

After Shahwali had made and set aside a sum of money, he and his father sold some of their farm animals and wheat to purchase a house in Kabul. Shahwali and his father furnished the home with everything a young bride would need. They selected and purchased kitchenware and dishes, as well as a rug, sofa, love seat, side chair, and coffee table for the formal living room and a table for the dining room, both of which were reserved for guests. They also selected a bright hand-knotted rug and red velvet mattresses and pillows for the family area. These would serve for seating as well as sleeping.

In Afghanistan, wedding dates were, and generally still are, set by the father of the groom. Especially in rural areas, young men had to work the farm to save money for marriage, both sets of parents wanting to be confident that the couple would thrive. Though Shahwali was past thirty-five, his father determined when Shahwali had sufficient means to be responsible for a family and the time was right for the ceremony. With all that a man had to do be-fore marriage coupled with the appeal of a young woman for a bride, the age difference between Shahwali and Qurisha was not uncommon.

With everything in place, his father told him, "You are ready."

After the ceremony, Shahwali packed up his young wife along with her ten-year-old brother, Fazel, and took them to live in the house in Kabul. Clearly, Qurisha was too young to stay alone in the house. A young wom-an couldn't go to the market by herself. If she needed something to cook for dinner, Fazel would be there to fetch it for her. If she needed to buy cloth or a household item, she could go to the marketplace with Shahwali when he came home from work.

To Qurisha, it wasn't a nuisance that her little brother would be coming to live with her and her new husband. The truth was that she was more than a little apprehensive about the whole situation. Having Fazel with her was a comfort. She was a little less afraid because she knew he would be there. She was also a little less homesick.

Though they went from Wardak to Kabul in style, the ride was rough. Instead of taking the bus, they undertook the journey in an older-model taxi. As they bounced along the rutted, unpaved road, they dodged men on donkeys and the occasional man on foot. The year was 1961. King Mohammad Zahir Shah oversaw the building of improved roads in the '60s, but they weren't yet completed for this most momentous journey in young Qurisha's life. (Parts of the highway that eventually became circular, from Kabul in the eastern part of the country to Kandahar in the south, Herat in the west, Mazar-e Sharif in the north, and back to Kabul, were never paved.)

Partly because the roads were so bad, owning and driving personal cars were relatively new ideas to people in small Afghan villages. One of Shahwa-li's duties in his government job was to travel to remote populations to teach people about car ownership. He taught male villagers to drive, register their cars, obtain licenses, and maintain their vehicles. He traveled to Baglan, Mazar-e Sharif, Kondoz, Meymaneh, and other villages and cities around the country—all on those same rough roads. While this government job didn't make him wealthy, he earned enough to maintain the Kabul home well.

When the demands of Shahwali's job pulled him away from home for several days at a time, Shahwali invited his brother, Qader, Qader's wife, and their children to live in the Kabul house with Fazel and Qurisha. Even though Qader and his wife were there to watch over the household, Shahwali never forgot about Qurisha and Fazel when he was away. Wherever he traveled, he bought local specialties to send home to Qurisha—from Mazar-e Sharif, dried raisins or mulberries; from other places, necessities such as rice, oil, flour, lentils, and sugar.

But young Qurisha and Fazel were no match for greedy Qader and his wife, who seized the packages when they arrived, and led Qurisha to believe they owned the house and all of its contents.

"Don't touch that," Qader's wife screamed at Qurisha. "Those dishes aren't yours," or "That banana is for our children."

None of these claims were true. The house and everything in it belonged to Shahwali. Though women didn't "own" anything, as his wife, Qurisha should have had access to everything.

"Just get out of the house until you learn not to touch my things!" Qader's wife sometimes screamed at Qurisha, pushing her out the door. She also had been a young bride, but an opportunity was an opportunity.

The turmoil escalated. Eventually Qader and his wife forced Fazel out of the home, put him on a bus, and sent him back to the family's village in Wardak. Now Qurisha was isolated from the only contact she had with her family. Qader occasionally threatened to beat her, and once he pointed a gun at her, telling her he would kill her if her family came to visit.

When Shahwali returned from his business trips, Qurisha dared not complain about the way she was being treated. Women weren't supposed to complain, and Qurisha had been taught not to whine. She did not want to upset her husband, but more, she knew if she told Shahwali what was happening, when he left, Qader and his wife would double their cruelty toward her.

On one of his trips home, Shahwali noticed his young bride had lost weight and asked her about it.

"Are you not eating?" he asked her.

"I think I just miss my family," she told him. "I must just be homesick."

Clearly he understood neither the situation nor the severity of it.

"When I'm gone, why don't you visit your family in Wardak?" Shahwali asked Qurisha. "I will pay for the bus, and then you won't be so homesick."

"I can't go visit my family because if I leave, Qader won't let me back into the house," she told him.

Her answer should have been a clue to Shahwali about what was happening in his absence, but he didn't pick up on it until later.

It was a hopeless situation for which there didn't seem to be options, so Qurisha bore the living arrangement as well as she could, though she was miserable.

Shortly after her first menstrual cycle, Qurisha became pregnant with her first child. By now, she had reached the age of fourteen. She was young and alone, and the pregnancy was hard. If only she could have lived in the village where her mother and father were, her mother could have helped her through the birthing process. But she wasn't in Wardak.

For the birth of her first child, Shahwali's older brother Zaher's wife, along with Qader's wife—who happened to be sisters—assisted her. When Qurisha's beautiful baby girl was born, Zaher's wife named her Shaima.

Realizing how hard the situation was for Qurisha, Shahwali finally requested and obtained a transfer to Kabul so he could be with her. With Shahwali at home, there was no longer a need for Qader and his wife and children to stay, so they prepared to move out of the house. On the day they packed their belongings, Qurisha stayed in the background, relieved they were leaving. But something was odd: they took only their clothing and a few other personal items with them.

"Why are they leaving all of their things here?" Qurisha asked Shahwali.

"What things?" Shahwali asked her.

"Everything—their dishes, their mattresses, their pots and pans."

Finally, Shahwali began to realize what had been happening under his roof. Finally, he understood the trauma his young bride had experienced. "This is all ours," he told her, with a sweeping gesture of his arm. "This is my house, not theirs. And so it is your house too."

Qurisha was happier after Qader and his family left, but that's not to say the couple settled into marital bliss. Fourteen-year-old Qurisha had difficulty with breastfeeding the newborn Shaima and she had no one to mentor her. Both of Qurisha's breasts had become infected, resulting in burning and bleeding each time she fed her baby daughter.

As Shaima fussed because she needed to nurse, Qurisha fretted. Without her mother, Qurisha had no one in whom to confide or from whom to seek advice. Afraid Shahwali would yell at her, she didn't mention her agony, suffering in silence.

As a parting gesture of ill will, Qader and his wife used black magic to cast an evil spell on Shahwali and Qurisha, turning them against each other.

"Your father wasn't a good husband then," Qurisha told her daughters when they were young. "Every day when he came home from work, he yelled at me."

"What did he yell about?" the young girls asked.

"I don't know. Anything. When he looked at me, I could see hatred in his eyes," she told them. "I just tried not to upset him."

On top of worrying about breastfeeding Shaima, the young mother was now fearful of her husband. She tried to do everything that would be pleasing to him—to prepare nice meals, to keep the house clean, to be respectful—but she always felt as if she needed to tiptoe around him, to be careful not to anger him.

Coworkers began to notice changes in Shahwali. He began to show physical signs of the stress he was under at home. He lost weight. He had trouble concentrating. He was depressed and moody, his brooding temper just below the surface.

The stress was so apparent that Karim, one of Shahwali's coworkers, approached him about it.

"You don't seem like yourself," Karim said to him one day. "You forgot to schedule maintenance on your government car last week. You missed an important meeting this morning. Is everything all right here at work?"

"Yes, of course," Shahwali answered.

"Then what's wrong?"

"I'm having trouble with my wife."

"Is she a good mother?" Karim asked.

"Yes, very good. She loves our little girl and always keeps her fed and clean. Shaima's a happy baby."

"Is your wife a good cook?"

"Yes. Qurisha always serves dinner on time and prepares food exactly the way I like it. And she's not wasteful. She's careful to measure out what we have so we don't run out of rice, flour, and tea."

"Does she keep the house clean?"

"Yes. It is perfect. The rugs are always clean, the dishes are always put away, and the rest of the house is spotless."

"Does she gossip with other women?"

"No. She doesn't have women friends. She stays at home and takes care of the house and baby."

"Does she behave badly when she goes with you to the marketplace?"

"No. She wears a scarf over her hair, doesn't talk to anyone she doesn't need to, and doesn't look anyone in the eye."

"Then, what?"

"I don't know," Shahwali said. "When I am away from home and think about Qurisha being home alone with the baby, I worry about her. She's young and away from her family. Unless a relative comes from Wardak, she's alone with only the baby for company. But the closer I get to our house after work, the angrier I get. I squeeze my hand into a fist and I want to beat her."

Karim immediately recognized what had happened to Shahwali and Qurisha: black magic had been used against them.

"There are only two people who could have done that," Shahwali responded after Karim shared his belief. "It had to be Qader and his wife. No one else has been around us since we moved to Kabul, and they weren't happy when I told them they had to move out of the house."

"Let's go," Karim said, abruptly standing. "Come with me," he motioned to Shahwali. "I know someone who can help."

Shahwali and Karim set out late in the morning on a steamy midweek summer day and walked from the government office building a few blocks into one of the city's busiest—and oldest—marketplaces. The streets teemed with vegetable carts loaded with grapefruit, tomatoes, and melons. The two men dodged merchants carrying stacks of colorful rugs over their shoulders to their shops, where more rugs were piled as high as ten feet on makeshift tables. Other shops held sheepskin products, leather goods, and furniture. The smell of the leather mingled with the odors of ripening fruit and vegetables, cooking meat, the silk and wool of the rugs, and animals—and their waste—in the street.

Men in traditional white turbans haggled over prices with shop owners, and women in light-blue burqas walked together through the dusty streets. Here there were no sidewalks, so humans shared the walking space with horses and other animals. Drivers of rundown pickup trucks and vans impatiently honked their horns to clear a path to drive.

The old and the new coexisted on this busy thoroughfare. The storefronts were rickety, almost makeshift. Electricity was delivered by wires strung from rooftop to rooftop or from poles added to the tops of the buildings. The street activity was set against the backdrop of newer buildings, some several stories high. Beyond these buildings, row after row of sand and pastel-colored homes sat at the base of—and partway up—the beautiful and rugged Hindu Kush mountains.

Shahwali and Karim passed a familiar food vendor from whom they often bought naan or a kebab for their midday meal. Even though the smell was intoxicating, they didn't stop. They were on a mission.

They walked by the tomb of Emperor Babur, stepping around a man sleeping on the stone floor. Both car and foot traffic began to pick up as they approached the center of Kabul and passed the eighteenth-century Pul-e-Khishti mosque, the largest in Kabul. Its proximity to the main commercial area made it a popular place for midday prayers, and hundreds of men were already placing their small carpets on the dirt outside.

Shahwali and Karim hustled so they could return to the mosque for prayers as soon as they accomplished what they set out to do. They sought a holy man, a spiritual healer, who would be able to cast off the spell put on Shahwali by his brother and sister-in-law. A good place to find a holy man was in one of the small shops near the mosque. While Islam doesn't embrace it, the practice of black magic is so accepted in the Muslim world that leaders often look the other way.

Shahwali started to enter one of the shops, but Karim held him back. "No, no. This isn't the man," Karim insisted, guiding him away. "My brother told me the man's shop is on the other side of the mosque."

So they walked a little farther around the mosque. "There! This is the one," Karim said, pointing to a small shop with a makeshift, faded red awning.

"What can I do for you?" the owner, who was also the holy man, asked.

"My friend and his wife have had a curse put on them by his brother and sister-in-law. They've made my friend turn against his wife. He and his wife are not happy, and he's even afraid he might hurt her," Karim said. "You helped my nephew get a better job when he needed it. Can you take this spell off my friend and his wife?"

"I hope so. Exactly what is the problem?" the holy man asked.

Shahwali repeated his story: When he was away from home, he loved his wife—even worried about her. He wanted to treat her well. But each day when work ended and he came closer and closer to home, his resentment of her became greater and greater. By the time he walked in the door, his feelings were more like hatred than love. He wanted to hurt her.

"This is a very evil spell. It's powerful, and you have been hurt badly," the healer told Shahwali.

"How did I get hurt?"

"Your brother and his wife put a very strong, very evil spell on you. But it's not too late," he assured Shahwali. "I know how to break the spell, but I can't do it here. We will have to go to your home. Your wife must be there. We will also need a young virgin girl. We should do this today before it's too late."

"How much do you charge?" Shahwali asked.

"You can pay me whatever you feel comfortable with."

The request for a young girl seemed strange to Shahwali. He had no idea how a young girl would be useful, but that afternoon he took a bus to Kote angi where Qader and his family now lived. He brought his niece, Aziza, home with him. If he thought of the irony that the key to breaking the spell Qader and his wife had cast on them was their own daughter, he didn't mention it. He didn't know many young girls.

When Shahwali, Qurisha, Aziza, and the spiritual healer were assembled in the living room, the healer read from the Koran. Through the spirits, he induced a trancelike state in Aziza, transforming her right thumbnail into a window into the spirit world.

The room, the people, seemed to fade away for Aziza, she later said. Gradually she felt alone, unaware of the healer, Shahwali, or Qurisha. Afterward, she told Qurisha she could see the whole room in her fingernail, describing it as an out-of-body experience.

The healer put a scratch mark on her nail. "What do you see?" he asked Aziza.

"I see green grass and a tree," she responded.

Meanwhile, Qurisha felt as if she had stepped into a hot oven. She could feel her body becoming hotter and hotter. Shahwali's body began to burn as well.

The healer continued to read from the Koran, then again asked Aziza what she saw.

26

"A woman wearing a scarf," Aziza said. "I can't tell who she is because the scarf is covering her face."

The healer read on. "Now can you see who the woman is?"

"That's my ana," she said, referring to her grandmother.

As the healer resumed reading, Aziza came out of her trance and slowly returned to a normal state.

The drama wasn't over. A ball, something tied in fabric, dropped from the wood ceiling to the floor in front of Qurisha and Shahwali.

"Open it," the healer instructed Shahwali.

Inside the fabric was a piece of paper on which had been drawn the outline of a human body, a needle piercing its heart. Also inside was a very small white stone and around it, a piece of animal fat. The stone had turned partially black.

"You are very fortunate you came to me in time," the healer told Shahwali. "If the stone had turned completely black, one of you would have killed the other. Wash the stone and throw it away, as far away from you as you can."

The process of breaking the spell was completed in about fifteen minutes. Immediately, both Qurisha and Shahwali were almost overcome as an icy cold knifed through their previously burning bodies. Shahwali turned to Qurisha, hugged her, and apologized.

"I am sorry I have been so angry and cold toward you. You are my wife. I love you. I don't hate you," he told her.

The relevance of having Aziza present, of the green grass and tree, the woman in the scarf, or recognizing her grandmother, wasn't quite clear, but those details didn't matter. The evil spell had been broken. Shahwali gave the healer five hundred Afghani, the currency of Afghanistan.

In short order, the household became more harmonious. Shahwali noticed that breastfeeding was painful for Qurisha. He took her to a doctor, who gave her a topical prescription for her breasts and explained to her how to give the baby cereal to supplement her breast milk. Her breasts healed, and little Shaima flourished. As was customary and as she did for her future children, Qurisha continued to breastfeed Shaima for several years.

Lailoma never learned who named all of the children, but one thing is almost certain: Qurisha didn't have the honor. As they had been for Shaima, naming rights for Qurisha's eight children to follow were reserved for others. When Lailoma was born three years after Ahmadwali, Hawa—one of Qurisha's stepsisters—decided she would name her.

"If you have a daughter, I'm going to name her Lailoma," she told Qurisha. And so it was. In the Koran, *Lailoma* means night and moon—"lai" for night and "ma" for moon.

Little Lailoma was barely out of the womb when her first suitor was proposed. Hawa was certain her one-year-old son would be the perfect match for Lailoma. "Lailoma is going to be my daughter-in-law!" Hawa told Qurisha, excitedly.

When she was older, Lailoma realized she was glad her father hadn't been present when Hawa claimed her as her daughter-in-law. Her father might have agreed to the engagement, and her fate would have been set the minute she was born.

As Lailoma was growing up, her mother occasionally repeated the story to her. "No way!" young Lailoma would scream. From her adolescent point of view, the cousin was a loser. "He stays home and takes care of the house like a woman," she told her mother.

Maybe Shahwali never learned of Hawa's proposal. Maybe he and Qurisha were swayed by Lailoma's disdain for her cousin. For whatever reason, the union never occurred.

As Shaima, Lailoma, and her four younger sisters grew up, Qurisha shared the story of her early marriage with them. "I'm not telling you this story so you will know how hard my life was and feel sorry for me," she said. "I'm telling you about my experience so when you get married and life becomes hard, you will know you have to be strong and never give up. Face life; don't run away from it. Always be strong. I want you to learn from my story."

Her words resonated in her daughters' lives again and again, shaping their courses, giving them strength.

CHAPTER 2

KABUL, 1970S

After the black magic episode and the death of their second child, Gulwali, at age two, Shahwali and Qurisha's family settled into a comfortable pattern. They weren't wealthy, but Shahwali's earnings provided a good life. Soon he was able to make it even better.

To increase his income, Shahwali started a private transportation company that was the first to provide regular bus travel to Kabul from Hamza, their village in Wardak. By now the roads were improving, and the bus made life for the villagers better. It also meant that Qurisha and Shahwali's family could visit with relatives on a more regular basis. At the same time, he maintained his office job in Kabul for the transportation division of the government.

Their home was in an area of Kabul near Bagh-e Bala, a hill on which sits the beautiful Intercontinental Hotel and also the blue-domed summer palace of Amir Abdur Rahman, who ruled Afghanistan in the late nineteenth century. Sometimes on Fridays, when Shahwali didn't work because it was the holy day, he took the family on a picnic across the street in Bagh-e Bala.

Lush with grapevines and apple, walnut, and almond trees, the park was Kabul's main picnic spot and a joy to visit. Oh, the delicious aroma of the ripening apple trees and the enormous roses of every color. The fruit and nuts were off-limits for the family to eat because the park was government-owned, but there was always enough in the picnic basket that Qurisha and Shaima—and later Lailoma—had packed. The women filled it with naan, mulberries, cheese—if they had it—and sweetened tea.

"Catch me!" one child would call while taking off on a run up the hill, and the others would spring into action to give chase. If they made it to the top of the hill where the palace sat, they had a view of all of Kabul—office buildings, marketplaces, and homes, even their own. When the children were tired from play, they gulped the water that ran fresh and cold from the mountains that surrounded the city.

In the evenings, Shahwali loved to take the younger children for a walk in the park. From an upstairs window, as they finished their homework, Lailoma and Ahmadwali watched the joyous play of their siblings. Occasionally Qurisha accompanied Shahwali and the younger children, but more often, she and Shaima prepared the evening meal during this time.

The family's white, flat-roofed, mud-brick home was typical of the homes around theirs. The first floor was dedicated to food. It held a pantry, which was stocked with staples such as rice and flour, the kitchen, and a room in which they stored charcoal for cooking as well as wood for winter. Several chickens made their home just inside the front gate. As each child was born, Qurisha's mother, Kobra, brought a chicken as a gift, so the family almost always had several chickens to provide eggs.

By 1971, when Lailoma was born, the political culture had changed, the rules regarding women loosening somewhat. Now Qurisha could go to the market by herself or with Shaima. Often they left their home two or three times a day for fresh fruits, vegetables, and meat.

In the kitchen, Qurisha instructed her daughters: "Peel another layer off those onions! Wash those potatoes again! Those apples aren't clean enough!"

Any attempt by the shopkeeper to make his produce appear clean was negated by the fact that he could be seen swishing his vegetables and fruit through the water of the same river where others were bathing and washing clothes and animals were taking a cooling dip.

The home's outdoor stairway provided entrance into the high-ceilinged main living area on the second floor. The entire family slept on the floor of this room, and with each child born, it seemed to shrink a little. Every evening, they took their narrow, cotton-stuffed mattresses, pillows, and blankets from the closet and rolled them out onto the concrete floor to sleep side by side. Just as Qurisha had learned from her mother, she taught her daughters to fold the blankets, roll the mattresses, and put everything back into the closet each morning.

Another door led to their formal living room and dining room. The living room was furnished with a sofa, love seat, and chair, and the spacious dining room featured two big windows and a large table. The built-in glass-front china cupboard contained the family's dishes, and its turquoise paint matched the frames of the windows and door, adding color to the otherwise white room. Both rooms were reserved for guests. Qurisha and Shahwali's family, as is customary among Afghans, sat on the floor in the family room for dinner.

Shaima always cooked with her mother. When dinner was prepared, Qurisha returned to the upstairs. This was the signal for Lailoma and Ahmadwali to go downstairs to help their older sister carry the big platter of food up from the kitchen and present it to their parents.

The family assembled on the floor around the dastarkhan, which had been spread like a tablecloth on top of their burgundy carpet. One of the girls then took their everyday silver pitcher and basin first to their father and then to their mother to wash their hands. One girl poured the water over each parent's hands, and the other held the basin under them to catch the water. Soap was offered as was a drying cloth. After the parents had washed, the pitcher was taken to the oldest child and continued down the line.

Shahwali and then Qurisha served themselves, spooning food onto their plates, before food was served family-style to the children. Having been passed, the big platter of the main dish and any accompaniments was placed in the middle of the dastarkhan. When everyone had their food, they dug in with their hands, using pieces of naan as scoops. The use of utensils was rare.

Dining on the floor came with a few perils, especially for small children. Once, when Laila, one of the younger sisters, was a toddler and just learning to walk, she tripped and fell onto the hot teapot on the floor. This was a common experience among Afghan children—tea was served morning, noon, and night. Laila screamed as her hand went into the hot tea, her burned skin immediately breaking into big blisters, producing scars that remained with her in adulthood.

The formal living area contained a leather sofa, coffee table, and side tables. These, like the dining table, were used only to entertain guests, places for serving tea, fruits, and maybe cookies or cakes, which Qurisha and her daughters prepared in the kitchen below. Guests were welcome any time. If they arrived after two in the afternoon, Qurisha and her daughters served a cold drink—perhaps a Pepsi, if they had it, or a glass of juice. If it was later in the day, they made tea and served it with some dried fruit. If they had cardamom, they might add just a pinch to the tea for flavor. But cardamom, like saffron and vanilla, was very expensive and not a staple in their pantry.

Family life revolved around this room, where they watched television or maybe a movie on their VCR. Western culture was brought to the family courtesy of Sylvester Stallone and Arnold Schwarzenegger. For movie time, they lined the room with their mattresses on the floor and arranged their pillows to lean against the wall as they watched and rewatched Rocky prepare for the ring and the Terminator go back in time to kill the resistance leader's mother before she gives birth.

Close by was a bathroom that was used for bathing only; it had no toilet. Family members carried warm water they had heated over charcoal downstairs in the kitchen up the outside staircase to this room. The water they poured over their heads from their pitchers drained through a hole in the middle of the concrete floor. The toilet was located in an outhouse behind the home. This building could get cold in the winter, and they moved a charcoal and wood-burning stove inside to warm the outhouse when they needed to, depending on the season.

In good weather, toward sunset, Qurisha swept and scrubbed the concrete patio outside the kitchen, and Shaima placed a carpet on it. Lailoma's job was to carry out the pillows and mattresses, and this became the gathering spot for afternoon tea. Sometimes on a nice evening, the family took the TV outside.

For the children, afternoons were filled with laughter and play. The tomboyish Lailoma loved to play outside with Ahmadwali—whether flying kites, playing baseball with a stick of wood as an improvised bat, or practicing her volleyball serve. These were all much more interesting than playing inside with Shaima, who was not only older but also more inclined toward traditional girl activities—playing with the doll her mother had made out of fabric scraps for her or helping with the cooking and cleaning.

So much like my sister and me, I thought as Lailoma told me about her childhood play. I liked dolls for a time, but my sister was the girly one, and I was the more outdoorsy, tomboyish one, at least in my mind. Growing up in a rural area, I didn't have a multitude of ready-made playmates, so my outdoor activities usually involved my bicycle. Or sometimes I played a game I made up where I would throw a ball onto the roof of one of the farm buildings, trying to hit the same height every time, just to the peak of the roof without letting it go over and down the back side.

BABA AMIN

"I wish you were my brother," Ahmadwali had told her more than once when they were growing up in Kabul.

Sometimes Lailoma wished so too. Mostly she wished she were his brother when Baba Amin visited from Wardak. Baba Amin was her mother's father. He was strict. More accurately, he was harsh. He was that way with every member of the family, but especially so with Lailoma, whom he saw as a somewhat rebellious, and certainly impertinent, child.

"Get down off the roof!" he would scream at her. "You can't play up there with the kites like a boy."

She had been taught to respect him, but she hated when he visited.

As for most Afghan boys, kites were Ahmadwali's obsession. Lailoma, his shadow, loved them too. Every day as soon as they got home from school, the boys raced up to the roofs of their houses to see if there were already kites in the air. Play was spontaneous. If one boy launched a kite, others put their kites up too. Kites of every size and color danced across the sunny blue sky. In December, January, and February—the three months of winter—when there was no school and if it wasn't freezing cold, they played more kites.

Kite "flying" in Afghanistan is really kite "fighting." The object isn't just to launch the kites, but to attract other kites and fight them, to break the string of another kite and send it dashing to the ground.

Ahmadwali and Lailoma lived in a perfect house for kite flying. The long, flat roof ran its entire length, and sometimes when Ahmadwali's string got cut, he would run to the far end to try to catch it. But usually that was to no avail. Once a kite gets away, it becomes a prize for smaller children on the ground below, who run as fast as they can after it. Whoever gets there first keeps the kite.

Ahmadwali was a skilled kite and string maker, taught by Mama (maternal uncle) Khalid, who was legendary in his string-making ability. Preparing the string was crucial, and kite makers have different methods for this most critical procedure. For Mama Khalid, and later Ahmadwali and Lailoma, it was almost a culinary event.

Mama Khalid taught Ahmadwali to use syrup he made from tree resin and ground-up glass. In the downstairs kitchen, they melted the resin over a small gas burner, and then soaked the ball of string in the syrup and ground-up glass. When it was wet through, they took the string outside and looped the ends around two trees to let it dry. The resin strengthened the string, and the glass provided its cutting ability.

"Ouch! Ouch! Ouch!" Ahmadwali occasionally screamed, grabbing at one of his fingers. Then Lailoma knew what had happened. The string had become so sharp he cut himself on it. This was a good sign, and both knew what it meant: the string was strong enough to slice through another kite's string.

Lailoma was proud of Ahmadwali. She was even prouder that he included her in this process.

"Sit here," he would tell her, motioning to a chair by the little burner as the liquid warmed. "You're in charge of letting me know when it's time to take out the string."

Occasionally, Ahmadwali made a small kite for Lailoma too.

A young girl playing in the open on the roof raised eyebrows. Even in Kabul, girls were not supposed to play out in the open, except maybe at a park when they were with their parents or several older brothers. Even more, they were not supposed to play with boys who weren't their brothers, let alone on the rooftop.

While Qurisha and Shahwali allowed Lailoma to join Ahmadwali in the kite-flying fun, others in the family weren't so tolerant, especially Baba Amin. He was quite certain Lailoma's playing on the roof doomed her—and their entire family—to a life of disgrace.

In their Wardak village, Amin had now become one of the elders, a respected man who often sat with his peers in the mosque and considered the disputes of men who came to them for advice. Sometimes the issue was marital; sometimes it had to do with paying debts or encroaching on someone's property. The elders would consider the problem at hand and produce a solution. Acutely aware of his standing in the village and that everything his family and extended family did was a reflection on him, Amin took his responsibility for their behavior very seriously.

Each time he called to say he was coming for a visit from Wardak, the message brought a round of complaints from the children—to each other, that is, not to their parents. They didn't anticipate his visit as one from a loving grandfather; to them, his visits were more like a visit to the principal's office.

"Are you happy Baba Amin is coming?" Qurisha would ask the children.

"Oh, yes," they answered. Then Ahmadwali and Lailoma would look at each other, their expressions saying the exact opposite: *Oh, no.*

When Baba Amin came, even Ahmadwali's play was restricted. Baba Amin interrogated him interminably. "What are you learning in school? Have you done your studies? I'd better not hear of you getting into trouble."

While Ahmadwali squirmed, Baba Amin's inquisition droned on and on. Sometimes, when he saw an opening, Ahmadwali managed to slip out of the room and sneak up to the roof anyway.

Not Lailoma. Her behavior was monitored even more diligently than Ahmadwali's by their grandfather. If she laughed out loud, he yelled at her.

"Stop that right now! You're a girl," he'd say sternly. "You can't laugh like that. You can't call attention to yourself like that. What will people think?

They will start talking about you, and that will be a poor reflection on me. That will be a poor reflection on our family honor."

Ahmadwali hated Baba Amin's harshness toward Lailoma almost as much as she did. Once, when Lailoma had just turned ten, she and Ahmadwali had worked diligently to make the perfect string and attach it to a new kite. The kite was a masterpiece, a beauty—red, green, bright blue, and yellow. They had just sent it soaring into the sky when they looked down and saw Baba Amin walking toward the house. His stern eyes locked on Lailoma's. Her heart sank. She didn't want to lose the kite, but she knew she had to come down off the roof or she would be in major trouble.

"Hold the string!" she shouted to Ahmadwali, shoving it into his hands before she ran downstairs and scooted into the house just ahead of Baba Amin.

"I saw you!" Baba Amin screamed at her as he stormed into the house. "I don't expect to have to keep telling you this: You can't play with the kites! You can't be up on the roof."

"Adai (mother), Baba won't let me play with the kite," Lailoma cried to Qurisha, hoping to gain her support.

"Go into the bathroom and stay there," Qurisha told Lailoma.

Qurisha knew she couldn't contradict her father, but she made an attempt to defend her daughter. Trembling, Lailoma put her ear to the door and listened as her mother pleaded her case.

"She's just a young girl," Qurisha told Baba Amin. "Let her play. She doesn't play with other boys; she's just with her brother."

Baba Amin wouldn't soften his stance. "Nothing good can come from her playing on the roof. First one neighbor boy will come, and then another. Then she's the only girl playing with the boys. She has only her brother to protect her. She will get a bad reputation, and it will be a reflection on me. It will be a reflection on our family. What will people in Wardak say? We could be ruined."

Lailoma stayed safely in the bathroom, her tears flowing as she sat on the smooth, cool concrete floor, her arms wrapped tightly around her knees. Finally, she heard her father arrive home from work.

She again pressed her ear to the bathroom door and listened as everybody said hello to her father.

"How was your day?" Shahwali asked Baba Amin.

When is he going to ask me how my day has been? she thought bitterly. *What kind of day does he think I've had? Who is going to stand up for me?*

In her heart, she knew no one, not even her father, could contradict Baba Amin.

Qurisha nodded to Shahwali, indicating by a tilt of her head that Lailoma was in the bathroom.

Shahwali opened the bathroom door to find his ten-year-old daughter sobbing. "Why are you crying?" he asked, as he hugged her.

"Baba Amin is here, and he won't let me play with Ahmadwali on the roof. He won't let me play with the kites," she said. "He's so mean. He yelled at me again. He always yells at me. He hates me. He's so mean!"

Shahwali went into the closet, changed his clothes, and came back to the bathroom. He held out his arms and hugged her as he brought her into the living room. She shielded her face with her hand and wouldn't look at Baba Amin. But her father couldn't reverse his father-in-law's decision. Even he was subject to the patriarch's stern rules.

"You know our village policy," Baba Amin yelled at his son-in-law, slapping him. "If somebody sees her on the roof, they are going to say everywhere that we saw the granddaughter of Amin playing on the roof with the boys. How are you going to answer that?"

Baba Amin yelled at everyone. He intended to keep his family above reproach. He didn't explain to the young Lailoma that his demand that she not play on the roof with the boys was his attempt to keep her safe—and, thereby, to preserve family honor.

Even later, when his sons were grown men in the army, old enough to understand right from wrong, his word was still the final word. His discipline wasn't just verbal. Sometimes it was physical. When his sons were adults, he slapped them when he felt they were out of line. They might not have liked it, but they accepted his harsh treatment as his way—and that of most patriarchs—of taking care of his family. It was his obligation. It was also his right.

But Baba Amin was a complex man. In spite of his harshness, there was no limit to what he would do to protect his family. In particular, his relationship with Mama Khalid, his fourth son, is a testament to the depth of his love.

Mama Khalid seemed to attract bad times throughout his life. In the '70s, he was an army lieutenant under President Mohammed Daoud Khan. He and the rest of his seven-person unit were stationed in the province of Helmand, part of the greater Kandahar region in the south of the country. Their job was to protect Helmand from the constant fighting among various mujahideen, opposing sects of guerrilla fighters who fought Daoud Khan's army—and each other—for control of Afghanistan. But the seven men could not hold back the mujahideen.

One of the first things the mujahideen did was to close the schools in Kandahar. Who knew what the children might learn at school? Who knew what propaganda the teachers might feed their young minds?

Since the schools were closed, as a favor to the villagers in Helmand, Mama Khalid, along with three others in his unit, quietly taught the children to read and write. A family would invite the school's former headmaster and the soldiers into their home and gather children from the area along with what books they had. "School" was in session for the afternoon.

These impromptu classes came to the attention of the mujahideen, and they took aggressive action, ambushing Mama Khalid and his three fellow soldiers. The four were captured. The mujahideen grabbed Mama Khalid and the three others by their clothing—or whatever they could hold onto—and forcibly shoved them into one room of a house they had commandeered, throwing them to the floor. Singling out Mama Khalid, they yanked him back to his feet and cuffed his hands.

"You want a lesson? Here's a lesson for you," they said. "Watch closely." Then they viciously stabbed and killed Mama Khalid's three comrades.

"Leave this pig alive, and we'll wait for the other pigs to come to rescue him," the mujahid in charge ordered his men, tipping his head toward Mama Khalid.

The "other pigs" most certainly were the school's former headmaster and the general. "When they arrive, we'll kill all three pigs at once."

Mama Khalid spent two long, sleepless nights on the floor of the room with the three corpses. Their congealing blood was everywhere. Each night he could hear as the mujahideen armed themselves and went out to find the other soldiers, especially the general, and the headmaster to ambush. But they didn't leave Mama Khalid unguarded. Two mujahideen sat outside the door around the clock.

To relieve themselves, the guards entered the room and urinated on Mama Khalid; they'd then spit on him too for good measure. At one point one of the guards grabbed Mama Khalid's hair, pushed his face into the blood of the other three, and made him lick it off the floor.

"You're not Muslim; you're a pig," they taunted him.

The guards returned every half hour to beat him with their guns, with the ends of their knives, with sticks, or with their fists. Apparently, they had no instructions to kill him at this point. They were just toying with him. Mama Khalid knew that, but their beatings were so violent he found himself hoping to be killed so the torture would end.

Late on the second night, he heard a car. He pushed himself to the window and turned around to knock on it with his hands, which were still cuffed behind his back. *If it's the army*, he thought, *they will rescue me; if it's mujahideen, they will kill me.* Either possibility was acceptable to him.

As he turned around, he lost his balance in the slippery blood and crashed to the floor where he lay for a few minutes, not having the strength to get back up immediately. Finally, he mustered the resolve to pull himself up onto his wobbly legs. He pressed his back to the unlocked window and slowly, quietly, pushed up with his legs, opening the window ever so slightly. Through the opening, he could see the car a little more clearly, and what he saw gave him a glimmer of hope. It was the army.

Three soldiers from Mama Khalid's unit overcame the guards at his door and, supporting him under his arms, helped him from the room to the safety of their car. They then returned to the room and brought out the three bodies, loading them into the car as well.

For the next three months, Mama Khalid and what was left of his unit worked to rebuild their base in Helmand. But the mujahideen attacked again. And this time they captured the general, the headmaster, and another soldier along with Mama Khalid. On the way to their headquarters, they shot the soldier, opened the car door, and pushed him out, leaving him like roadkill along the side of the road. They did the same to the headmaster.

They had other plans for Mama Khalid and the general. They took them to their headquarters, where they pummeled the pair with their fists and the butts of their guns and then separated them into adjoining cells. For two nights Mama Khalid listened in agony to their violent torture of the general—the sounds of kicking, beating, and shouting. From the general, he could hear only muffled groans.

As Mama Khalid lay on the floor, a new odor seeped into the room. *What is that?* he thought in a daze. Then he recognized the familiar smell: gasoline.

"You've been holding chalk in your hands and turning children against Islam," the mujahideen screamed at the general, referring to the makeshift school lessons. "You won't do that anymore."

Mama Khalid could see a shadow of fire outside his window, and soon the general's groans turned to screams. Around midnight on that second night, the sounds stopped. The eerie silence was unnerving. Mama Khalid didn't know if the general had passed out or died. He never found out. He knew for certain, however, that the general's hands had been destroyed. The mujahideen had been correct: even if he were alive, which was unlikely, the general's hands would never hold chalk again.

Tomorrow night will be my night, he thought. *Tomorrow they will torture me.*

Eventually word filtered back to Baba Amin that Mama Khalid was missing. Knowing the mujahideen were headquartered in Kandahar, Baba Amin began his search for his son there. He located their facility and asked the guards if they knew of Khalid.

"No," was their answer.

He gained admission to the office and inquired there about Mama Khalid. "We don't know of him," was again the answer he received.

Amin was distraught—and desperate—to find his son. He threw himself at the guards' feet; he kissed their hands.

"If he's hurt, just tell me," he pleaded with the mujahideen. "If he's dead, just tell me."

The mujahideen answered his pleas only with jeers. "Surely your son doesn't need his old baba to take care of him. Surely he can take care of himself."

As it turned out, Mama Khalid was no longer in Kandahar, but the mujahideen weren't going to share that information with Baba Amin.

The night after the general's voice went silent, it was indeed Mama Khalid's turn. But his fate was different. The mujahideen dragged Mama Khalid into a truck and drove west out of Afghanistan into Iran, where they held him hostage in a house. When daylight came, Mama Khalid began studying those around him, trying to gain an understanding of where he was and who his captors were. One face looked familiar, and Mama Khalid remembered where he had seen the man. He was someone he had known in Wardak. On that first day in Iran, their eyes met in acknowledgment, but their instincts told both men not to speak to each other. The next night, the mujahid quietly said to Mama Khalid, "I will help you, but I don't know when. Be ready, but act as if you don't know me."

The third evening, it was the Wardak mujahid's assignment to guard Mama Khalid's door. When no one was around to observe him, he left the door slightly ajar. Mama Khalid quietly seized the opportunity to escape.

Hopefully he got away too, Mama Khalid thought as he ran. *If he didn't escape, they will kill him.*

Who were the good guys and who were the bad? Who knew? Often by day men went about the business of normal living—they worked in their shops, they talked with others in the marketplace. By night some picked up arms and fought. Some never put them back down.

Knowing whom to trust was dicey. Fortunately, when Mama Khalid escaped the house in Iran, he fell in with a group of mujahideen who were returning to Afghanistan. For his safety, he had to assume he couldn't trust them—were they Sunni, as he was? Were they Shia, a different sect of Islam? A different group altogether? One thing he knew: traveling alone wouldn't be safe, so he just blended in and pretended he was part of the group.

They walked part of the way and took a car the rest of the way, all under cover. When they reached Afghan soil, they separated, each going to his own city or village. Mama Khalid headed toward Wardak. Kabul wasn't an option. Now, sneaking back into the country, he might fall under suspicion by the Afghan government, which could accuse him of being a spy sent by the mujahideen. It certainly looked that way. No one would realize he was just using the mujahideen for cover.

Meanwhile, Baba Amin continued his search for his son. When he lost hope after pleading with the mujahideen at their headquarters in Kandahar, he began to search in the surrounding desert. Maybe they had killed Mama Khalid and thrown his body under the bushes. His arms and legs became raw with scratches as he desperately looked under the prickly desert shrubs. In the process he touched the dead bodies of many who had met the fate he feared for Khalid. Later he wished he could have recovered the bodies and returned them to their families.

The Helmand River runs through the mainly desert Kandahar, supplying it with water for irrigation of the area's farming operations. In his despair, Baba Amin saw the river offering another option. He was so distraught when he didn't find Mama Khalid that he threw himself into the water. Like most Afghans, he couldn't swim. Fortunately, two men who did know how to swim were nearby and able to rescue him.

Dejected, not even able to end his life by drowning, he returned to Kabul. His arms were bloody and his skin was blistered and peeling, burned by the scorching sun. He arrived at Qurisha and Shahwali's home just two or three days after their ninth child, Susan, was born. His face was tear-stained and his hands were shaking as he leaned on his cane. Though three months later he would learn that Khalid was in Wardak and go to join him, for now he was a worn-down, tired, and broken old man.

By the time Lailoma told me this story, we were several months into our Saturday routine, and she no longer spoke in the carefully controlled voice she had used when we first started talking. Clearly the memory of Baba Amin's distress weighed heavily on her. She was still a little girl at the time but old enough to appreciate her grandfather's pain. As I was driving home that forenoon, I thought about the pain my own maternal grandparents must have felt when they lost one of their sons during World War II. We rarely, if ever, discussed the loss, but my mother kept a bundle of letters from her brother until the day she died. After my mother passed, I read through that bundle of letters, discovering a sweet young man who would have been my uncle.

KAKA ZAHER

In Qurisha and Shahwali's generation, family often represented the whole of an individual's social interaction. Although Qurisha did the daily shopping and Shahwali took the children to the park, some women and children, especially in the villages, never left the walled compounds of their homes, as Qurisha had not when she was a child. That remained true as well for some women in Lailoma and her siblings' generation. But Qurisha and Shahwali's children were lucky: life in Kabul was more progressive than life in the villages, and right next door they had cousins to play with.

Zaher, Shahwali's older brother, had eleven children from two wives. Before he moved to the house in Kabul, Kaka (paternal uncle) Zaher had lived in one of the small villages in Wardak. His first wife was a second cousin to him, and she bore him three daughters. Unfortunately, she didn't have a son. Kaka Zaher moved from the village to the northern province of Kunduz, where he bought land as well as a big house. But that was six hours away from Wardak, where he kept his wife and their three daughters.

Essentially maintaining two homes, on one of his many excursions from Wardak to Kunduz to tend to his property, Zaher fell in love with another, much younger woman. He was prosperous and handsome and her parents weren't wealthy, so they gave their daughter to him, a fairly obvious decision and a simple transaction.

Deciding to consolidate his family, he took his first wife and their daughters to live with wife number two in Kunduz. He overlooked just one important detail: he hadn't told wife number one about marrying wife number two. When his first wife arrived at the big home and saw his second wife, she screamed at her husband.

"Who is this woman in our home?" she demanded. In the back of her mind, she knew there was a strong possibility he had married the woman.

"She's my friend's wife," Zaher lied to wife number one. "She's just come to stay with you for a while until you get used to living here in Kunduz."

When the next morning, wife number one saw the other woman taking a shower, getting dressed, and applying makeup, it was clear that her stay was more than a visit.

"Who is she?" she screamed again at Zaher.

This time Zaher decided to come clean. "You cannot have a son, so I married her," Zaher confessed.

With this second wife, Zaher had four daughters and four sons. Because she bore him four sons, he treated wife number two better than he treated his first wife. He doted on the sons and daughters from wife number two. He bought them more—and better—clothes than he bought for the first wife's daughters.

Eventually Zaher rented out his land and house in Kunduz to a farmer and moved his large brood to Kabul, right next door to Qurisha and Shahwali's home. Zaher and his family lived in what was the original home on the property (and the only one actually in the deed, which Shahwali held). Shahwali had built a new home a little higher on the mountain behind it, which happened not to be on their property—a fact that either was not known by the authorities or was overlooked. The houses were separated from each other by a common wall that ran the length of the yard. From the children's point of view, Kaka Zaher was definitely their wealthy uncle.

Shahwali and Qurisha's children were close with their cousins. In fact, because the cousins were slightly older and called Shahwali "kaka," his own children called him kaka too.

The yard was filled with laughter as the cousins, all close in age, played hopscotch and volleyball together, or raced each other from the front of the yard to the back. They also played *danda*—a game a bit like baseball. For equipment, they improvised: they made a bat out of a long piece of wood and used another four-inch piece of wood as a "ball." They took their jackets off and these became scoops to catch the flying wood. Only the volleyball, which Shahwali had bought for Lailoma and which was a source of pride and joy for her, was not homemade.

Eventually, Shahwali and Zaher put a small door in the wall between the yards so the children could go back and forth without having to go outside their property. For the children, it was a happy scene.

Once a year, Zaher made the trip to Kunduz to collect money from the farm and bring it back to Kabul, where he sold furniture and appliances in a small shop. All was seemingly well in the house next door—with its eleven children, two wives, and Kaka Zaher—but at night, Lailoma would lie on her mattress and hear loud crying as Zaher beat his first wife.

First she would hear her uncle yelling, then she would hear her aunt—sometimes both of her aunts—yelling back. Then the sound of slapping and kicking. Then screaming. Then sobbing. Since Lailoma's entire family slept in the same room, others in the family must have heard it too, but no one spoke about it. For Lailoma, lying there in the dark, the experience was frightening, and so lonely. Each morning after the first wife was beaten, she came over to Qurisha and Shahwali's house covered with bruises—her legs, her back, her face—from where he had kicked her, with his shoes on.

Around four o'clock one afternoon when Lailoma was ten or eleven years old, her mother and Shaima performed their ritual of washing the patio and laying out the carpet and then the pillows for afternoon tea. Lailoma was doing one of her favorite things, playing volleyball in the yard with Ahmadwali and their cousins.

Suddenly, Kaka Zaher's second wife burst into the yard, with Kaka Zaher right behind her. "Your brother is so mean to us. He kicks us. He beats us. He won't leave us alone!" she screamed to Shahwali.

At that, Kaka Zaher proved her right. He shoved his second wife into the concrete block wall, banging her head and causing her to stumble, barely catching herself before she fell. Wife number two was no shrinking violet. When she regained her footing, she kicked him—where it hurt.

Kaka Zaher's face turned white. "You bitch!" he screamed at her. "Are you trying to kill me?"

She turned on her heels and ran back to their house.

"It hurts, but you're not going to die," Shahwali consoled his brother, giving him some water.

The next day, wife number two came over to Qurisha and Shahwali's house, declaring that Kaka Zaher wouldn't be hitting either her or the first wife again.

"How do you know? How can you be sure?" the young Lailoma asked.

"Men are very sensitive there," she explained, laughing. "If you get married and he hits you, just grab him there," she said, gesturing and making fun.

After that incident, the first and second wives presented a united front against the violence of Zaher. And he learned—somewhat—to control his rage.

He may have had a temper and been violent, but Kaka Zaher's children, his four sons and seven daughters, were each enrolled in school. He was educated, and he had lived away from Wardak long enough to realize that young women as well as young men needed an education. In Kunduz there was a school for girls, and he had enrolled his daughters in it. When he moved to Kabul, it was natural for him to enroll them in school there too. Compared to that of other families, including Lailoma's, his thinking was progressive. Of course Ahmadwali went to school, but most families didn't allow their daughters to attend. In the '70s, education for girls was a relatively new concept in Afghanistan, especially for conservative Sunni families. Qurisha had no education, nor did any of the females in her family before her. It never occurred to Shahwali to enroll Shaima in school. Instead, like most girls of her generation, Shaima stayed home to help with the cleaning, shopping, cooking, and sewing. No one taught Shaima to read and write. Who could? Not Qurisha.

As the older brother it was generally accepted that Kaka Zaher had authority over Shahwali, and he exercised it. One day when Shahwali was away from home for a few days on government business, Kaka Zaher decided that Lailoma, who had just turned seven, should attend school, so he took it upon himself to enroll her. When Shahwali came home, Qurisha trembled, so afraid to tell him that Lailoma was now going to school. She couldn't bring herself to even broach the subject. Then the phone rang. It was Kaka Zaher. Qurisha answered it.

"Did you tell Shahwali that Lailoma is in school?" he asked in a voice that demanded an answer.

"No," she answered nervously.

"Give the phone to Shahwali," Kaka Zaher barked.

In very clear terms, Kaka Zaher told Shahwali that enrolling Lailoma in school was his idea, not Qurisha's. "I enrolled your daughter Lailoma in school, and she is there right now," he said. "Don't yell at Qurisha. I did this. This was my decision. I did it. It's not Qurisha's fault, and it's not Lailoma's problem."

Animated arguing followed. Shahwali screamed at his brother. "The whole village will point at me, calling me a bad father for putting a girl in school," he yelled.

Although they lived in Kabul, what the villagers in Wardak thought about them was still important to them. But the older brother Zaher stood by his decision. "If the people in Wardak yell at you, they will have to answer to me. Tell them the truth: I did it."

Later, as Lailoma brought her reports home from school, Shahwali saw that she was very bright and a quick learner, and he took her education seriously. He checked to see if her homework was completed daily, provided the necessary uniform, books, and paper, and was proud that she was a good student. After Lailoma, her four younger sisters all attended school along with Kaka Zaher's children.

At first, Lailoma and her girl cousins were something of an oddity. Sometimes when the cousins played at the park, other kids would point at them and say, "There are the girls who go to school."

But the comments never bothered Lailoma. She and her cousins loved school so much they played "school" at home. Once, using a found piece of charcoal, they pretended the living room wall was a blackboard—or maybe it was the original "white board." Qurisha was furious.

"What have you done? Why did you mark up the wall? Go get some water and clean it!"

They made a good effort, but Qurisha ended up scrubbing the wall, not trusting that the children could actually get it clean.

Lailoma learned to cook, clean, and sew along with Shaima, but school was a priority and her mother only made her perform these tasks when she had no homework.

In addition to raising eight children, making two or three trips to the market daily, cooking, and keeping the house clean, Qurisha took in sewing to make a little extra money, and she saved the leftover pieces of fabric in a bag. Lailoma, her sisters, and her girl cousins loved to play house and make little dolls from the scraps of fabric, stuffing the dolls' bodies with cotton and forming their faces with thread. For hair, they used black thread.

At first they sewed only by hand, not allowed yet to operate their mother's hand-crank sewing machine. "Make sure you don't lose the needle," Qurisha warned. "Needles are expensive, and so is thread. Don't waste them!"

Later she taught the girls to operate the handwheel slowly and cautiously, guiding the fabric carefully through the machine.

Life was different for Shaima. While Lailoma—and every sibling, boy or girl, after her—went to school and learned skills that would help them navigate the modern world, Shaima stayed home with her mother. In the winter, from the time Shaima was very young, she crocheted, helping her mother make things for Lailoma and her cousins. To Shaima, Lailoma and her other sisters were the oddities. She didn't realize the doors that would open for them and not for her. She didn't realize until many years later that the book skills they were learning would eventually become survival skills.

SCHOOL DAYS

"Lailoma, wake up!" Her mother's hand gently rocked her shoulder. "Get out of bed! It's time to eat your breakfast and get ready for school."

Lailoma's inner clock told her both of these events should happen much later. She hated getting out of bed in the morning, but she liked school, and she knew Ahmadwali and her cousins would be waiting to walk down the dusty path behind their home toward the two-story concrete elementary school about twenty minutes away.

Breakfast, as always, consisted of sweetened tea and naan. Oh, how Lailoma would have loved to have milk with her bread, but that never happened. Milk was expensive, especially in Kabul. The villages and farms were so far away, and transportation was spotty. Even if milk arrived in the city on a consistent basis, most people didn't have refrigeration. "Oh, Adai, please buy milk for breakfast," Lailoma wanted to plead to her mother, but she held back. While she dreamed of milk, she knew it wasn't a possibility.

Attending school came with an additional set of expenses for the family: books, uniforms, pencils. Most classrooms had one wall painted black for a blackboard—if not, usually there was a small chalkboard in the room. Twice each month each student contributed a small amount of money for chalk.

Happy-go-lucky, easygoing Ahmadwali was ten when Lailoma started school. Ahmadwali traveled light. Sometimes he carried a notebook in his hand or in his back pocket, but he didn't take his books and supplies home from school. Taking them home meant he would just have to carry them back the next day. If he got behind in his homework, with his winning personality he could often coerce a classmate to let him copy his or her finished assignments. Lailoma, on the other hand, took her schoolwork seriously right from the first day. She carried her schoolwork, books, and pencils in a bag her father made for her from Persian carpet. Throughout elementary school she carried the same bag, slinging it crossbody over her left shoulder.

Sometimes while she sat with her thirty-five or more classmates on the concrete floor of the schoolroom, there would be a tap on the door. Ahmadwali needed something.

"Lailoma, do you have a pencil I can use?"

Lailoma would feel around the bottom of the Persian carpetbag and usually come up with an extra pencil.

Finally, noon would arrive and it was time to go home for the day. As they reversed their morning walk, the smells of cooking food wafted from the homes they passed—meat, kebabs, vegetables. Their mouths watered at the wonderful smells. Oh, they were so hungry by then. The breakfast of sweetened tea and naan had been hours earlier.

"I hope Adai is making kebabs!" Lailoma might say.

"Or rice pudding with raisins," Ahmadwali would add.

At their home, Qurisha and Shaima were cooking, but generally there was nothing elaborate and usually no kebabs or meat of any kind. Almost always there was only one dish, though their mother was creative and prepared something different each day. By now their father had many mouths to feed and keeping Lailoma and Ahmadwali stocked with school supplies pressed the family's finances.

So lunch for them might be a cooked vegetable. Or soup with a little rice, ground lamb, beef, or chicken. Sometimes their mother chopped onions and fried them with potatoes in oil. The smell drifted out the windows to welcome Lailoma and Ahmadwali home. That was a simple but tasty dish when she didn't have a great supply of food in the house. Qurisha might also combine the fried onions and potatoes with yogurt and naan—or just with naan—and it was delicious. If they had rice, they ate that with the onions and potatoes.

By noon, Ahmadwali was so hungry he would eat anything; sometimes Lailoma was pickier. But her mother might have leftover chicken to give her or just cook an egg for her. Lailoma loved eggs, and she had her own source right downstairs! Each child either ate his or her own chicken's eggs, or sold them for a little extra money. For that reason, she didn't want to eat too many eggs, but if she didn't like what her mother and Shaima made for lunch, she had an option.

ARIZONA, 2013

"Pizza tonight!" Lailoma announced to Maiwand as she entered the condo through the patio door into their living room. "It will be here by the time you've showered."

Maiwand, still in his workout clothes and sweaty from weight lifting, grinned. Like his mother, he had become an American. Like Maiwand, Lailoma had become Americanized.

Because Lailoma called her before she ordered the pizza on the way home from her award-winning day at work, Qurisha had already resigned herself to the fact that there wouldn't be lamb on this night, but she clearly wasn't quite as happy as Maiwand. Nevertheless, she took the large square dastarkhan off the kitchen counter and spread it out on the burgundy area rug in front of the fifty-five-inch big-screen television in the living room. Then she went into the kitchen to make tea. Bigger is better, Maiwand had told Lailoma when they had shopped for the TV.

Lailoma made a beeline for the upstairs bedroom she shared with her mother and changed from her conservative black pants and jacket into the pajama pants and T-shirt she typically wore around the condo. Yes, she was tired, but what a big day it had been. She couldn't wait to share the news of her Neiman Marcus Best award with Maiwand and her mother.

"Sit at the table tonight," Maiwand said to his mother and grandmother, whose insistence on sitting on the floor to eat made him impatient. Sometimes he joined them, but he didn't feel like it tonight. Lailoma wanted her mother to be happy and so she always obliged her. The doorbell rang. "Food's here!" he called out.

Lailoma had begun to anticipate the smell of warm pizza nearly as eagerly as Maiwand. Maiwand's first experience with pizza came from the elementary school cafeteria when he first arrived in America at age nine. As for most young children, it was love at first bite. "Mamo," he would call to her enthusiastically when he burst into the apartment from school on pizza day, "we had pizza today! It was so good!"

Lailoma had been a little more cautious, but with Maiwand's urging and a discount coupon a fellow refugee gave her for Domino's Pizza, she learned to enjoy it almost as much as Maiwand did.

"What kind did you order?" he asked, beginning to open the lid.

"Just cheese," Lailoma replied.

"Ah, Mamo," Maiwand started to protest, but then he saw that she was teasing.

"OK. It's mostly mushrooms and onion, but I had them leave a couple of pieces plain."

She set the pizza box in the middle of the dastarkhan and lowered her tired body to sit across from her mother on the floor. Maiwand eagerly put the largest two pieces—with mushrooms—on his plate and took a seat at the table. Lailoma put one of the plain cheese pieces on a plate for her mother and one on a plate for herself.

After prayer, Lailoma ate, but her mother just pushed her pizza around on her plate. Finally, Qurisha stood up and went to the kitchen. Within a couple of minutes, she returned with an egg she had boiled earlier in the day. The reality of having an egg whenever she wanted—without even owning chickens—was still a remarkable phenomenon to Qurisha.

"How was your day, Adai?" Lailoma asked as they ate.

"Fine," her mother replied in Pashto.

Since she had joined Lailoma and Maiwand in the United States earlier that year, Qurisha's activities were limited, and her answer was always the same.

She didn't watch much television because she didn't understand English well, but she knew about the Kardashians and learned a few words from the shows. Even if she had had books in Pashto, she didn't know how to read. When she left the condo, occasionally she walked around the pond at the nearby park, watching people fishing or the ducks as they swam in the clear water. Sometimes she sat on a bench to watch golf at the course within walking distance of Lailoma's condo. She actually made a friend while she was watching there, an older man, who suffered with symptoms similar to Parkinson's. He spoke no Pashto, and her English was limited, but somehow they communicated and she looked forward to their visits at the golf course.

"How was your test?" Lailoma asked, turning to Maiwand.

He grinned. "Yes! An A in physiology! After my exam tomorrow, this semester is over."

"Have you studied for it?"

"Yes, Mamo."

Maiwand was a good student and Lailoma knew she didn't need to ask these questions, but she was his mamo. Maiwand had an eye toward medical school—sports medicine—and she badly wanted him to get in.

"How was your day, Mamo?" Maiwand asked, turning to Lailoma. Distracted by the pizza, neither Qurisha nor Maiwand had noticed the flowers she put in a vase on the coffee table.

Though Maiwand had asked the question in English, Lailoma responded in Pashto so her mother could understand the conversation. Her eyes shining, Lailoma told them about her award, how excited and nervous she was to stand up in front of everyone to receive it, and how proud she was. But now she was tired.

"I'm just going to lie down on the couch for a little nap," she said. "If I'm not awake by nine, wake me up. I have a lot to finish tonight. Mrs. Peters is coming by tomorrow morning to pick up her jacket before I leave for work."

"All you do is work," her mother complained. "I want you to sit and talk with me. I'm lonely. I have no one to talk to. I might as well go be with the rest of the family in Pakistan."

"Adai, in America, everyone works," Lailoma responded, a little irritation revealed in her voice. "All of you think that just because we're here, we automatically have lots of money. Yes, people here have a lot, but they have to work for it. That's how we have this condo. That's how we have this pretty furniture. That's how we have good food and a nice car." Sometimes her patience with Qurisha ran thin.

Lailoma woke up from her nap at about nine fifteen and headed upstairs to finish the extensive alterations on the designer jacket Mrs. Peters had bought two sizes too large because it was on sale.

"I'm going to study with John," Maiwand called to her.

Qurisha retired to the patio, her long fingers wrapped around a Marlboro.

Lailoma settled in front of the industrial sewing machine she had bought used from her former employer. She threaded it with navy blue thread that matched the fabric of the jacket and began to sew the back darts and side seams where she had pinned them on Mrs. Peters. Then she reworked the shoulder seams.

Two hours later she began the laborious job of replacing the elaborate beadwork that had been disrupted to alter the jacket. By two thirty in the morning she was finished, a little earlier than on some mornings. She steamed the jacket, hung it up, and lay down on the floor—not wanting to disturb her mother by going into the bedroom they shared—to snatch what sleep she could before it was time to get up for another day at work.

At seven the next morning when the alarm went off, Lailoma got up, quickly showered, dressed in her black pants and jacket with a fresh blouse, and put on a touch of makeup. By seven forty-five she was downstairs making a pot of tea with cardamom for breakfast. Her stomach hurt again, as it often did, perhaps from stress, so she just ate a little bread with her tea. Costco, it turned out, sold pretty good naan.

Where is Mrs. Peters? she wondered as the clock approached eight thirty. She had promised to be there by eight o'clock.

She had met Mrs. Peters at a bridal shop where she moonlighted in the evenings when she didn't work late at Neiman Marcus. She didn't know her well enough to know if she would arrive on time so she wouldn't be late for work. Finally, there was a knock. It was 8:40.

"Sorry I'm late," Mrs. Peters said, without offering a reason.

"It's OK." Lailoma said patiently. "Let's just try this on so we can be sure it's right."

At 8:50 she got into her car for the eight-minute drive to the store. Hopefully, there wouldn't be any traffic delays on the way.

The day had gotten off to an iffy start, but at least the extra money from Mrs. Peters's alterations would help toward the monthly expenses. Often when we met, she seemed tired. I knew she worked into the early morning hours almost daily. Sending six hundred dollars each month to Ahmadwali to help him support the family in Pakistan definitely took its toll on both her energy and her budget, but if she failed to send it, how would they pay for even the basics—rent, food, school tuition and supplies for the children, and any necessary medical supplies? She could survive on just a few hours' sleep each night if it would help her extended family.

CHAPTER 3

KABUL, 1979

Kabul is thought to have been established between 2000 BCE and 1500 BCE, and since 1776 it has served as the capital of Afghanistan. Throughout Afghan history, tribal conflict has threatened government stability, but there were years of relative peace and progress, particularly during the forty-year reign of King Mohammed Zahir Shah. Shah's rule lasted from 1933 until 1973, when it ended in a bloodless coup. Relative peace and prosperity also existed when President Mohammed Daoud Khan, who had been prime minister under Shah, took over in 1973. Khan did away with the monarchy and was popular, especially among the Pashtun majority. Under Khan's government, an electric trolley-bus system provided public transportation across the city for the first time. The roads were good and the parks were well-maintained, as were ancient monuments that reflected the many cultures that had influenced Afghanistan, a country situated between Pakistan to the east, Iran to the west, and the Soviet Union to the north (before its breakup in 1991, when it became Turkmenistan to the northwest and Uzbekistan to the north in central Asia).

As president, Khan instituted a republic and was known for his progressive policies, which emphasized education and improving the rights of women. He sought to remove Communists from his government and as he shifted away from the Soviets, he looked to Islamic nations and the West for aid. The progress and reform were slow, however, and frustrated the Western-educated upper class and Russian-trained army officers, who were accustomed to a more aristocratic lifestyle than he was able to achieve. Dissatisfaction ultimately led to the Saur Revolution on April 27 and 28, 1978. The People's Democratic

Party Army, led by Nur Muhammad Taraki as general secretary of the People's Democratic Party, killed Khan, his family, and many of his supporters.

Taraki then assumed the presidency and the position of prime minister. Under his lead, the country again patterned itself after the Soviet Union. Private businesses were nationalized and education was modified to be more Soviet. In reaction to Taraki's secular government, rural guerrillas (mujahideen) took up arms in the name of Islam.

None of this spelled stability for Afghanistan. In September 1979, Deputy Prime Minister Hafizullah Amin, who had been one of the main organizers of the Saur Revolution, seized power during a palace shootout in which Taraki was killed. But Amin's tenure as leader was short-lived. Just three months later, in December 1979, he was assassinated by the Soviets.

Lailoma was eight years old and in second grade at the time. Her days had revolved around flying kites (when Baba Amin wasn't in Kabul), footraces with her cousins, picnics with her family, and homework. But even a child could sense there were changes afoot. The carefree days of walking with cousins and other neighborhood kids, talking and laughing, making fun of neighbors in the surrounding houses, and kicking stones along the dusty roads were now gone. The atmosphere seemed heavier, more serious. Another revolution had started.

The Soviets invaded Kabul on December 24, 1979. From the beginning of the Soviet occupation, thousands of armed soldiers (some estimates indicate as many as thirty thousand soldiers) and tanks flooded the streets. Shahwali now accompanied Lailoma, Ahmadwali, and their cousins on the morning walk to school, and he returned to the school at noon to walk them home.

On the third day of the revolution, December 26, Lailoma came home from school and sensed that something was different. Her mother was nine months pregnant, and all signs were that it was time for the baby to be born. Qurisha was worried because, except for when Shaima was born, her mother had traveled from Wardak to help her deliver all of her children. This time all the streets in Kabul were closed and the trip from the village wasn't even a remote possibility.

Amid the chaos created by the removal of Taraki from power, Hafizullah Amin's short reign and sudden assassination, and the arrival of the Soviet army, Sonita was to be born. She would be Qurisha's seventh child and Lailoma's third sister.

Outside there were tanks in the streets and planes in the sky on their way from one mountain to another to secure Kabul. Flying low, they created a strong, hot, smelly wind that blew in the faces of those who dared to step outside.

While it was common to give birth at home, most expectant mothers had a special woman—a daiee or a relative—with them to help. This time, Qurisha was on her own, so to prepare she gathered the things she would need—a new razor blade, thread to tie the umbilical cord, clean bandages, clothes for the baby, and a bar of soap to wash the newborn. She took these items to the downstairs bathroom, which, thankfully, Shahwali had by then connected to the rest of the house, and put these supplies, along with two large cooking pots, on the steps that led to the top of the two tall water drums in the room.

"Fill both pots with water," she instructed Shaima, "and take them down to the kitchen so you can heat the water when it's time."

Shaima didn't know why they needed hot water, but she quickly took first one pot and then the other up the steps to the water drums, filling each and carefully carrying it back down. Then Shaima and Lailoma each took a pot to the kitchen and set it on the stove.

Lailoma knew her mother was in a lot of pain but, at eight years old, couldn't understand the intricacies of childbirth. Her mother couldn't be still. She was in and out of the bathroom, walking in the yard, then stopping to hold her back and stomach, sometimes crying out. Then she would start walking again. Her only help—Shaima and Lailoma—stayed by her side. Shaima was sixteen. Neither knew the first thing about delivering a baby.

"What's wrong?" Lailoma asked Shaima. "Why is Adai so upset? Why does she hurt so much?"

Both girls were scared.

"Ana isn't here," Shaima said, more than a little panicked. "Ana always comes to help. What are we going to do?"

Their father was in the upstairs living room. Delivering babies was women's work. But he kept in touch by calling down the stairs. "What's going on? How is your mother? What's she doing?"

"She's walking! She's in terrible pain!" Lailoma called back upstairs.

Really, she didn't know what to say. The afternoon wore on in agonizingly slow fashion. Kaka Zaher and his two wives lived right next door, and the wives certainly would have known how to help Qurisha, but she didn't want their help.

"No, they can't be here!" she insisted to Shaima, when Shaima suggested she go get them. "I want this child to be born quickly!"

That line of thinking didn't make much sense to either Shaima or Lailoma, but Qurisha was adamant about not having them help her. She believed, as every woman in their community did, that when people enter and leave the house, they take the pregnant woman's labor pains with them. That may sound like a good thing, but it also meant her labor would slow down and the birth of the baby would be delayed. Better to stick it out without outside help. In this case, pain was a good thing.

In spite of the impending birth, the rest of the family still needed to be fed. Shaima prepared shola rice, a traditional Afghan food, carefully soaking and parboiling it before draining and steaming it. After pouring the soft, fluffy short-grain shola rice onto a platter, she used a serving spoon to make a hole for yogurt. Then she poured a ground beef sauce she had made over the shola. As she served the dish to the rest of the family, she dipped each spoonful in the yogurt before placing it on the plates. Even with the army outside the walls of their home, fighter jets overhead, and Qurisha walking the yard in labor, Shaima served the meal with great care. The family dug into their food enthusiastically, scooping it up with their naan and eating the rice with great relish.

Only Shaima, Shahwali, and Lailoma knew Qurisha was going to give birth. Ahmadwali and the younger siblings had no idea of the drama in the yard and downstairs bathroom.

"Why doesn't Adai eat?" Ahmadwali asked. "Is she sick? Did she have a fight with Father?"

"No, there was no fight!" Lailoma answered him sharply. "Mother is crying for Mama Fazel," she said, improvising. Her uncle had recently joined the Afghan army to fight against the Russians. "She's worried he might be killed."

Her explanation must have satisfied Ahmadwali because he stopped questioning her.

After dinner Shaima and Lailoma gathered the platter and individual plates and took them downstairs to the kitchen. As Shaima washed the dishes, Lailoma made tea, carefully putting the hot pot along with a cup and saucer on a tray to carry up to their father. By 10:30 p.m. Ahmadwali, Naim, and Laila were fast asleep on their mattresses for the night.

Qurisha called for Shaima and Lailoma to set water to boil and as soon as it boiled to bring it and a little rug—which she would sit on to have the baby—to the bathroom. She then instructed Lailoma to bring in a cement block from the yard.

"Why is she asking me for that?" Lailoma asked Shaima.

Shaima looked as baffled as Lailoma was. "Just bring it."

With the block in place, Qurisha then directed Shaima to wash it.

Lailoma pelted her mother with questions. "What is the block for? Why do we need a razor blade? Why do we need hot water?"

Qurisha explained her requests to her daughters as she gave them—to a point. Finally, she sat down on the cement block and turned to Shaima.

"Sit behind me," she said, "and hold my back down low."

Then she turned to Lailoma. "Leave the room."

With her ear pressed against the closed door, Lailoma soon heard the cry of a baby. When she went back into the bathroom, her mother used the fresh razor blade to cut the cord and tie it off on the baby. The other end she wrapped around her toe to hold it until the afterbirth was delivered.

It was all astonishing to Lailoma, but her mother seemed to know exactly what she was doing. After all, this was her seventh birth and all of Qurisha's children were born at home.

Using the clean cloths she washed her new baby girl with the soap and warm water, letting Lailoma help. Then she wrapped the newborn in a towel and gave her to Lailoma to take to her father. If Qurisha had gone to the hospital or had a daiee, a nurse or the daiee would have delivered the news of whether the baby was a boy or a girl to Shahwali, who would have been in the waiting room. If a boy was born, Shahwali would have given presents to the nurse or daiee. If a girl was born, he would have tipped the nurse but nothing else. A boy was more cause to celebrate. However, when Lailoma handed him his newborn daughter, he was ecstatic.

"Who do we have here?" her father asked, when Lailoma came up the stairs carefully holding the precious bundle.

"A baby sister," Lailoma said, still in wonderment at all she had witnessed.

He called to his other children. "Ahmadwali! Naim! Laila! Wake up! You have a new sister!"

By the time Lailoma went back into the bathroom, her mother was folding the placenta into a clean cloth. "Go give this to your father," she instructed Lailoma. "He will put it into the garbage."

Because no other family was around, Shaima, Ahmadwali, Lailoma, Naim, and Laila were allowed to name their new sister. They chose the name Sonita, a popular name at the time. Shahwali didn't object, so that was that.

Lailoma climbed the stairs to the top of one of the water drums in the bathroom and used a green marker to write Sonita's birthday on the ceiling. She and her siblings didn't know the exact days on which they had been born, but they didn't want to forget Sonita's birthday.

The next day, December 27, 1979, the Soviets promoted the communist revolutionary and politician Babrak Karmal to leadership as chairman of the Revolutionary Council and chairman of the Council of Ministers.

ARIZONA, 2010

"Do you know what day today is?" Maiwand texted Lailoma in the spring of his first year at the local community college.

What is today? Did I forget to do something? she thought.

"No. What day is it?" she typed.

"Today is February 16. Wasn't yesterday my birthday?" he texted back. "You forgot my birthday!"

Of course, Lailoma knew when her son's birthday was, even though she didn't know the exact date of her own birthday. Afghan calendars bear no resemblance to the Gregorian calendar on which most of the world keeps time. The country has its own solar calendar, which counts years from when Mohammed migrated from Mecca to Medina. Other Islamic countries use their own version of the same calendar.

When Sonita was born, Lailoma had written the date on the bathroom ceiling. No one had recorded Lailoma's birthday. To keep track of the current year, Lailoma related the year to how old she was when Maiwand was born in 1991, when she left Afghanistan in 1996, and when she arrived in America i n 2000.

Especially during the long years of fighting from the 1980s on, the Afghan government didn't have a way to track births. For that matter, there were no ID cards and very few driver's licenses. This lack of recordkeeping extends back centuries. Additionally, historically home births were not recorded regularly and many Afghans don't use a surname. As such, keeping any sort of national registry would be a bureaucratic nightmare. As refugees such as Lailoma came to the United States, they were required to list their birthdates. While January 1 isn't New Year's Day in Afghanistan, it became nearly everyone's birthday, some think because it was easy to remember.

Maiwand was among the lucky: Lailoma made certain he knew his birthday. Because of the calendar difference, had they remained in Afghanistan, they would have celebrated his birthday on March 27. In the United States, his birthday is in February. Especially after they arrived in America, she celebrated the day with Maiwand as most Americans do—with toys and cake, and as he got older, with gifts of new clothes. But, yes, the year he turned nineteen, he good-naturedly reminded his mother of the day. She was so busy that she had forgotten to wish him a happy birthday.

KABUL, 1979 TO 1989

A day or two after Sonita was born, about five days after the Soviets arrived, the tanks left the area. The soldiers were gone, and the Soviet fighter jets no longer flew low overhead. A semblance of normalcy returned—if only for a brief while. What had happened politically—the Soviets assuming control of Kabul—was of less interest to the children than the fact that they could once again walk to school safely with their cousins and friends. Once again they could play in the yard without the ugly hot wind created by the planes.

Prior to 1979, Afghanistan had already been among the world's poorest countries. When the Soviets arrived that year, things went from bad to worse. Shahwali's friends warned him that the Russians would decimate their country. "They aren't here to help us. They are here to help themselves," they warned. But Shahwali hadn't believed them.

The Russians claimed they wanted to build up Afghanistan when they invaded Kabul, and for a short while things actually seemed better, especially for women, as the Russians encouraged education for both genders. But in the end, Shahwali's friends were right: Russia rained terror on families, schools, and the government.

The ten-year conflict between the Soviet-allied government and mujahideen from the country's rural villages began in 1979 when Lailoma was in second grade, the year Sonita was born, and Shahwali's friends' prophetic words were soon realized. In the countryside, the Soviets shot farmers in their fields. Who knew who was who? The farmers wore the same style clothing as the jihadis—could they be jihadis in hiding? Crops were lost because crucial irrigation systems were destroyed by bombing. Soviet or government troops shot livestock. The mountains became dotted with white—the robes and turbans of farmers who fled with their families for safety. Often they died there.

"Our daughters and wives won't be safe," Shahwali's friends had told him.

They were right. Soldiers stormed villages and raped the young girls. Sometimes they took them back to the army base to rape them and then left them in the desert. Or they might see an attractive woman or young girl during the day, take note of where she lived, and return at night to pull her from her home and take her to the army base, sometimes keeping her there for two or three days. They made the girls dance for them, and then they raped them. They might take them back to their homes, but just as often, they abandoned them on the streets. Even if the soldiers returned the young women, many families considered them disgraced and wouldn't take their daughters back. Some of the young women became homeless. Some turned to prostitution in Kabul, or a jihadi killed them because they had been with another man. Lailoma recalls stories of some young women choosing death by throwing themselves from a window to avoid the humiliation.

Kabul broke down as many public services were closed. Electricity and running water became sporadic. As a consequence of the poor maintenance and bombing of the electric network, the popular trolley-bus service was terminated.

During this time, no one was truly safe. Upward of a million civilians in addition to Afghan troops are estimated to have lost their lives as a direct result of the Soviet invasion. Thousands of prisoners—civilian, military, political—were executed. For those who could leave—five million to ten million fled—Pakistan and Iraq offered refuge. By 1988 more than three million Afghans were housed in Pakistan alone.

For the several years that Babrak Karmal was in power, the walk to school was not disrupted. The big change for Lailoma was the timing of her school day. Because the building couldn't accommodate everyone at once, the students were on a staggered schedule. The younger children attended in the morning, leaving at noon, and the older students arrived at noon and were dismissed at six in the evening. Now, thankfully, since Lailoma hated to get out of bed in the morning, she ate her lunch at eleven, before she went to school. By midafternoon, most of the students were hungry. If Lailoma had a piece of naan and tea with sugar, she would take it for a snack during break. When she didn't have anything to take for a snack, the afternoon dragged on. Then, she just waited until dinnertime to eat. During these middle school years, the classroom was coed, and some of Lailoma's male classmates became like brothers to her. They played together at school, studied together, and helped each other with their homework.

Karmal had introduced several reforms, among them amnesty for previous political prisoners, but by 1986, his policy failures displeased the Soviets and they removed him from power, replacing him with Mohammad Najibullah as secretary general of the People's Democratic Party of Afghanistan. At the time, Lailoma and Ahmadwali were in high school. Except for the constant whir of rockets overhead as the rivaling mujahideen tried to overthrow Najibullah, life went on as usual.

The camaraderie Lailoma had experienced with her male classmates in middle school came to a screeching halt when she reached high school, which was not coed. Lailoma and her classmates wore their black skirts and pantyhose with a blue denim shirt and long white scarf. Some of the girls put the scarf on their heads as they were supposed to, but most, including the free-spirited Lailoma, just tied it around their necks, especially when they were away from the watchful eyes of their parents. Ahmadwali and his classmates chose whatever color pants they wanted, but their shirts were denim like those of the girls, and they also sported white ties.

In the late '70s and early '80s, females were allowed to work outside the home, and some were teachers. Lailoma and her girlfriends were awestruck by their female teachers. They wore professional clothing—unlike their mothers and aunts, who were at home in their shapeless dresses. Like the students, teachers had a uniform that was specific to the school in which they taught. In Lailoma's school, the women wore long olive-green coat-style dresses. And they wore makeup. To their teenage students, they were beautiful.

In each classroom there were thirty to forty students, all dressed alike, some sitting on chairs and others on the floor because there weren't enough seats. Lailoma and her friends tried to get to school early so they could sneak a chair from another classroom into theirs. Especially when exam time rolled around, nobody wanted to be stuck with their papers spread out on the floor.

While Lailoma and Ahmadwali were in high school scrounging for chairs to sit on as they took their exams, Qurisha often stood by her window looking toward their schools. Even though their home was only two streets up the mountain on which they lived, it was elevated enough that she could see most of the area below. Higher on the mountain were more houses, but below them were shopping areas, mosques, office buildings, and schools. Sometimes she would see smoke rising above a particular area, causing her to fret for the rest of the afternoon that one of the schools had been hit by a rocket.

Qurisha had other worries as well. Buying two or three sets of uniforms for each student to have a fresh one daily wasn't in the budget for many families, including theirs. By now she and Shahwali had several children in school, so Qurisha washed their shirts by hand when the children got home, or sometimes she just rinsed them and hung them out to dry, not using detergent every day to save money.

The children thrived in school. Ahmadwali was a whiz at history and geography, and Lailoma loved anything science-related, especially chemistry and biology. If she found a frog in the park, she would scoop it up and take it to school so she and her classmates could dissect it. The once-a-week chemistry lab was her favorite.

From the first grade through her high school graduation, Lailoma was one of a trio of Lailomas, best friends who were inseparable. Their teachers referred to them as the three musketeers. They went to each other's houses after school to do their homework together. They listened to the romantic songs of Ahmad Zahir on the radio or a cassette player, and sometimes played volleyball in the yard. When one of them was sad, they cried together. If the home economics teacher gave them a cooking assignment for the next week, they cooked together. Sometimes they sewed together. Their circle of friends expanded in high school to include classmates Nabila and Salma. All of these young women were good students, but especially the three Lailomas.

In their high school classroom, students were seated in three long rows that extended from the front of the room to the back. On test day, to discourage cheating, each row was given a different version of the exam. At the front of each row sat the students with the best grades. The rest of the class loved it when the Lailomas sat at the front, which was fairly often, as the three generous musketeers nudged their papers to the side of their desktops or sometimes, when the teacher left the room, they held them up as if they were reading them, giving the students behind them an opportunity to see their answers. When the teacher returned, they quickly lowered their papers. If she left the room again, they held them up again.

Meanwhile, the streets were becoming increasingly chaotic. In 1988, when Lailoma and her peers were sixteen and seventeen years old, with so much resistance from the mujahideen, the Soviet troops began to withdraw. Within a year, the Soviets had pulled out of Afghanistan entirely, but they had left behind a country primed for civil war. Rival mujahideen factions fought each other outside Kabul.

When the militant mujahideen groups, loosely united but still at odds, came into Kabul, they cut the electricity across the city. For Lailoma and her siblings, cousins, and friends, that meant studying by candlelight or, in Lailoma's family, by their one small gas lamp. Qurisha and Shaima sometimes cooked by candlelight. These activities had to be done quickly to save the candle or the gas for the next time. A slender little candle lasted about a half hour, and while less expensive than gas, it was still pricey. *Study faster and harder* became Lailoma's mantra.

CHAPTER 4
AN AFGHAN FRIEND, 1988

In a place where some women rarely leave their homes or the extended compound where they live surrounded by family, friendships with other women are hard to come by. With so many languages and dialects of languages, language itself also creates a barrier to making friends. Lailoma's family spoke Pashto, the national language spoken primarily in the eastern, southern, and southwestern parts of the country, but nearly half of the population, especially in the city, spoke Farsi (later called Dari).

The fact that school lessons were taught in Farsi meant that Lailoma and her siblings learned Farsi and were able to make friends outside the circle of their siblings and cousins. As a result, school was a game changer for their social lives, and Lailoma treasured her friendships and cared greatly for each of her girlfriends. Unfortunately, things didn't turn out well for all of them.

Among her closest friends, Salma was everything a girl could want to be. She was beautiful and smart, and her family was wealthy. They owned a car long before other families did. In school, when she went to the little room that served as a cafeteria, she was able to purchase her lunch—something the others never could afford to do. Like Lailoma, if they had it, the other students snacked on a piece of naan they brought from home. But Salma would buy a hamburger on pita bread with tomato, cilantro, and onion, or she might buy a piece of fruit or a container of milk. Her friends looked at these luxuries with a bit of yearning.

Salma's parents selected a wealthy young man for her to marry, but—unintentionally and against all the rules—she caught the eye of a young man named Fazel. Fazel attended the same boys' school as Ahmadwali, just down the street from the girls' school.

When both schools let out at 6 p.m., the teens had sly opportunities to chat with each other, especially if they just "happened" to miss the bus to take them home. Lailoma would talk to the boys occasionally, but mostly fear held her back. If Ahmadwali saw her, even though the two siblings were close, he might tell their parents, who would be embarrassed by such scandalous behavior. Lailoma would be in deep trouble.

That Fazel happened to notice Salma isn't hard to understand. Her thick brown hair hung in glossy curls down to her waist. The girls were supposed to tie their hair back with their white school scarves, but Salma rarely did. And sometimes instead of wearing her uniform to school, she dressed in beautiful, stylish clothing her father bought for her on one of his many international business trips. She carried pricey handbags made in Germany, Japan, and France. Her black school shoes were new, and expensive. If the teacher reprimanded her, her parents complained. Beautiful, rich Salma lived life on her terms—exquisitely dressed and lovingly pampered.

Fazel was lovestruck, crazy in love with Salma. She didn't return his affection and gave him no encouragement, if for no other reason than that his family was poor. And, of course, she was already engaged. Fazel's parents operated a bakery where women could take the bread dough they made at home to be baked. He was not the sort of young man Salma wanted to be with, and he certainly was not what her parents envisioned for her.

Ultimately, lovesick Fazel's obsession with Salma nearly destroyed her life. Almost every day as soon as he saw Salma board the bus after school, he hopped onto his rickety bicycle and followed the bus to her home. When he learned Salma was engaged, he stalked her, warning her that he might kidnap her. Salma rarely was able to walk home for fear of an encounter with him. While other girls "accidentally" missed the bus with the thought that they might talk with some of the boys, Salma almost always rode the bus, only walking when other students were around to walk with her. Her goal was to avoid any risk of impropriety—and Fazel. At night he lurked in the yard around her house or just outside the compound walls. Somehow Salma's parents didn't know what he was doing, and if Salma knew, she didn't tell them for fear they would think it was her fault.

One day after the school bus dropped her off in front of her home in the evening, Fazel accosted Salma.

"I love you, Salma," he declared, throwing his arms around her and kissing her.

The incident created quite a buzz the next day at school, casting shame on Salma. Her mother was understanding, but her father was infuriated—not at Fazel, but at Salma. To him, the incident was Salma's fault; Salma must have encouraged him. Her worst fears had been realized.

"Why did you do that?" her father screamed at her. "I've given you everything, and you are ungrateful. Now you have ruined my name and my family."

Though Salma was allowed to continue going to school, her reputation was ruined and her fiancé broke the engagement. Eventually, her parents selected another, older man for her to marry. After a year, they divorced.

AN AMERICAN FRIEND, 2013

Lailoma had sewn into the early morning hours, but even if she was tired, she always looked forward to Friday, her day off from the department store. Sometimes she spent the day catching up on her moonlighting jobs; sometimes she made a morning call on a Valley woman to help her go through her closet to find things that needed to be altered or purged. This morning she took a quick shower and planned to go to the mall with her friend Samira.

By chance, Lailoma and I had arranged to talk on Friday that particular week, and I arrived early so she could enjoy the rest of her day off. I was glad I was there to meet her lively Afghan American friend, Samira. She was about ten years younger than Lailoma and had come to America as a twelve-year-old, several years before Lailoma and Maiwand arrived. Samira and Lailoma chuckled as they told me how she made her way to the United States.

As for many immigrants, Samira's path to the US required some careful, and a little bit of creative, negotiation. Her parents had left Afghanistan in the late '80s before the Russians vacated the country and the mujahideen began their reign of terror. The family was living in Pakistan, but they wanted to send Samira, their oldest child, to America for her education. Unfortunately, they had left behind whatever slim documentation they had for her in Afghanistan, and they couldn't just put her on an airplane without papers. Not least of all, she was only twelve, and her Afghan documents wouldn't have been useful anyway. So her parents forged a document that listed her age as eighteen and her marital status as the fiancée of a cousin who was already living in America with his family. With this document, Samira arrived in America ahead of her immediate family, finished her high school education while living with her cousin's family, and found a job working in a dental office where another of her cousins worked. When she gained her American citizenship, she applied to bring her father and mother to America as well. Later, their other children, who were all under the age of eighteen, were able to leave Pakistan too, and finally the entire family was in the United States and moved together from New Jersey to Arizona.

Lailoma met Samira by chance when she arrived in America. Samira's mother had learned about Lailoma through other Afghans in the US, who told her that Lailoma regularly sent money to Pakistan. Because she had family in the city where Ahmadwali now lived, she asked Lailoma if she could send money to her family as well. Her daughter, Samira, delivered the money to Lailoma to send. Though Lailoma was nearly a decade older than Samira, almost immediately the two became friends.

Sometimes when the workweek ended and Samira left her job as a dental assistant, she drove straight to Lailoma's condo. They might just sit and talk or go browse the stores in one of the area's many malls, but they also went out to restaurants or to see movies, especially before Qurisha arrived to live with

Lailoma. With Qurisha in the condo, they often stayed home with her so she would have someone to talk with. Or they took her with them to buy groceries.

The American supermarket, especially the refrigerated cases piled high with fresh produce, never stopped being a source of wonderment for Qurisha. "The fruits and vegetables are so clean!" she said each time she lingered in the produce department. No doubt she had visions of the Afghan and Pakistani shopkeepers who dipped their produce in the streams where people swam, women washed clothes, cows waded, and the shores were lined with garbage. The warehouse store Costco was nothing short of shocking to her.

"You can find anything here!" she often declared.

"That's true," both Samira and Lailoma agreed.

And there was another bonus of supermarkets, Lailoma explained to me. In the United States, if you want something in particular, you can call the store to see if they have it. In Afghanistan, the stores often did not have a telephone, so you might walk or take the bus from one store to the next for the better part of a day and still not find the item you wanted.

On this day when Samira arrived, she made herself at home, chatting with Maiwand and me as she waited for Lailoma to come downstairs. "Welcome," Qurisha said to her in Pashto, extending her hand.

"Thank you," Samira, who does not speak Pashto, replied in English.

Today was one of Qurisha's bad days. Often depression settled on her as she missed her family and longed to converse with someone other than Lailoma and Maiwand, who had a reasonable grasp of Pashto. Sometimes she had panic attacks and stopped breathing. At night, if she slept, she had nightmares about the sufferings of her family—a nephew who was killed, a brother who died.

On this Friday morning, she had tried to tell Lailoma her vivid dream about her fourteen-year-old nephew who had been killed. But, as always, dreams are difficult to articulate.

"We were at a wedding," she told Lailoma. "And there he was, coming at me with open arms. 'Aunt, I'm so hungry,' he told me. Someone brought him a plate of food and he ate with his dirty hands. My brother Fazel rented a plane and said, 'Let's go.' I looked outside and saw all the air was coming out from the wing. 'How is the plane going to fly?' I asked my brother. But we all got on the plane, and we flew away."

In telling Samira and me the story, Lailoma explained that Qurisha's dream was about something that had happened twenty-five years earlier. Qurisha's brother Fazel had been killed in Logar Province, and later a rocket hit near his home in Kabul, killing her nephew.

"I've never dreamed about him," she told Lailoma. "Why after all this time, do I dream about him now? Why was he hungry? I've always wished for him to come to me in my dreams, but why did he come now?"

Lailoma understood her mother's despair because Lailoma battled her own inner war daily. While Lailoma kept herself so busy she didn't have time to dwell on her devastating past, Qurisha didn't have that luxury. She was by herself all day long. Lailoma went to work. Maiwand went to school, to the gym.

In addition to her young son Gulwali, Qurisha had lost so many: her brothers Anbar, who lost his leg in Mazer-e Sharif and later died; Ashraf, who died of stomach cancer; Fazel; Fazel's son and three of her brother Khalid's children. "I don't have anybody," she told Lailoma. "I don't have the strength to handle this anymore."

"Don't think like that," Lailoma told her mother. But Lailoma's words couldn't quiet her mother's demons any more than she could quiet her own.

Samira's outgoing personality brightened Qurisha's spirits. Qurisha busied herself in the galley kitchen of the condo, washing and wiping out three cups for tea. The cups had already been washed in the dishwasher and stored in the cupboard, but neither Qurisha nor Lailoma could resist rewashing them, a habit of a lifetime, stemming from the dustiness of their native land—and their skepticism of the dishwasher.

She poured frozen mulberries into a bowl and walnuts into another and brought them to the living room, where Lailoma, Samira, and I were now seated on the sofa with our tea.

"Aunt," Samira said, respectfully addressing Qurisha, "how are you doing today?" Samira asked the question in English and then Lailoma translated it for Qurisha.

Speaking rapidly in Pashto, Qurisha told Samira about an upsetting phone conversation with Ahmadwali she'd had the previous evening. One of her grandchildren, young Reza, son of Naim, was very ill with leukemia. They lived in Pakistan, where both Lailoma and Qurisha felt the medical services were better than in Afghanistan, but the necessary treatments were well beyond Naim's ability to pay. Lailoma had sent money for the first two treatments and was saving her moonlighting money for more.

"What will we do?" she asked before turning to address Lailoma. "You have to send more money. We can't lose Reza!"

"Adai, I will send money to Naim. Don't worry. We'll do everything we can for Reza," Lailoma said, trying to calm her. In her mind, Lailoma knew she couldn't work any harder than she already was.

"She constantly worries about Naim and Reza. She can't think of anything else, and she makes herself sick," Lailoma said in English to us. "Of course I care so much about Reza, and I want to help Naim get the best treatment possible for him. But sometimes I get so tired of her never-ending worrying about it. Now she wants to go back to Pakistan. I'm saving money for a ticket for her, but she doesn't understand how much it costs. 'Things aren't free,' I tell her. If I send her to Pakistan, I don't want her to change her mind in a week or two and want to return to the US. I can't afford to keep buying airline tickets and still send money to Naim."

But how could Qurisha understand the economics of the situation? She had never worked beyond taking in a little sewing and mending when she lived in Kabul. She had never had a mortgage, paid for a car, or written a check for an electric bill. To Qurisha, everyone in America just had money. Everyone had enough. Of course that wasn't true, but her world was confined to what she saw in the condo complex, at the supermarket, and at Costco. America, to Qurisha, was the land of plenty. She didn't comprehend that the reason Lailoma had a nice condo and was able to send money to Pakistan for her brothers' families was because she worked so hard.

Maiwand tried to be patient, but, like Lailoma, he easily tired of hearing his grandmother complain. "Ana," he said, "Mamo is doing her best."

Maiwand helped where he could as well. Finding he had his grandfather's knack and love for automobiles, he bought a used car, worked on it to make minor repairs, and sold it for a small profit. "Here," he said, extending his hand and giving his grandmother a hundred dollars, "you can send this to Naim."

"Aunt," Samira placed her arm on Qurisha's shoulder, "you are strong. Afghan women are strong."

Qurisha nodded as she grabbed her pack of Marlboros off the arm of the living room love seat and opened the sliding door to the patio.

As I closed my computer and gathered my things to leave, Samira turned to Lailoma. "Do you have a shopping list?" Samira asked. "I was thinking we could drive to Tempe and shop at Whole Foods. Do you want to see a movie this afternoon?"

"Let's do it," Lailoma said. She needed a diversion. And she was glad to have her American friend.

THREE ENGAGEMENTS, KABUL, 1988

By the time Lailoma and her girlfriends were in tenth grade, the jihadis had circled the perimeter of Kabul. The factions shot rockets at each other from one mountain to the next and had even cut the electrical wires, but they hadn't yet entered the city.

Lailoma, along with her girlfriends and younger siblings, continued her studies. Shaima continued to cook and sew. Ahmadwali prepared to graduate from high school. Qurisha and Shahwali began to think about marriages for their three older children, especially for Shaima and Lailoma. The year was 1988. The times had changed. Societal traditions had softened, but the Soviets were still in Afghanistan and there was growing concern over the infighting mujahideen. It was time to secure their children's futures.

While Lailoma found friends among her classmates, and therefore social engagement outside of the family compound, Shaima didn't have that opportunity. A big outing for Shaima was mingling with other women when she took dough she and Qurisha had made to the bakery to be baked.

Occasionally on a weekend, Lailoma helped Shaima by taking the dough to the bakery for her—or she would go with her to keep her company. For stay-at-home women, the visits to the bakery were a social time, a time to see who was out and about—a near-daily occasion to chat and maybe gossip a bit with someone outside of their families.

Shaima was twenty-five when Lailoma was in tenth grade, and she was neither married nor engaged. By the standards of the time, she had no life. Lailoma felt for her—and was so glad she wasn't her. Qurisha and Shahwali were well aware that the marriage opportunities for Shaima were fading.

On one particular Saturday when Lailoma volunteered to take the dough to the bakery, the mother of one of her classmates was there. The woman remembered she had seen Shaima with Lailoma on a previous trip, and that afternoon she watched Lailoma go home to see where she lived. Later she stopped by the family home in Bagh-e Bala to inquire about Shaima.

After she introduced herself as the mother of one of Lailoma's class-mates, the purpose for her visit became apparent.

"Our family owns prosperous farmland in Helmand," she told Qurisha and Shahwali. "I know you have an older daughter who isn't married, and my broth-er Ghlamwali would make a wonderful husband for her. Ghlamwali is so smart and accomplished! He has finished high school, and now he is ready to study in Russia."

The story was plausible. Geographically the largest province in Afghanistan, Helmand is located in southern Afghanistan, west of Wardak, and is known for its rich farmland. It not only is one of the largest opium-producing areas in the world but also produces tobacco, cotton, sesame, wheat nuts, and myriad fruits and vegetables. A large farming operation could be prosperous indeed. Livestock was also a popular source of farm income.

Her own husband had been killed in the war, the sister explained. Now she was living with her brother-in-law's family in Bagh-e Bala and raising her three sons and one daughter. She was pleasant, respectful, and very traditional. Qurisha and Shahwali liked her immediately. Could her brother Ghlamwali be the perfect match for Shaima?

"Thank you for your visit," Shahwali told her. "I will talk with my brother Zaher and then give you an answer."

Kaka Zaher not only loved Shahwali's children as if they were his own, but also had a responsibility as Shahwali's elder brother to verify that Ghlamwali was a good man for Shaima. Over the next few weeks, he inquired about him among his friends and business associates. Was everything he had been told about Ghlamwali true? Was he educated? Did he work hard and was he prosperous? Would he be able to provide a good life for Shaima and any children they might have?

He learned the answers from Ghlamwali's sister's brother-in-law—the one whose house sheltered her and her children. He stopped by Kaka Zaher's resale shop to warn him: "Don't engage your niece to Ghlamwali. The family is not as prosperous as his sister says. They are too lazy to make their crops flourish, so they make just enough money to get by. Ghlamwali is not the nice, industrious person she describes him to be. He doesn't know how to work hard. He's selfish and self-centered. He uses people for his own advantage."

Unwittingly, Qurisha and Shahwali had already proceeded with plans for the engagement. Zaher called Shahwali to his shop to break the news on the very day that friends and relatives had been invited to their home for the big announcement. They had bought the traditional chocolates, flowers, and everything festive associated with this wonderful occasion.

"I'm not authorizing you to give my niece to Ghlamwali. You don't have my blessing. He is not good; he is not prosperous. He's lazy. His sister has not told you the truth about him."

"But we've invited everyone to our home. It will bring us shame if there is no engagement," Shahwali answered Kaka Zaher.

Later, at home, Qurisha agreed with Shahwali. "We have to go through with this," she told her husband.

That evening the guests began to pour into their home. Ever vigilant, Ghlamwali's sister noticed her brother-in-law talking with Shahwali.

"Don't listen to him!" she told Shahwali. "I know he's telling you bad things about my brother. They are not true. He's just saying these things because he's jealous. We're a good family. My brother is a good man. He and Shaima will be very happy."

The party proceeded. Guests were feted with kebabs, salads, rice pudding, cookies, cakes, and tea with cream. Two people who didn't attend were Shaima and Ghlamwali. This "party" was transactional between the two families and didn't involve the future bride and groom. The engagement announcement was finalized, and negotiations were started for the engagement party and the wedding. Shahwali listed his requirements for the engagement party—how much money the groom's family needed to provide, what food would be served, how many guests would be invited. Ghlamwali's family readily—maybe too readily—agreed to everything he wanted, and so Shaima became the first child of Qurisha and Shahwali to be promised in marriage. The expected order of events had been fulfilled. What did Shaima think? No one asked. This was the life path that had been planned for her. Lailoma was glad she wasn't the chosen one. This time.

Ahmadwali completed high school that same year, and upon graduation it was mandatory for him to join the Afghan army. By this time fighting between the various mujahideen groups was prevalent throughout most of the country, and Ahmadwali's army unit was constantly on the move trying to quell their activities. Qurisha and Shahwali prayed for him wherever he went. As was customary, they killed an animal each time they prayed, giving the meat to the poor. Every time they performed this ritual, Ahmadwali returned home alive, uninjured, and in good health.

But one day, disturbing news came from Khost, the last location the family had known Ahmadwali's unit to be. The city was just over ninety miles from Kabul in eastern Afghanistan near the Pakistani border and lodged between mountains eight thousand to ninety-eight hundred feet high to the north and another chain of ninety-eight-hundred-foot peaks to the west, thereby putting military units there at high risk for ambush.

The news that reached Lailoma's family was that the mujahideen had captured Khost. It was the ninth month of the Afghan calendar, the month of Ramadan, when Muslims fast during the daylight hours. In 1988, Ramadan began on April 18.

For three days, the mujahideen surrounded Ahmadwali's unit, trapping the soldiers and causing them to run out of bullets, food, and water. Each evening, when the fast ended at sunset, all Ahmadwali and his comrades could do was bring their injured soldiers back to the base and hope for intervention from Kabul.

Feeling pretty certain Ahmadwali was still in Khost, the family continued to pray and sacrificed more animals. They hoped for the best but as the days went by the reality set in that they had no concrete information as to whether Ahmadwali was dead or alive. Finally they received a phone call from the army hospital in Kabul.

Ahmadwali was alive, but he was very ill. A rocket had literally knocked his worn, ill-fitting shoes off him, causing him to have to continue his tour of duty barefoot. One foot had become infected, sending red streaks up his leg. The army had flown him back to Kabul for treatment. Ahmadwali was one of the few lucky ones. Of the three thousand soldiers in his unit, only about a third survived.

When they learned Ahmadwali was alive and in Kabul, the family was ecstatic. "Now," Qurisha told him, "it is time for you to get engaged and married. I'm sick, I'm old, maybe I'll die and won't see your wedding. I want you to get engaged."

Qurisha was in her midthirties. She cajoled and cajoled until her son agreed.

Ahmadwali had his eye on a girl he had noticed from Lailoma's school—maybe she had accidentally missed the evening school bus.

This could work out, he thought. He told his mother to engage him and the girl.

Two factors, however, conspired against this pairing. First, the young woman spoke only Farsi. Qurisha said, "No. We don't speak Farsi."

Like Lailoma, Ahmadwali spoke Farsi as well as Pashto, but Qurisha didn't.

And second, mother knows best. She wasn't going to allow Ahmadwali to randomly select a girl she didn't know.

"I will pick the girl for you," Qurisha told her son.

So that was that. The girl of Ahmadwali's dreams was not going to be his wife.

Qurisha and Shahwali had relatives who also lived in Kabul and visited in their home often, and they had a daughter about Lailoma's age. She was a stunning girl named Ojeie (pronounced O-zhay). She kept her shiny black hair a little shorter than most of the young women her age, and her black eyes and even, white teeth shone in her lighter-skinned face. Qurisha chose Ojeie for Ahmadwali.

To announce the engagement, Qurisha and Shahwali invited family and other guests to Sitara, an upscale hotel nearby, for a party. What could be more fun than your big brother's engagement party?

Lailoma dreaded it.

Mindful that she was already sixteen and still not promised to anyone, she tried to stay in the background as much as possible. Who knew who would be there, see her, and think she was an eligible candidate for engagement? In fact, she had established a habit of declining all of her father's invitations to attend even family weddings and parties.

"I'm not feeling well," she would say. Or, "I would love to go, but I have homework to finish."

But on this night, ducking out wasn't an option. And not being seen was nearly impossible. Who wouldn't notice the eligible young woman she had become? Her thick dark-brown hair hung to her waist, her face was appealing, and her sparkly eyes revealed an intelligence that made her even more attractive.

Certainly the boys who followed her to the school bus stop had noticed, as they sometimes called after her. "Lailoma, you're so pretty," they'd say. "Your hair is so beautiful."

It's a curse, she thought sometimes. *I don't want boys to think I'm pretty. I don't want someone's father or mother or aunt or uncle to want to engage me to someone. I want to go to the university and become a doctor. I should cut my hair. Then they wouldn't notice me as much.*

But no, short hair was forbidden in her conservative Sunni family. Her mother and father never would hear of her cutting her hair, and Baba Amin, well, who knew what he would do if she cut it?

Despite her best efforts to stay in the background, on the night of Ahmadwali's engagement party, one of Shahwali's coworkers took note of her. According to hearsay, he remarked to his uncle later, "I saw a beautiful girl at Ahmadwali's engagement party. I work with Shahwali, her father, and her family is from Wardak, like ours. She goes to school, and she's very pretty. I think you should arrange to engage your son to her."

Everyone, it seemed, was a matchmaker. Just a few days later as Lailoma was getting ready for school at about 11 a.m., somebody knocked on the gate. Her heart sank. They had come for her. She just knew it. Someone wanted her to get engaged.

These negotiations can happen quickly, she knew, recalling how readily her parents had agreed to Shaima's engagement.

Qurisha was sitting outside in the front courtyard when she heard the knock on the front gate. Because the gate wasn't locked, the visitor opened it partially. "Aunt!" she called, to get Qurisha's attention.

As Qurisha stood, two women opened the gate all the way and just walked in. Lailoma watched from the upstairs bathroom window.

Qurisha spoke to the guests in Pashto, and learned the women were from Wardak Province. Now they behaved as long-lost friends, hugging each other. As Qurisha and the two women passed by the bathroom, Lailoma stood on the other side of the door, frozen in fear, the same fear and anxiety she had felt all those years ago when she hid in the bathroom to avoid Baba Amin when he caught her playing with kites on the roof. Her heart was pounding, and she was filled with dread.

One of the two women introduced herself by explaining that her father, Abdul Nabee, was a cousin of Shahwali. The families didn't live in the same village, she explained, but they were indeed cousins.

Ah! A relative! That was their entrée. The three women then sat down to talk.

"I didn't know I had an uncle living here in Kabul," one of the women said, referring to Shahwali.

"We heard about your son's wonderful engagement party," the other woman said. "We came to congratulate you and your son. Do you have pictures from the party? We would love to see them."

Lailoma wanted to stay and listen to the rest of the conversation, but she had to leave for school. After the women were seated, she quietly slipped out of the bathroom, down the stairs, and out the door.

Qurisha brought out the photos the professional photographer had taken and spread them on the table. The women picked them up one by one, examining the attractive family.

"Who is this?" they asked pointing out one guest after another. "And what is this handsome young man's name?"

Qurisha obliged with answers to each question. The women also showed great interest in the gifts displayed around the room: the big bouquet of flowers, the candy, the gifts for the groom, the suit fabric, the shirts, the personal grooming items.

Qurisha was eager to share because she was so happy she finally would have a daughter-in-law. She was proud of the prosperous display of gifts.

"This is my oldest daughter, Shaima," she said, pointing to Shaima in one of the photos. "And this is my second daughter, Lailoma. She's in school right now."

Just like that, the women had what they had come for—not only the name of the beautiful girl they had heard about, but also the potential for a picture they could take back to their family.

"Could we borrow this picture?" they asked. "We want to show our family in Wardak what a nice party it was and what a beautiful family you have."

Qurisha gave them two photos, one of Ahmadwali and Ojeie, and a group photo that included Lailoma.

At school, Lailoma could barely concentrate on what the teacher was saying. The afternoon seemed as if it would never end. Lailoma couldn't take her mind off the unexpected visitors. Shaima, because she didn't go to school, was the only one at home whom she could trust to tell her what had happened, and she couldn't wait to talk with her.

"Shaima, who were those people?" she demanded as soon as she opened the front door.

"They want you," Shaima replied. She then explained that one of the women who had visited was the daughter of one of their father's cousins. "All they had to say to Adai was that they knew Baba Amin in Wardak, and that one of their fathers was a cousin of our father. They were in," Shaima told Lailoma, who rolled her eyes.

Qurisha later admitted to Lailoma that she thought the way the women walked right into the courtyard was a little pushy. She said that it was only out of politeness that she invited them into the house to sit and talk—and look at the engagement party photos. Even though they said they were originally from Wardak, she didn't know them. Nevertheless, she had to be courteous.

After that, every day for a month, the two women came for a visit. To Lailoma, this behavior was worrisome. She knew it could only mean one thing. No matter how much she cried and pleaded with her parents that she didn't want to get engaged, her parents gave these women serious consideration. By now, Qurisha and Shahwali knew quite a lot about Abdullah, the potential groom's father, and his family—much more, for instance, than they knew about Shaima's fiancé's family. The women seemed more concerned about establishing Abdullah's wealth than in discussing his son's qualifications as a suitor. As it turned out, his qualifications were considerable.

"Lailoma," her mother told her, "they are good people. They have money."

"I don't want to get engaged," Lailoma, said, sobbing. "I don't care if they have money."

"Maybe you're in love with someone else, and that's why you don't want to get engaged with this family," Qurisha said, teasingly accusatory. She knew this was unlikely because Lailoma was so interested in her studies, but she put it out there. Lailoma might have noticed a boy or two, but she certainly wasn't interested in getting engaged to any of them.

"I want to finish school. I want to be a doctor. I don't want to get married," she beseeched her parents repeatedly.

As is typical of this particular Afghan social convention, for a few weeks, only the women visited. When the talking became serious, the men in the family began to visit as well. Qurisha and Shahwali talked with them, but still they remained uncommitted. Then Mama Rahim, one of Qurisha's older half brothers, entered the picture.

Mama Rahim knew Abdullah as the owner of Doostiee, the only restaurant in Kabul that served alcohol. Doostiee became very popular with the Russians after they arrived in 1979, and Abdullah was happy to serve them liquor. He made a lot of money from them, considering that the Soviets were in Afghanistan for ten years.

Mama Rahim, who worked at the radio station in Kabul, sometimes went to Doostiee for lunch and had become acquainted with Abdullah.

Qurisha and Shahwali were torn. They knew Lailoma wanted to finish school. They knew how badly she wanted to become a doctor. Finally, after much consideration, they told her they had decided they were going to decline the proposal. For a few days, Lailoma relaxed. But then Mama Fazel weighed in. He had worked with Abdullah's son, Mussa, in the army when they were on duty in Logar Province not far from Wardak. Up to this point, not much had been said about the potential groom.

"I know Mussa," Mama Fazel said. "He's a good man, and he's gaining a lot of attention from the top, rising through the ranks of the military."

With Mama Fazel's stamp of approval, Qurisha and Shahwali changed their minds and agreed to the engagement. For a brief moment, Lailoma thought she might have a way out of it. Kaka Zaher voiced the opinion that they should say no, because in Afghanistan if the older sister isn't married, the younger sister can't get married. What he didn't consider was that Shaima was engaged, even if it had been against his better judgment. She just hadn't married yet. Engagement counts.

Lailoma sobbed. She was heartbroken.

Her engagement shocked just about everyone. Not because she was so young (at sixteen, she wasn't considered young for engagement, or marriage for that matter). Not because she wanted to finish her education before even thinking about marriage. The shock was who her fiancé was: Mussa was a highly placed general in the army of Mohammad Najibullah, the man who had become president of Afghanistan just one year earlier. After graduating high school, Mussa had gone to military school in Russia and studied in Germany and England as well, paid for by the Afghan government. He had traveled with the army for a few years, and then settled in Kabul. At this point, his family felt it was time for him to marry.

His accomplishments might have impressed others. They didn't impress Lailoma.

Unlike Shaima's fiancé's family, Mussa's father was indeed wealthy, mostly because of the Doostiee restaurant. When it came time to shop for engagement-party clothes, Abdullah paid for almost everything—shoes, purses, makeup. Mussa was the first child, and everyone in his family was excited and happy he was getting married. But when the women in Mussa's family came to take her shopping, Lailoma made her last stand: she refused to go with them.

"You pick out whatever you want me to wear," she told them. "I will wear whatever you want me to."

Soon it would be New Year's Day, and Mussa's family told Qurisha they would bring *nowrosei* for Lailoma. Nowrosei is a New Year's Eve present for the bride-to-be, a basket full of everything from clothes and makeup to shoes and a purse. It also contained freshly cooked fish, seasonal and dried fruits—whatever the groom's family could afford to give.

Mussa's family could afford abundant gifts, and when New Year's Day arrived on March 21, there wasn't just one such basket. Everyone in the groom-to-be's family who came to introduce themselves to Lailoma's family brought a basket, and the parade of guests turned it into a party.

After Mussa's family left, Kaka Zaher's family and Mama Rahim's family arrived for the opening of the baskets to see what Mussa's family had brought to Lailoma. The baskets were a family occasion—not simply a gift for the bride. Qurisha gave both families a share of all the food. As their extended family left the home with their bounty, they spread the word that Lailoma was engaged.

Soon—too soon for the sixteen-year-old bride-to-be—the day came for Mussa and Lailoma's engagement party at the Sitara Hotel, a return to the scene of Ahmadwali's engagement party. Lailoma and Mussa had not yet met.

That morning at about 8 a.m., three women from Mussa's family, plus Shaima, the girl cousins, Ahmadwali's fiancée—Ojeie—and Lailoma arrived at the beauty salon to spend the entire day in preparation, all paid for by Abdullah, Lailoma's future father-in-law. While the hairstylist put rollers in Lailoma's waist-length hair, the other women were also getting their hair styled. At lunchtime, Mussa's family brought shish kebabs for the entourage of women.

Lailoma's hair was so long and thick that it didn't dry very quickly under the bonnet-style hair dryer. "Can we trim your hair a little bit so it will dry faster next time?" the hairdresser asked.

"Oh no, my mother wouldn't allow that," Lailoma told her.

Roya, Mussa's sister, who was to become a good friend, was quick to say no as well.

"Then on your wedding day you have to come in earlier," the stylist told Lailoma. "The electricity sometimes goes out, and if that happens, we wouldn't be able to dry it."

After every strand of hair had been wound around a roller, it was time for makeup, a new experience for the bride-to-be. The application was quite a process and seemed to take forever.

"Here," the makeup artist said to Lailoma, handing her a mirror. "Look."

When Lailoma saw her reflection, she was shocked. The day before, she had gone to the same salon to have her eyebrows shaped with a thread. The dramatic face she now saw in the mirror surely wasn't hers!

It was nearly time to leave the salon and go to the Sitara Hotel. The hairdresser took the rollers out of Lailoma's hair, styled the top with curls to hold a tiara and veil, and left the back down in a wavy dark-brown mane. In the next hour before the car arrived to take the women to the party, the curls relaxed, making Lailoma's hair seem to grow longer and longer by the minute.

When the women helped Lailoma into her baby-blue ball gown, a slight smile came to her lips and a sparkle returned to her eyes. She felt beautiful.

At 5 p.m. a car stopped outside the salon. The burgundy Toyota that Mussa had rented for the occasion was decorated with flowers. An abundance of flowers. Fresh flowers covered the bumper. Bright plastic and silk flowers ran the length of the car from the front to the back. Following the flower-bedecked Toyota was a minivan to transport the rest of the wedding party from the salon to the party. Leading the parade was a pickup truck, carrying a videographer in its bed to capture the entire procession on videotape.

From the salon, Lailoma watched the Toyota's arrival and soon she heard additional commotion outside: the groom-to-be had also arrived.

Lailoma had kept her composure during the long day at the salon, but now she fell apart. She peered out the window to get her first look at Mussa and drew back, aghast at what she saw. She tried to conceal her shock, but it was hard. He was so old! At least twenty years older than she was! *And*, she thought, *he doesn't have much hair.* To her sixteen-year-old eyes, he appeared almost bald.

Shaima took her sister's hand. "Don't make a scene. Don't embarrass him." Shaima knew their mother, who was already at the hotel, was nervous about this moment.

"This is what's going to happen," Shaima, who had been through this experience, told Lailoma. "He's going to come into the salon. He will give you a bouquet. You need to take a small flower from it and put it into his jacket pocket. Then you shake hands."

Lailoma followed her sister's instructions to the letter. After those formalities, Mussa helped Lailoma into the back seat of the car and sat down beside her. The videographer in the pickup truck started the camera rolling, recording the journey from their departure at the salon to their arrival at the Sitara Hotel. Hiring the videographer had seemed like a good idea at the time, but the reality was that there wasn't much to record as Lailoma sat awkwardly in the back seat beside Mussa. Everything about this day was unfamiliar to her—the makeup, the hair, the baby-blue gown, and now Mussa.

Later, she screamed at her mother, "Why did you do this to me? Why did you engage me to such an old man? He's bald. He's ugly. He's as old as my father!"

Actually, Mussa was considered quite handsome, but Lailoma couldn't see that. He certainly wasn't one of the boys at the bus stop, but he wasn't as old as her father either.

The ride from the beauty salon to the hotel was long, quiet, and very strained. Lailoma didn't utter a single word during the entire trip. Mussa started to get a little worried. "Are you mute?" he asked her.

She shook her head. To herself, she was thinking, *What will my friends think when they see this old man?*

"Can you say any words?" he asked.

She couldn't look at him for fear that she would cry, so she just stared straight ahead or looked down.

"Are you happy?" he asked.

What was he thinking? Of course she wasn't happy. She didn't answer. If she answered, she knew the tears would start. And then her makeup would run down her face. And then her mother would know she hadn't behaved well.

Their arrival at the hotel created quite a stir. Bodyguards in military uniform lined both sides of the entrance, and when the wedding party entered the hotel, they never left Mussa's side.

Well, maybe he's OK, Lailoma conceded to herself. *He seems to be pretty important. He might be a good man.*

Relatives whisked the bride into a room by herself, as she was not allowed to mingle with the guests until after dinner. The groom was free to chat with those who had gathered for the party. Qurisha came into the room where Lailoma had been seated and asked her daughter, "Are you OK?"

Lailoma just stared at her. She knew her mother knew how she felt.

Then her cousin Zobaida came in and asked Lailoma if she was happy. "Do you like him?" she wanted to know.

How would I know? Lailoma thought. She dared not answer the question aloud because Mussa's family had come into the room to see her. She would never knowingly hurt their feelings.

The elaborate party Mussa's family hosted included dinner and dancing, and lasted until two or three in the morning. The couple cut the cake and shared fruit punch with each other, but they weren't allowed to join the dancing because they weren't yet married. Both of their Sunni families were very strict about this custom.

Traditionally, this is the time when young women receive their first jewelry, jewelry that has been part of the families' negotiations upon arranging the engagement. This jewelry becomes the bride's insurance if she should fall on hard times.

Lailoma was showered with lovely adornments. Abdullah, her future father-in-law, gave her sparkling emeralds—a bracelet, earrings, choker, and ring. Her mother gave her a gold necklace, a ring with a big round ruby, and matching ruby earrings, all jewelry that had been given to her when she became engaged in Wardak. Her father presented her with an aquamarine ring. Plus each member of Mussa's family gave her jewelry. She had so much gold— earrings, rings, bangles, chokers. Every finger had a ring, and the bracelets stacked up almost to her elbows. Then additional family members brought still more jewelry, and she removed the first set of rings to make room for the next.

When the party ended, Mussa and Lailoma went back to Lailoma's parents' house. Mussa stayed the rest of the night with her, which was customary, though sex, of course, was taboo. An Islamic bride is expected to be a virgin on her wedding night. Instead, Mussa talked and talked.

Won't you ever stop talking? Lailoma thought.

Won't you ever start talking? he must have thought.

"Tell me about your school," he said to encourage her. "Do you take a bus to school? Do you have friends at school?"

On and on he talked, trying to learn a little bit about her, trying to make her more comfortable. She was so nervous she didn't say anything until morning.

She was sixteen, in tenth grade, and had never been alone with a man other than her father or brothers. Of course, Mussa would have known this. But, of course, he was also anxious to get to know her.

The next day, Mussa arrived at their home in the burgundy Toyota and took her to an upscale restaurant for lunch. This should have been a treat, but she was so nervous her hands were shaking. She accidentally dropped her spoon. Then she picked up her fork and dropped it.

"Why are you so nervous?" he asked.

She had no answer. Wasn't it obvious why she was nervous? He was an older man, like her father, and she was so shy. They took a walk in the park and then he took her home.

Two days after the engagement party Mussa came to her home to say goodbye to everyone. President Najibullah had ordered him to go to Kandahar for two months.

Oh, thought Lailoma, *what a relief! Now I can continue my life as usual. I can go to school and study with the Lailomas, Salma, and Nabila.*

When Mussa's two-month duty in Kandahar ended and he returned to Kabul, he came to Lailoma's house every Friday. They went out for lunch or dinner, or sometimes somewhere for a night or two. Slowly she became more comfortable with him and gradually she learned to talk with him. Occasionally he stayed in her parents' house. Their engagement lasted more than two years.

During those two years, Abdullah also came to visit her in her parents' home every Friday, even when Mussa was in Kandahar. Abdullah and his brother, a doctor, were business partners. Before they opened Doostiee, they had started a business that imported pharmaceuticals from Germany and exported Afghan products such as rugs and nuts to Germany. They also owned a little convenience market in their neighborhood.

In those days, businesspeople, and only businesspeople, put their money in the bank. As a businessman, Abdullah was an exception, keeping most of his money at home. He only used the bank for transferring money he sent to Germany as payment for the pharmaceuticals. Then they would wire money back to the bank when he sent the rugs. When they opened Doostiee, he still kept his money at home.

Every Friday he took money from his stash at home and put it into his left breast pocket for Lailoma. "This is your school money," he told her, giving her sixty or seventy Afghani—a lot of money during that time, and a lot of money for a young woman who previously had little to no spending money. Her parents were right: Abdullah was wealthy. And though she didn't admit it to anyone, it was fun to suddenly have money to spend.

One day Abdullah came with a handkerchief full of beautiful Russian gold. Qurisha stepped in at this point and told Lailoma she couldn't keep it. "You have enough," she said.

"No, thank you," Lailoma told Abdullah, knowing her mother was right. "I don't want it."

Abdullah somehow brought out the best in Lailoma. Where she might have been timid around Mussa, her future father-in-law made her comfortable. He trusted her with business information because he could see that she understood it.

"You're my boy," he told her.

He wasn't insulting her, only acknowledging her ability to comprehend matters of business. Ahmadwali had often suggested he wished she were his brother, and now Abdullah regarded her with the same esteem he had for his son.

Lailoma spent the money Abdullah brought her. "Save it," her mother told her. "One day you will need it."

But Lailoma was sixteen and in high school. She spent the money on clothes, shoes, and things for the wedding.

Her engagement gave her the opportunity to be out in the world as she hadn't been previously. She hadn't wanted to get engaged, and her father told her he didn't want her to get engaged either. But that's not how things worked out. She found the silver lining and enjoyed the fun her engagement afforded her.

A wedding dress—my daughter's—brought Lailoma and me together. Now, wedding stories have become a centerpiece of my understanding of the culture in which she grew up. When Lailoma explained the accepted—and expected—Afghan engagement rituals to me, I was alternately fascinated by the colorful celebrations and appalled by the transactional nature of the proceedings. I always assumed I would marry one day. After college. Possibly after I had started a career. What I knew for certain was that the groom would be the person of my choosing. The same would be true for my daughters. Lailoma's story made me realize that that luxury isn't afforded to everyone. Like life everywhere, her family's history is part joy and part disappointment. For her family, it was also part tragedy.

TRAGEDY, 1988

Qurisha knew the minute she opened the door that something had gone terribly wrong. The previous night she'd had a dream that Fazel was killed. She had woken up in a frenzy and hadn't been able to coax herself back to sleep because she didn't want to be sleeping while her brother was being killed. She had spent the rest of the night with her hookah on the second-floor balcony of their home. She told Shaima her dream in a panic.

"No," Shaima reassured her. "Nothing has happened. Everything is fine."

But it wasn't. Instinctively, Qurisha knew. In 1988, Mama Fazel, who lived in Kabul with his wife and children, was in the military and had traveled to Logar City, just fifty miles south and slightly east of Kabul, for a meeting at the army base. When he stepped outside the meeting facility for fresh air, a sniper, who had been concealed by the cluster of trees at the edge of the base, pumped a barrage of thirty or so shots into Fazel's stomach.

Meanwhile, in Kabul, Lailoma's extended family was enjoying a celebration. Shaima and Qurisha had taken the bus to visit Mussa's cousin in the nearby neighborhood of the Macroyan. Mussa's cousin had been promoted to general, and family had gathered to celebrate, taking with them flowers and chocolates. Possibly because the cousin was connected to the military, that call a family never wants to receive came to his home. When the phone rang, Mussa's sister Roya answered it. Knowing how close Qurisha was to her brothers, especially Mama Fazel, Roya couldn't bring herself to tell Qurisha that her younger brother had been killed. So she endured an agonizing hour or more having tea with Qurisha and Shaima and keeping the news to herself before they finally left.

Around the same time of day, at the family's home in Bagh-e Bala, there was a knock at the door. Shahwali was at work and the younger children were in school. Only Ahmadwali and Lailoma were home. Ahmadwali answered the door to find a military representative, whose shocking news caused him to faint, hitting the wall and dropping to the floor. His collapse made such a thud that Kaka Zaher's second wife heard the commotion and came running from next door.

"What happened? What happened?" she demanded.

Because Fazel and his family had moved recently, the address the military had on file was Qurisha and Shahwali's home. Ahmadwali and Lailoma gave the representative his current address, and he left to inform Fazel's wife.

The word spread, and soon the house was filled with relatives from all over the city, who came so that Qurisha, who experienced occasional panic attacks throughout her life, would not be alone when she returned home and learned the news. To her, Fazel was still the little brother who had traveled the dusty road with her from Wardak to Kabul all those years earlier after she and Shahwali married. He was still the young man who had been her companion in the lonely house with Kaka Qader and his wife and children.

"Mama Fazel has been killed, hasn't he?" she asked Lailoma as soon as she walked into the full house.

"No," Lailoma lied. "He's been injured." Because of her mother's panic attacks, Lailoma felt she should give her mother a little time to rest from her trip from the Macroyan before she learned the truth.

"Tell me the truth," Qurisha insisted.

Kaka Zaher's wife stepped up. "Yes," she told Qurisha, "Fazel has been killed."

Family members quickly went to Fazel's house to be with his wife. In addition to his wife, Fazel left behind two little girls and one boy.

The year 1988 had begun with engagements and parties, and now it was also marked with death and grief.

CHAPTER 5

WEDDING SEASON, 1989 TO 1990

In 1989 Soviet rule came to an end. Now the mujahideen—the militant Islamic sects from the hills of Afghanistan—saw an opportunity to seize Kabul. Tens of thousands of Afghan civilians were killed as tribal factions fought each other, holing up in the mountains and firing rockets across the city at each other. Many of the rockets that were intended for rival factions, or for government areas, landed instead in the residential areas. The Soviet withdrawal certainly hadn't improved the lot of women. The Afghan fighters treated women to more rape and plunder.

Mussa was a member of the military while Najibullah was president from 1987 to 1992, first as a commando and eventually as a general. He and his family supported Najibullah, who still received Soviet economic and military support, and wanted to make peace with the mujahideen. The mujahideen wanted Najibullah—along with Soviet influence—to leave Kabul to them. Najibullah predicted that if he left, chaos would ensue, and that's exactly what happened, as civil war broke out.

Amid this turmoil, Ahmadwali and Ojeie married. In spite of the political climate, their wedding was a joyous occasion marked by all of the customary traditions and pageantry. A tinge of disappointment mingled with sadness, however, hung over the couple. Just weeks before the big day, Ojeie's father had passed away, and the family was still in mourning. A monumental celebration was out. Instead of the elegant affair Ahmadwali's family had planned to take place at Sitara Hotel, a simpler ceremony was performed at home.

Ojeie's family lived about a mile from Ahmadwali's family, but Ojeie's family's yard was bigger, so that's where the festivities took place. A chef arrived the morning before the wedding, dug a hole for a cooking fire, and labored throughout the day to produce the elaborate menu. The celebration lasted a week because extended family who wanted to attend had to travel from Wardak. The chef just continued to cook.

When Lailoma's family arrived at Ojeie's house on the evening before the wedding, they brought a large platter decorated with flowers, candy, and candles. The centerpiece of the platter was a bowl of henna, and all the items were beautifully tied up with a large tulle bow. The occasion was heightened by the delicious aroma of the chef-prepared foods wafting over the yard and into the home through the open doors and windows. A DJ kept everyone on their feet as they danced to the lively music. The celebration was grand, and guests didn't leave until midnight, when the bride-to-be went to bed to rest before the big day.

For Ojeie and Ahmadwali's sisters and female cousins, the wedding day would be long as the young women would spend hours at the local salon preparing for the evening. Ojeie was a beautiful young woman, and as a bride she was stunning. Both sides of the family were exceedingly pleased about the union.

Shaima was still a bride in waiting. Her fiancé, Ghlamwali, was said to be studying in Russia and hadn't been in touch with the family for quite a period of time. Did Shaima have her doubts? If so, she kept them to herself. Lailoma didn't voice her suspicions either, but she knew Kaka Zaher was very disturbed by the situation. Since Qurisha and Shahwali wouldn't allow Shaima's engagement to be broken, he offered to take her into his own family as his daughter, but they wouldn't hear of it.

In spite of the fact that Shaima wasn't yet married, Abdullah decided it was time for Mussa and Lailoma to marry, and not long afterward, the reluctant Lailoma began preparations for her own marriage. This time, Abdullah would be the host.

The marriage between Lailoma and Mussa took place after Lailoma's first semester of twelfth grade. She was nineteen, give or take. She had no idea how old Mussa was. The year was 1990. The American embassy had closed in January of the previous year, and the diplomats had left the country. President Mohammad Najibullah had been in power since 1987.

The evening before the wedding was henna night, and just as Lailoma's family had hosted a party at Ojeie's family's home, Mussa's family hosted a party at Lailoma's family's home. On display around the room were all of the beautiful presents Mussa's family had given Lailoma. Close friends from both families came for the occasion, and the lively party lasted well into the morning hours.

Following a traditional ritual to symbolize beauty, luck, and good health, Mussa's aunts decorated Lailoma's feet with henna tattoos, and, also according to custom, seven young female family members who were not yet engaged painted her hands with intricate henna designs.

Dancing by women was prohibited in public, but oh, the lively dancing that took place at family gatherings! The older women supplied cassettes with traditional music, or sometimes one of them sang. All the women wore traditional floor-length dresses of velvet, silk, or satin atop leggings that complemented the colors of their dresses. The brightly colored gowns were intense hues of red, green, blue, yellow, and hot pink, and trimmed in the traditional gold ribbon. Some were embroidered with colorful flowers or patterns. Some were loose-fitting, while others had trim waistlines accented with embroidery or beads. Lailoma's festive dress was purple and yellow. All of the women dressed their heads in colorful scarves or even a sparkling barrette. Multiple generations joined in the fun of the intricate dance steps. The men retreated to another room during the rambunctious frivolity. This part of the party belonged to the women!

Abdullah spared no expense. Shahwali had a pit dug in Kaka Zaher's yard next door, and a chef had labored over it throughout the night, producing meatballs, rice, and kebabs. An assortment of food was brought into the home throughout the evening: *salata* (a chopped salad similar to Mexican pico de gallo), a garden salad, artfully arranged fresh fruit, rice with raisins, cooked spinach, cauliflower, meatballs, and kebabs. And then the desserts: white pudding seasoned with rosewater and cardamon, *firnee* (pudding sprinkled with pistachios and decorated with kiwi), and *jalebi* (fried dough dipped in honey and sugar). The younger brothers and male cousins went from room to room, carrying the steaming food piled high on large platters, and guests helped themselves.

The meal was followed by an extravagant tea. The chef boiled water in a huge kettle over the backyard fire, and after the young boys had taken a teacup and saucer to each guest, they delivered the tea with dried fruit. Finally, everything had been served, and the boys helped clean up and wash the mounds of dishes. Then it was their turn to enjoy the bounty. They sat with the chef in the yard and enjoyed some of the delicious food they had been carrying to the guests throughout the evening.

It was then time for the grand entrance of the bride- and groom-to-be. One of the aunts inserted a cassette of the traditional "Ahesta Boro" into the boombox. "Walk slowly on my side," crooned Sarban, the Frank Sinatra of Afghanistan.

When Mussa entered the room, Lailoma stood up and held her right hand above her head in a fist, her eyes closed. In Afghan tradition, the groom tries to pry open the bride's closed fist—some brides make it really difficult— to place a gift of gold or diamonds in her hand, to the delight of the applauding guests.

As Mussa opened Lailoma's hand, he slipped a diamond inside. The women then resumed their dancing, pictures were taken, and Mussa escaped to the other room with the men. By the time the rented buses returned to take the guests home, everyone was a happy tired. As is traditional, Mussa's family selected a representative to stay at Lailoma's house until morning. Mussa's aunt was chosen, and in the morning Lailoma's family gave her a gift of printed silk fabric to make a new dress. Lailoma's extended family and friends spent the night as well. Some continued to party; others caught a few hours' sleep where they could.

Lailoma, like brides all over the world before their wedding day, slept very little. The hours seemed to pass slowly as she was lying awake, but then suddenly the time arrived for her to shower and get ready for another long day at the beauty shop.

Early in the morning on Friday, the wedding day, Mussa's cousin brought a car to pick up Lailoma and her two gowns (one in traditional green and one in white with a veil), her jewelry, the still-unmarried Shaima, three of her cousins, and Mussa's cousin's wife. His assignment was to deliver the entourage safely to the salon.

The scene was an emotional one as the time had come for Lailoma to say goodbye to her parents. Tears streamed down her face. She didn't want to leave her family. She didn't want to marry. Though no one had told her she couldn't attend school once married, she worried her husband and father-in-law might not allow it. Everything was wrong.

In fact, everyone cried, though for different reasons. Qurisha cried. Shahwali cried. Shaima cried. Laila and Sonita cried. Only Sitara's and Susan's eyes were dry. They were too young to understand. Even Mussa's cousin's eyes became a little misty. Some of the aunts teased him a little for crying, but then they backed off, knowing this was an emotional time.

After several hours of getting her hair and makeup done at the salon, Lailoma left with her entourage for the Lucky 5, the hotel where the wedding was to be held. There, the couple remained apart. Mussa, in his chocolate-brown suit and emerald-green shirt and tie, waited in one room, and Lailoma, in her emerald-green dress with its intricate lace, waited with some of her family and friends in another.

When the guests had enjoyed their dinner and the bride and groom had been served in their separate rooms, the elders from each family met with the mullah, the religious leader who would perform the ceremony. The mullah also presided over the tradition of appointing guardians for the bride and groom. The families sent three men as witnesses to Lailoma. They asked, "Who is your guardian?" Tradition dictated that she not answer.

Then they went back to the assembled elders with the message, "The bride doesn't answer."

They sent the witnesses back to her a second time. "Who is your legal guardian?"

Again she wasn't allowed to answer.

They returned to the family elders a second time. "The bride doesn't answer."

The third time they asked the question, she was allowed to answer. "My Kaka Zaher is my guardian," she told them.

If things went terribly wrong in the marriage—abandonment or death—Kaka Zaher would be her representative in any negotiations that resulted. Mussa's uncle served as his guardian. Both bride and groom indicated they had personally chosen their guardians, but of course, they hadn't. The selection had been determined by their parents.

Lailoma's guardian, Kaka Zaher, made a list of assets that would be hers in case of divorce or death. Then he gave the list to Mussa's guardian. The two conferred and signed the agreement. Then the mullah read from the Koran, as the elders held their hands up for a blessing and congratulated Mussa. The men returned to the party area, and Mussa came back to Lailoma, letting her know all the formalities had been finished.

She changed into her rented white gown—the tulle, ruffles, and lace transforming her into a fairy princess—and he changed into a black suit, then together they entered the party room to much fanfare and sat as guests of honor on the stage in front of the beautiful cake table. On the table were two glasses of sweet orange punch, the tiered white cake, a holy mirror, and a basket of triangular handkerchiefs Qurisha had made for each guest at the wedding. Also on the table were jewelry boxes from both families. These contained the jewelry from the engagement party. The bride and groom cut the cake together, fed each other, and drank the sweet punch.

The traditions continued. Family members draped one long green shawl over both Lailoma's head and Mussa's head as they peered into the holy mirror on the table with the cake. With the shawl over their heads, nobody could see the mirror but the couple. They looked at each other in the mirror and then it was removed from under the shawl. Mussa and Lailoma read from the Koran together, still under the shawl. When they read, Mussa put money inside the Koran, later to be distributed to the poor.

Mussa's uncle, as is traditional, put henna on Lailoma's hand, as well as on Mussa's little finger, and then used one of the triangular handkerchiefs to cover her hand and Mussa's.

After the ceremonial cake cutting, all the guests were served cake and tea. Henna and the handkerchiefs Qurisha had made were offered to everyone. The rituals complete, at last it was time to celebrate.

The evening was festive indeed. Abdullah's younger brother had been in charge of selecting the singer, and he chose Abdullah Maquri, who performed the entire night. Maquri wasn't Lailoma's favorite, but she wasn't part of the decision. The guests enjoyed his music, though, and more than two hundred relatives, business associates, neighbors, and friends filled the dance floor throughout the evening, the women dancing on one side of the room and the men on the other. Proud big brother Ahmadwali videotaped the happy occasion. That evening, thoughts of the fighting around them took a back seat to their celebration.

Immediately following the wedding, Lailoma and Mussa went to Abdullah's house for a continuation of the wedding traditions. Before they entered the home, they put blood from a rooster's comb on Lailoma's shoes. (Modern brides might use blood from another animal—or even red nail polish—to fulfill this ritual.) They stepped into the yard and then to the front door. Lailoma was given a hammer with which to pound a nail into the door, summoning good luck and a long, happy life. Then she and Mussa walked into the home, and she kissed the stove as a sign of respect for her new father-in-law. They spent their first evening and several after it in Abdullah's home. Gradually, Lailoma had become comfortable with both Mussa and his father.

The next week, Abdullah hosted yet another party, and the same guests were invited to return. This was the occasion for friends and family to bring gifts. Some brought cash; some brought jewelry, housewares, or clothing.

Following this party, Lailoma moved into the apartment where Mussa had been living. Delivered by her family, all of the gifts and anything she had designated to take with her awaited her in her new home.

The excitement—and trauma—of the wedding behind her, Lailoma turned her attention to some unfinished business. The second semester of her all-important senior year started, and it was time to go back to the books for Lailoma and her friends. Occasionally, they studied together at Lailoma and Mussa's apartment, but their homes were no longer close by, and Lailoma's time with her girlfriends grew more and more limited after the wedding.

Lailoma finished twelfth grade and took her qualifying exam for higher education as a married woman. On the day the scores were to be posted, she and her friends met and went together to the university, where the qualifying exam had been administered and the test scores would be posted. Oh, the anxiety of knowing you did your best and feeling you had known the correct answers, but not knowing the results. Until they actually saw their names and scores on the list, they kept up nervous chatter, trying to ignore the pits in the bottom of their stomachs.

At the university they joined other students who had crowded around the wall where the scores were posted. Lailoma wanted so badly to receive a high score that would qualify her to study medicine, and there it was in black and white: Lailoma's name at the top of the list, a perfect score. Lailoma number two was just a little farther down the list and Lailoma number three was a little lower. Each had not only passed the test; each had excelled.

The three serious students, giddy and high on their accomplishments, spent the rest of the day planning for their classes at the university. "What will we wear on the first day?" Lailoma number two asked. "Let's shop together!"

But in spite of the frivolity and excitement, a cloud hovered over the newly married Lailoma's head. She had earned acceptance into the university to study medicine, but she knew there was a formidable obstacle in her path: her new family. Abdullah's oldest brother's daughters-in-law hadn't gone to school past twelfth grade. She knew Abdullah didn't want his brother to be upset that his daughter-in-law might be allowed to go to the university.

"I don't know if I can go to the university because my father-in-law doesn't want me to have more education than his brother's daughters-in-law," she said, worrying aloud to her friends.

"But if your husband says it's OK, how can your father-in-law say no?" one of the other Lailomas asked.

When Mussa came home from work the night Lailoma learned her test scores, he beamed with pride at the good news.

"I'm so proud of you," he said, picking her off her feet and twirling her around. "I knew you could do it!"

"But what if your father and your family won't allow me to attend the university?" she asked.

"Don't worry, honey," he told her. "I can take care of them. This isn't their business; this is your business and my business. This is our business. If you can't go to the university here in Kabul, we will go somewhere else so you can study. I will support you until you finish and graduate. Don't worry."

"But I respect your father, and he's been so good to me. I don't want him to be unhappy," Lailoma said.

As it turned out, university wasn't in the cards anyway. By the time she graduated from high school, still more turbulent times were on the horizon. In fact, the very day after she received her exam scores, Lailoma woke up and looked out the window to see soldiers and tanks in the streets. She went back into the bedroom and told Mussa about them.

"I know, I know. I saw them," Mussa said with worry in his voice. He picked up the phone and dialed his office, but there was no answer.

"Where is the president?" Lailoma asked.

"I don't know," Mussa answered. "Maybe he went to the UN office. Maybe he's dead."

Najibullah wasn't dead yet. But daily life had begun a downward spiral.

With the Soviets out of Afghanistan, the rivaling mujahideen had the opening they needed. Fighting was everywhere as each faction sought to gain control. It was hard to say who was fighting whom as bullets and rockets were omnipresent. When the mujahideen entered Kabul, the social rules changed quickly. Females were barred from all the schools in the city. Professional women lost their jobs, and no women were allowed to work outside the home, including the beautiful teachers in their olive-green dresses. Lailoma's dreams were dashed.

The three Lailomas and their friends had entered high school with high hopes—the Lailomas to be doctors and Salma to be an architect. They knew they had to achieve exceptionally high scores on their admission tests for the university, and each did. Unfortunately, for this group of promising young Afghan women—and for many men too—achieving their goals wasn't to be. Graduation day was the last time Lailoma saw any of the other girls.

For a few months, she was upset, but then she told herself, *Forget it. Just move on. It's not meant to be.*

Instead of studying medicine, Lailoma used her time to teach. To help women who had been widowed by the war, the UN canvassed neighborhoods to identify women who could sew to serve as instructors. Lailoma eagerly volunteered. The UN supplied her with a sewing machine similar to the one on which her mother had taught her, and they paid her a small wage to teach. This was not what she had expected to be doing, but she felt productive. Each morning the women came to her apartment for their instruction. Another lady had been hired to teach the women how to knit and crochet. The activity gave the women skills and became a short-term means of survival. At the end of each month, the UN exchanged whatever the women had produced for pantry staples—beans, grains, and especially oil.

For a while, Lailoma had something to occupy her time. With the mujahideen in the city, however, electricity wasn't consistently available. The UN representative brought her a little gasoline stove for heat, but after just three months, the classes had to come to a halt.

Every day, she saw killing all around her, and she followed her own advice. She forgot completely that she had ever dreamed of becoming a doctor. She simply blocked it from her mind.

Life had been pretty good until the times changed. Her husband treated her well and with respect, and her father-in-law, Abdullah, was good to her. It was the times, not Mussa or Abdullah, that changed her life.

✿ ✿ ✿

After their marriage, Lailoma and Mussa lived in the Macroyan, the same upper-class suburb in northeastern Kabul where Mussa's cousin—the newly appointed general—lived. In fact, the Macroyan was inhabited mostly by government officials. During the 1980s, this had been a Soviet quarter where the communist elite had made their homes.

Several-stories-high apartment buildings lined the streets, and they included amenities the average Kabul home didn't have. Toilets, for instance. Showers with running water. And twice each week, hot running water. On those two days, relatives came to bathe or wash clothes because none of them had hot running water. On the other five days, Macroyan residents had to heat their water over a fire or on the stove just as people in older neighborhoods did, but they still had indoor plumbing.

Although relatively peaceful days had come to a halt by the time of Lailoma's marriage, life still moved on. For one thing, her father-in-law, Abdullah, began to find more and more ways to pull her into his business affairs. Abdullah had succeeded despite the fact that he wasn't an educated man. His brother, a doctor, had run all of their business operations, but, perhaps because Abdullah was a little suspicious of his brother, he preferred to trust Lailoma, despite his stricture with the rest of the women in his family. Mussa was also educated, but as he rose through the ranks in Najibullah's army, he could be of little help to Abdullah with his business.

Soon after Lailoma and Mussa married, Abdullah transferred all of his money—a considerable amount even by today's standards—to a bank account in Lailoma's name, making her the only person who had access to his fortune.

Abdullah considered her family his and his hers. Her relationship with him was in many ways closer than her relationship with her own father. Sometimes she even thought she loved Abdullah more than she loved her own father.

As part of her marriage to Mussa, Lailoma also acquired a new pal, his sister Roya. Roya was lively and turned out to be something of a drama queen, but she was close in age to Lailoma and always had an idea of something fun to do.

One afternoon Roya breezed into the apartment in the Macroyan. "Let's go shopping! I want to buy shoes, and we need to get out!"

Lailoma, always up for some fun, welcomed the idea of shopping. Even though the mujahideen were visible everywhere, the young women felt the streets were safe enough and took off for an afternoon of girlish camaraderie.

Shopping was an all-day event. It was not as though the two could jump into a car for a quick trip to the mall. They wanted to go to Mandawi Market, a popular open-air shopping district in the heart of Kabul. You could find anything and everything there: fresh produce, clothing, jewelry, and yes, leather goods, including shoes. The drawback was that reaching the area required about a forty-five-minute bus ride from Mussa and Lailoma's Macroyan apartment. But the pair planned to spend the better part of the day, so the travel time was not a problem.

They dressed for the occasion. Neither owned a burqa, but since the mujahideen were everywhere, they did wear scarves over their heads. Roya had more finely tuned the art of covering her head than Lailoma had. Both pulled the scarves down over their foreheads and up over their mouths so that just their eyes showed, but Lailoma's scarf kept slipping off, leaving her vulnerable to the eyes of anyone nearby.

The evening before the shopping spree, it had rained heavily and the streets were muddy. As people—mostly men, but some women, all in burqas or scarves—gingerly picked their way through the mud, the hems of their gowns became dark and heavy. The girls, out on an adventure, didn't bother with caution. They ducked in and out of stores as they browsed the latest fashions and Roya tried on shoes.

The retail stores were located on the first floor of the commercial complex. The second floor was home to, among other establishments, a hotel and a men-only balcony restaurant that overlooked the street. As Lailoma and Roya walked along, chatting and laughing, Lailoma heard a thud in the mud behind her. Startled, she turned to see a man's shoe. Both girls glanced up, and there, seated on the balcony, were several mujahideen, recognizable by their long hair, long full gowns, scarves around their necks, black makeup on their faces, and automatic rifles over their shoulders.

Lailoma and Roya froze in place. Why would someone throw a shoe at them?

One of the mujahideen leaned over the rail and supplied the answer to that question. He looked Lailoma in the eye. "Cover your head," he ordered in Pashto. Her scarf had fallen off her head again and lay draped across her shoulders.

"Fix it!" Roya hissed at Lailoma, knowing she might resist the order.

"No," Lailoma whispered back. "I'm not going to put it back on."

"You have to," Roya urged in a little louder whisper. "We could be in so much trouble."

"No. All of them are watching me. If I put the scarf up, everyone will think I'm afraid."

When she didn't pull the scarf up, Roya snarled at her with a few curse words and an angry *"Dakhtar sag!"* calling her a dog. Then in a louder whisper, she cried, "You're going to get us killed."

Lailoma instinctively steered her into the nearest store. "Just act natural," she told Roya. "We're just two girls shopping. Pretend nothing happened."

After what seemed an eternity, but was probably no more than fifteen or twenty minutes, during which Roya tried on shoes to kill time, Lailoma thought they had hidden long enough. "Let's get out of here," she urged Roya.

"No! No! They're probably still out there. They're probably looking for us." Roya's face was white with fear.

Eventually Lailoma convinced her to exit the store. Both glanced up to the balcony as they passed, but the mujahideen were gone and no one seemed to be following them. A damper, however, had been put on their happy shopping trip, and both girls just wanted to get back to the Macroyan.

"Let's grab the bus and go home," Lailoma said.

"No! We can't get on a bus! They could find us too easily if we take a bus," Roya responded, shaking her head.

Finally they hailed a cab and had the driver take them to Abdullah's house so the mujahideen couldn't follow them to the Macroyan. From there, they called Mussa, who drove over and picked up Lailoma.

The rendition Roya gave of the episode to Abdullah and Mussa was dramatically embellished to the point that both father and son laughed. Yes, they had been in danger, but maybe not as much as Roya portrayed.

"She's always been this way," Mussa told Lailoma with a bit of humor in his voice.

The excursion was one of the last semi-carefree days left for Lailoma and her sister-in-law. Everyday life soon became miserable for Kabul residents, even in the Macroyan.

KABUL, 1990 TO 1991

The Russians had completely vacated Afghanistan by February 1989. Without them, there was no appetite for a restaurant that served alcohol, so Abdullah closed Doostiee and opened a bakery. Still, his medical drug import business with Germany provided a steady income that supplied food for his wife and children, and he couldn't resist showering Lailoma and Mussa with special treats in addition to what they already were able to purchase with Mussa's income. Granted, nothing was quite the quality they had enjoyed earlier, but they were still better off than most people.

Even though their home was well-stocked with good food, Lailoma began to lose her appetite. Maybe, she thought, this was due to the uncertainty around her. Food just didn't settle well in her stomach. And sometimes the smell was nauseating.

"Why aren't you eating?" Roya demanded to know one Sunday evening in 1990 as they shared a delicious dinner at Abdullah's house.

"I just don't feel that well," Lailoma told her. "I'm sure I have a touch of stomach flu or something."

"You're pregnant!" screamed the always flamboyant Roya. "I just know it!"

"No, I'm sure I'm not," Lailoma returned. "Don't get so excited. It's probably nothing."

To prove she was okay, Lailoma nibbled on a piece of naan, but soon put it back on her plate.

"Yes, you're pregnant," Roya said. "I'm taking you to the doctor."

"Let's give it a couple more days," Lailoma told her sister-in-law. "If it doesn't pass, I promise to go to the doctor."

A few days later, to surprise her, Mussa picked up kebabs on the way home. When he walked into the apartment, the smell, which she usually loved, sent her running to the bathroom.

"You're pregnant," Mussa told her.

And so it was. Lailoma and Mussa had been married just a little more than a year and now both families welcomed the good news that a baby was to be born. "If it's a girl, let's name her Fawzia," one relative said, "or how about Aisha?" Another suggested "Noman" if the baby was a boy.

Lailoma's appetite returned, and then all she wanted to do was eat. Eat well, she did. Mussa's family cooked good, nutritious food and sent it to her, including delicacies she wouldn't have otherwise had: *bolani* (a flatbread with a vegetable filling), *ahshak* (dumplings similar to wontons), and *kabuli* (a main dish featuring rice, carrots, raisins, and lamb). Sometimes they laughed at her amazing appetite, but they were generous and treated her solicitously.

Prenatal visits with a physician weren't common when Lailoma was pregnant—possibly one of the reasons Afghan women suffer from one of the highest rates of maternal mortality in the world—and Lailoma visited with a doctor just once during her nine months of pregnancy. Mussa and she planned a two-week vacation in India to escape the cold of Kabul during March, the Hamal month on the Islamic calendar (February on the Gregorian calendar), and she was concerned about whether flying would be acceptable so close to her due date at the end of the month. The doctor assured her she would be fine, so they enjoyed a two-week escape from the cold. They returned by Hamal, March 21, the beginning of the new year, and just six days later, their child was born. Unlike Qurisha's nine children, Lailoma's child was born in a hospital.

When a woman reaches her ninth month of pregnancy in Afghanistan, in-laws begin to arrive to help take care of her. In this case, Roya became a permanent fixture in Lailoma and Mussa's home. When Lailoma's contractions began early that March morning, she made the mistake of telling Roya.

"I think I might be in labor," Lailoma calmly told Roya. "But the pain is light, so maybe not."

Roya sprang into action. "You're going to have your baby!" she screamed, jumping up and down. "You're going to have your baby! You're going to have your baby!"

Her outburst was probably enough to wake Mussa, but still she went into the bedroom and screamed at him. "Get out of bed, Mussa. We need to go to the hospital now!"

In quick order, Mussa hired a taxi and the three sped off to the hospital. Like many first-time mothers, Lailoma arrived at the hospital before it was necessary. If she had had her way, she wouldn't have gotten there so early.

"You have all day before the baby is going to be born," the doctor told her. "You can go home and come back later when the contractions are closer together."

"OK," Lailoma said, turning to Mussa and Roya. "Let's go home."

Roya wasn't budging. "No, we are not going home!" she said with authority. "What if we don't get back here in time?"

As it turned out, they didn't have all day. By four that afternoon, Lailoma and Mussa's baby was born. The nurse ran into the waiting room to share the good news.

"A boy or a girl?" Mussa asked.

"Give me my gift first," the nurse said, teasing him.

In the meantime, Roya ran into the waiting room. "Give her something! Give her something! You have a boy! You have a boy!"

Abdullah had made sure Mussa was ready for this moment with a thousand Afghani. After giving some to the nurse, he pulled bills out of the roll for everyone in the waiting room.

The excitement wasn't over. At midnight, there was a fire in the security guard's room. Mussa, Lailoma, and Roya were so accustomed to hearing rockets and gunfire that they assumed someone had attacked the hospital. Fortunately, that wasn't the case. They never found out what started the fire, but it was extinguished within a half hour, Mussa and Roya went home for the night, and Lailoma was able to settle down for a little sleep, but not much. The room—typical for one of the area's hospitals—made Lailoma squeamish. The "hospital smell" made her queasy, and she couldn't look past the blood-stained brown wool army blankets the nurses insisted on using to cover her. There was no sheet between her and the stained blanket as each bed was outfitted with a bottom sheet only.

The next morning when Lailoma looked out the window and saw Roya and Mussa approaching, her heart jumped for joy. She knew she was going home. Maybe because Lailoma was so anxious to leave the hospital, the checkout process seemed to take an extra-long time. When Roya left her sister-in-law's bedside to help facilitate the process, Lailoma and Mussa had a brief moment alone in the hospital room, their first since the birth.

"It's good you have a boy," Mussa told Lailoma somberly. "He will help you. If I don't live that much longer, this baby boy will grow and become the man of your house.

"Make sure he studies. Just don't let him join the army. Give him any other education he wants, but don't let him join the army. Afghanistan will no longer be a good, safe place to live. There will always be war that robs our country of its young people. If I am not alive, leave the country. For his studies. For both of your safety."

"Why do you say that?" she asked, alarmed. "Please don't say that. You're going to live."

"Not with these people in power," he answered. "Our son will be the man of your house," he repeated.

On the third day after their son was born, Lailoma and Mussa invited relatives from both sides of the family to their home, and then the naming frenzy began in full force. Everyone offered a suggestion. One of Mussa's three aunts had chosen a name before Lailoma gave birth, and since she was one of Mussa's favorite people in his family and he was especially close to her, they agreed to give her the honor of naming the baby. Their son would be named Maiwand.

The nursery was ready, compliments of the women in Lailoma's family—her mother, sisters, and any other female who wanted to help—and when the time came to lay Maiwand in his crib for the first time, the honor went to Qurisha, not Lailoma. The custom didn't bother the new mother. She knew that when the first child is born, especially if it is a boy, the mother doesn't have much say in what happens. The nursery decor, the clothing, even the name are for others to choose. Whatever the family selects, that's the way it is.

Qurisha had lined the crib in baby blue as soon as she learned the child was a boy. But she was ready for either a boy or a girl. She had prepared everything—the clothes, the blankets, the baby bathtub, and more—in both pink and blue. Two of everything, one pink, one blue. The women brought out fresh fruit, chocolates, and other candies. They shared all of these with neighbors as a way to announce Maiwand's birth. As Lailoma looked at all the support from the two families, she thought to herself, *They are so happy.*

She was happy too. She had just given birth to a beautiful, healthy baby boy. The thought of medical school had been abandoned, but she recognized that she had a good life and was surrounded by people she loved.

Inside, the family celebrated. Outside, the shelling continued.

A short time later, in 1992, the mujahideen took control of Kabul—though they continued to fight each other—and President Najibullah's government collapsed. Mussa lost his job, but thankfully Abdullah was able to keep the young family supplied with enough food for themselves and to share with the people around them. Their neighborhood was home to many government workers who also lost their jobs, and as the times were uncertain for everyone, when Lailoma prepared a meal, she made more than she and Mussa could eat and invited the neighbors' children to come in for a good meal. Or sometimes she just took the food outside when it felt safe and called the children to come and take it to their homes or to a neighbor's home. Among the neighbors she shared food with were Mussa's friend Magid—who had also worked for Najibullah—along with Magid's wife, Shrifa, and their two children. Several years later, they would return the favor.

ARIZONA, 2012

"I have something for you!" Lailoma said when I arrived one Saturday morning.

I wondered what it could be, and then out she walked holding a lovely pair of crepe winter-white cocktail pants. "Wow! They're beautiful," I told her. "But why?"

I attended many formal events as part of my work life, and Lailoma knew that because she had altered so many of the things I bought to wear. She also knew my size.

"Someone returned these to the bridal shop," she told me. "The shop owner gave them to me because they had been altered and she could no longer sell them. I have nowhere to wear them, so I'm giving them to you! Try them on, and I'll make them fit."

Before we started our conversation for the day, I slipped on the pants, and she went to work with her pins. After tightening a bit of fabric here and there and making them a little shorter, she was satisfied. I had just become the lucky recipient of someone else's buying mistake, and I was touched by Lailoma's thoughtful gift.

That day, she told me the story of Ojeie, her sister-in-law. Maybe she had already been thinking about Ojeie and that's why she wanted to talk about her. Maybe the white pants made her think of her sister-in-law. Later, I realized that Lailoma's generosity almost always included something she had made or sewn for someone. The same turned out to be true with Ojeie.

OJEIE, 1992

After Lailoma and Mussa married in 1990, Mussa had secured a job for Ahmadwali as his personal bodyguard, but when President Najibullah was ousted and Mussa lost his position as general, Ahmadwali became unemployed as well. At this point, he couldn't afford to buy a house, so in 1992, he and his wife, Ojeie, moved back in with his parents.

Shaima, engaged but not yet married because her fiancé was still studying in Russia, lived in the family home, as did Naim, Laila, Sonita, Sitara, and Susan. It was a full house, to say the least. During this time everyone struggled—to find transportation, to purchase food. Buying a home was out of the question, but they were lucky. They had family.

Ojeie had become pregnant shortly after her marriage to Ahmadwali, but lost her first baby, a boy, within just a few days of birth. Now, a couple of years later, she was in the early months of a second pregnancy. Wanting her to have some fresh maternity clothing, especially since this time the baby was due during the hot summer months, Qurisha bought some pretty cotton fabric—blue with white polka dots—and asked Lailoma, the family's most talented seamstress, to make a dress for Ojeie. Lailoma wasted no time, happily deconstructing an older maternity dress for a pattern and quickly sitting down to sew.

Ojeie loved Lailoma's creation. When she tried it on, she twirled and danced around the room to show it off, but there was still a sadness about her. Even in her celebration, she seemed melancholy, as if she had a premonition of something bad to come. Later, Ojeie confided in Shaima, "Lailoma worked so hard on my dress, but I don't know if I will live to wear it. If something happens to me, here is where I've put the cleaning cloths and the detergent to wash the walls."

Her matter-of-fact tone sent an icy chill down Shaima's spine. "Don't say that, Ojeie. Nothing will happen to you," she consoled her, but Ojeie's gloom pervaded the room. Her words stayed with Shaima for the rest of her life.

With all of the fighting, travel outside Kabul had become nearly impossible, so visiting with family in Wardak was out of the question. But one summer day, three of Qurisha's brothers felt it was safe enough to drive into Kabul.

"Come over for dinner tonight," Qurisha told Lailoma on the telephone, "Your uncles are coming! Mama Rahim, Mama Naeem, and Mama Khalid are all coming from Wardak. It's the first time in so long! I want the whole family to have dinner together."

Mussa couldn't go out that evening, but he called a cab for Lailoma, who gathered up five-month-old Maiwand and a diaper bag and set out to visit with her family.

Ojeie donned her new blue-and-white polka-dot dress for the occasion. Nearing the end of her fifth month of pregnancy, she now needed the extra space the maternity dress provided.

As evening approached, the streets were filled with celebration over the triumph of Abdul Ali Mazari, who had led the mujahideen into Kabul. Soldiers shot guns into the sky, whooping it up with dancing and jumping. The mujahideen were joyous and rowdy.

Inside, Shaima, Ojeie, and Lailoma prepared a sumptuous meal of rice, lamb, and a green salad for dinner around 9 p.m. The family gathered on the floor around the dastarkhan and enjoyed the pleasure of the good food and each other's company. After dinner, the three young women cleaned and folded the dastarkhan and took it with the dishes outside to the downstairs kitchen. When Lailoma returned to the living room, there was a convivial family scene: the uncles were playing a lively game of cards with Ahmadwali and the room was filled with joking, laughter, and fun. In spite of the chaos outside, in spite of the gunshots in the air and uncertainty over the incoming regime, the family members felt secure and happy in each other's presence.

Shaima and Ojeie made the evening tea and brought it up to the living room. "Let's wash dishes in the morning," Ojeie suggested. "Tonight let's sit down and relax. We girls need to have some fun too."

Lailoma nursed Maiwand and after he fell asleep, she laid him on a mattress for the evening. Qurisha wanted to move the party downstairs—it would be quieter for Maiwand and Shahwali, who was ready to retire for the evening. Except for the baby and his grandfather, everyone took the outside staircase down and moved their gathering to just inside the door, nearer to the kitchen. Qurisha sat on a mattress next to the door and Ojeie sat down next to her.

"No, sit over there," Qurisha told Ojeie, indicating a spot more to the inside. "With all of the gunshots outside, it's not good to sit so close to the door."

"No, Adai, I want to sit close to you," Ojeie answered.

They left the door slightly ajar for the fresh summer air. When everyone was settled, Ojeie stood and served the tea, then rejoined Qurisha on the mattress.

About fifteen minutes later, Shaima brought another pot of tea from the kitchen. Suddenly, there was a loud "pop." At first everyone thought someone from the outside had banged into the door very hard. But what they heard wasn't a thump on the door. It was, instead, one of those moments in life when everything changes, one of those shocking moments you later want to replay, as if the outcome could somehow be altered.

Ojeie reached up, touched her shoulder, and looked blankly at Qurisha.

"What was that?" she asked, her eyes opening wide. These were her last words. Then she slowly slumped over onto Qurisha.

Qurisha screamed. "She's been shot!"

Ahmadwali, Shaima, and Lailoma tugged the blue-and-white polka-dot dress up to Ojeie's neck and saw a very small hole on the backside of her shoulder. That was all, and it was so small. But there was no exit wound in the front, and they could see no bullet. The bullet had entered her shoulder but not come out.

"It's deep," Ahmadwali said.

Suddenly the gravity of the situation hit him. "We're losing her!" Ahmadwali shouted. "The bullet is stuck inside her. It could be in her heart!"

Ojeie just gazed at her mother-in-law. Qurisha rocked her back and forth, calling to her, "Ojeie! Ojeie! Stay with us!"

A single tear trickled down Ojeie's check. Then she slowly took her last breath.

"The baby!" Qurisha said, placing her hand on Ojeie's abdomen. She could feel the child moving quickly. But soon it too quieted down and then, like Ojeie, the child became still.

Qurisha was still holding Ojeie and screaming when Ahmadwali tore out of the yard to run to a neighbor's house to borrow a car. With the mujahideen in the streets, it was dangerous to drive, but he had no choice.

Qurisha helped put Ojeie into the car, and Ahmadwali and Mama Khalid drove as fast as they could to the Red Cross hospital about ten miles away. The hospital was under the control of the Shias and their family was Sunni, but Ahmadwali had to take the chance that he could get help for Ojeie. The doctor assessed the situation quickly.

"I'm sorry," he told Ahmadwali. "It's too late."

The happy family celebration had changed in a split second. Ahmadwali and Mama Khalid took Ojeie's body back to the house. Those gathered at the home hugged Ahmadwali and told him how sorry they were, trying to console him. Because Muslims do not embalm their dead, typically they are buried within twenty-four hours of death. It fell to Ahmadwali to assure this happened. The young husband, who suddenly had so much to accomplish in a very short period of time, functioned in a state of shock.

In fact, the entire family functioned in a state of shock, and they were especially worried about Ojeie's mother. How would they tell her? Would she think Ahmadwali was responsible? Or that one of his uncles was?

Early the next morning Mama Rahim walked the fifteen blocks to Ojeie's mother's house to share the devastating news. Later, family members brought her to Qurisha and Shahwali's house, where they had laid Ojeie's body on the bed. Ahmadwali went out and bought the traditional white fabric in which to enshroud her, and a coffin. The women set about the process of preparing Ojeie for burial. Lailoma had made the pretty blue polka-dot dress for Ojeie. Now she sat down to make a white dress and pants in which to bury her.

Often a woman from the mosque—a daiee, the person who sometimes helps deliver babies—comes to wash the body. But Ojeie was shy and Qurisha knew she would have been embarrassed to have a stranger handle her body. Qurisha, along with the wife of one of her cousins—who happened to live on the same street as her—would attend to Ojeie's body. Ahmadwali, Mama Khalid, Mama Naeem, and Mama Rahim placed Ojeie's body on a board, covered her with a cloth, and moved her outside, where Qurisha and her cousin's wife slowly, gently, washed the body using a piece of the same white fabric Ahmadwali had bought for the burial clothes. Ahmadwali read from the Koran, and by 5 a.m., less than twelve hours after her death, Ojeie was prepared for burial.

Shahwali hired a chef from his office to come to the house. He and the chef dug five deep pits in the yard and built a fire in each to prepare lunch. The chef prepared large quantities of every kind of good food: a variety of delicious rice dishes, meatballs, and korma—a casserole made with sautéed onions, tomato sauce and seasoning, and small pieces of lamb. He made kabuli with rice, raisins, carrots, and pistachios. The meal was one the family might have chosen for a holiday, featuring some of the same dishes they had enjoyed at engagement parties and wedding feasts, but on this day the chef prepared the menu for a funeral.

At least 150 people came to the house to pay their respects. The women were somber as they stayed with the body, and Kaka Zaher opened his house to accommodate the men, who had their own special duties to perform.

Among the guests was the mullah, who prayed. Then the men placed Ojeie's body in the casket Ahmadwali had acquired that morning. They covered her face with a white cloth, which would be removed only for family members of the same sex. Ahmadwali would not be allowed to look at her face again because after a spouse dies, the vow has been broken. The mullah positioned Ojeie's face toward the mosque, and prayed for the forgiveness of her sins. When it was time, the men placed the casket in a hearse, and then boarded the two buses Ahmadwali had rented to transport them to the cemetery, following the hearse. Gravediggers had already prepared the site.

There the mullah prayed, declaring, "Allah is kind and forgiving," and placed a prayer he had written on a small piece of stone in front of Ojeie's face in the coffin.

After the graveside prayers, the men returned home and joined everyone in eating the abundant lunch. Then they went to the mosque for noon prayers. It was hard to comprehend that it was just noon, barely twelve hours from the time Ojeie had been struck by the random bullet.

At home, Qurisha and her daughters made halwa, cooking flour in oil with cardamom and sugar. When the oil rose over the halwa, they spooned it onto a long loaf of bread they had cut into ten pieces. They put the sweet treat on big plates and took it into the street to feed the poor. This would help nourish Ojeie in the afterworld. They also served sweet juice, water with sugar and lemon, to the children. This would keep Ojeie from being thirsty.

When everything required had been fulfilled on this day, Ahmadwali slipped away to the bedroom he had shared with Ojeie and sobbed.

For three days after Ojeie was buried, one of the men in the family went to the cemetery before sunrise. He knocked on the headstone and called to Ojeie, "Wake up, Ojeie! It's morning, and it's prayer time."

When the sun rises over the horizon, it is commonly believed to make a very frightening sound. The man's voice would keep Ojeie from being scared. The men continued this ritual for three days, knowing that on the third day, when Ojeie tried to rise and her head touched the coffin, she would realize she was dead.

Generally, women don't go to the cemetery because of a belief that they look naked to the dead person. If a woman decides to go, she modestly folds the right side of her skirt over the left side to cover her private parts. Qurisha, her daughters, and their other female relatives followed this custom as they paid their last respects to their beautiful Ojeie.

Every Friday during the following forty days, extended family members and close friends cooked for the family, alternating serving the meals at Qurisha and Shahwali's home and Mussa and Lailoma's. During these forty days, Qurisha continued to serve the sweetened lemon water to the children in the streets.

On the thirty-seventh day, the family invited to their home all the people who had attended Ojeie's memorial. The mullah came and gave a reading from the Koran. Then he took a pitcher of holy water to the grave and poured it over the place where Ojeie lay.

The mullah returned from the cemetery, bringing with him thirty Korans, and each of the men read from the book, making sure to complete the readings before prayer time at noon. The same elaborate food that had been prepared for the memorial service was shared again at this occasion.

After everyone left, the family took the remaining holy water to the cemetery. Each spoke a few words to Ojeie and then poured the water on the grave. They said their last goodbyes and went home.

CHAPTER 6

WINTER, 1992

In 1992 Abdullah still had some means, though somewhat altered. The winter after Ojeie was killed, he decided it was a good time to move the family out of Kabul for a while. Najibullah had been assassinated; Burhanuddin Rabbani, president of the Islamic Council of Afghanistan, had declared himself president of Afghanistan; and the civil war in Kabul was in full force. Abdullah owned property in Wardak and, because he was prosperous, he had built a country home outside the village walls. It was here, in what he considered a vacation home, that he hoped to keep his family safe until the dangers in Kabul lessened. Because he didn't often use this home, his sister and her family lived in it.

Having made arrangements to take his second wife, Rahima, his two young stepchildren, his daughter Roya, and his younger daughter, Naseema, to Wardak, he stopped by Mussa and Lailoma's apartment in the Macroyan.

"Pack your things," he told them. "We all need to get out of the city, and you need to leave the Macroyan because it's especially dangerous. There are more rockets here than anywhere else in Kabul. We're leaving tomorrow."

"No," Mussa answered. "I can't leave in case I'm needed here. I don't know what's going to happen here, how things are going to turn out. But maybe it's a good idea for you to take Lailoma and Maiwand with you."

Abdullah's nephew in the Wardak house had access to a minibus and was prepared to pick them up the very next day and drive them to Wardak. When Abdullah made up his mind, he moved quickly. "Get ready," Abdullah told Lailoma. "Pack some things for yourself and Maiwand. We'll pick you up first thing in the morning."

The entire family, save Mussa, made the trip together in the minibus, planning to stay for the two and a half to three months that remained of winter. Even though it was cold outside, the inside of the car was stifling. The women had to don burqas for the excursion out of Kabul, and Lailoma, who didn't own one, wore a short version one of her relatives had sent to Kabul to be repaired. It was too cold to open the bus windows, and there was no ventilation inside the vehicle. To take a sip of water, the women lifted the bottom edge of their burqas and raised the plastic cup under it to their lips. The younger children got carsick.

The minibus bounced along the same uneven road taken by Qurisha as a young bride with Shahwali so many years earlier. The road that had been bad then had deteriorated more with time. Abdullah's nephew still had to dodge donkeys, but now the problems were more significant. Because the Russians had used the road for transportation of their heavy tanks and other artillery, it was full of potholes. Sometimes the nephew had to pull off the road for a line of heavy equipment to pass. Along the way, there was the ever-present risk that travelers could be caught in the crossfire as the mujahideen shot at each other from the mountains. Cars broke down too, with drivers sometimes able to pull off the road and sometimes holding up traffic because they couldn't. It was common to see male passengers get out and try to push a stalled car out of the way.

Driving, at best, was a free-for-all: there were no road rules.

Afghanistan also had no car seat regulations—and still had not implemented them many years later. Maiwand, a toddler by this time, rode on Lailoma's lap; for a while, Roya held him. Sometimes he sat on the seat, but space was limited and it was hard for him to keep his balance as the vehicle made its way on the rutted road. When he finally nodded off after Lailoma breastfed him, she laid him on the seat beside her, tucking a blanket around him—not for warmth but to help hold him in place. Abdullah's two young stepchildren—one younger than Maiwand and one a year older—were also in the minibus.

The trip wasn't a restful one, to say the least. It was treacherous. What should have been a two-hour journey lasted fourteen. And places to make a stop were few. Along the side of the road there was an occasional makeshift stand where the entrepreneurial sold fruit, bread, or kebabs, and drivers pulled off to stretch their legs and get a snack. When Abdullah's entourage was able to make such a stop, they found fresh, hot kebabs. Abdullah and his nephew got out of the car and bought the welcome treats—enough for everyone.

The gesture was good, except for one thing: the women and children couldn't get out of the stifling car. Abdullah and his nephew sat outside on the ground to eat, but delivered a kebab on a long piece of bread for the women and children to share inside the car. All they could do was break pieces off the bread and pass it along to the next person. Lailoma pulled Maiwand inside her burqa, and they took tiny bites of the kebab under cover. Roya ate her snack the same way. Naseema was younger and wore only a scarf, so she was able to eat a little more easily. To wash down the bread and kebab, they took tiny sips of water. They knew there were no bathroom facilities along the way, so taking a deep, satisfying drink wasn't an option.

Finally, they arrived at the country home in Wardak around dinnertime. All Lailoma wanted was to use the bathroom, enjoy a long drink of cold water, and rest. But Abdullah's sister had other plans. She and her daughters-in-law, who had prepared a full meal for the weary travelers, laid out the dastarkhan and proceeded to serve dinner.

Dusty and tired, Lailoma's mind was on the family she had left behind. She felt she and Maiwand were relatively safe, but what about her mother and father and her sisters and brothers? What about Mussa?

And she worried about living here. The home was so unfamiliar to her, and she wasn't used to living among people who weren't her immediate family. She hated the idea of being a guest in another woman's house. To her, the homes in this area outside the village seemed castle-like, especially compared with the homes in the village. But while the home was large, to Lailoma it was crowded with too many relatives, and it was personally stifling.

Abdullah's sister and her husband stayed in one room with their daughter. Their two sons and their families each had their own rooms. On the other side of the home was one room where Lailoma, Roya, and Naseema put their things. Abdullah, his wife, and her two small children had a room on that side of the house as well. Three single sons stayed in another room on the second floor, which they had added to the home. This attic-like second floor, which had not been finished, had no window and no door.

The stucco home sat on an acre of land outside the village, with other large homes a short distance away. In the very conservative Wardak Province, Lailoma and the other women weren't allowed to walk outside the enclosed part of the yard, lest they be seen by jihadi who might be in the area. It was also taboo for a woman who came from another village and family to be seen outside the home.

In addition to all of this, Lailoma really was viewed as different by the rest of the family. Under the burqa she had worn for the journey to Wardak, she was wearing modern clothing and her hair in bangs. And, perhaps more than anything, it was well known that she had attended school, setting her apart from all of the other females in the home. Life in Wardak—even outside the village walls—came with a different set of rules.

One evening before dusk Abdullah said to her, "Let's go for a walk. I want to show you our land. If I am not alive and Mussa is not here, I want you to know about our property."

Both put on their coats and scarves and went for a walking tour. Abdullah showed her all of his farmland and his orchards. When they finally came back to the house an hour or more later, Abdullah's sister was beside herself with anger. "You have shamed us," she told Lailoma. "You went outside by yourself with my brother."

The entire household became embroiled in a boisterous argument. The women screamed their disapproval. The men yelled. Never mind that Lailoma was Abdullah's daughter-in-law. Never mind that he had initiated the excursion. But Abdullah didn't seem to be bothered by this breach of tradition.

"Stop!" Abdullah shouted over their angry voices.

"If you have a problem with my daughter-in-law, you come to me. She's not only my daughter-in-law; she's like my son. She can read and write. She understands money. She does my banking. I need her to know these things. I need her to know where our property starts and ends. This is none of your business."

He had a point. There were no official property lines. Mostly landholdings were marked by a stone or tree. If someone moved the stone or chopped down the tree, they could argue that the boundaries were different. Abdullah was in charge here, and the family learned to give Lailoma some space, however grudgingly.

In Kabul, Lailoma was used to dressing mostly as she wanted. In traditional Wardak, her clothing from Kabul was considered inappropriate and disrespectful, and she had every intention of conforming to their standards. One day a traveling fabric salesman came by the house. Piled high on his donkey were various folded fabrics, which he sold by the yard. The family let him into the yard, and all of the women clamored round him to select fabric for themselves.

"I'm happy to sew for everyone," Lailoma told the women.

Mussa's cousin's wife, Cobra, had a sewing machine, which Lailoma borrowed, and she began the task. It was a massive amount of sewing to undertake: two sets of clothing, each consisting of a dress and pants, for each woman. But she had nothing better to do, and the challenge kept her busy.

Even though she made clothing for Cobra too, Cobra became very "protective of her sewing machine. "Be careful with my sewing machine," Cobra would say. Then she would make an excuse to take the machine back to her room for a while.

When she wanted to continue sewing the next day, Lailoma, cautious and a bit shy about approaching Cobra, would send Roya to borrow the machine again. With the machine going back and forth between Lailoma and Cobra, making the dresses and slim pants to go under them took much longer than it might otherwise have.

Lailoma conformed to Wardak's conservative traditions in other ways as well. Since her engagement party, she had learned to pluck her eyebrows, but such primping was considered taboo in Wardak, so she stopped. In Wardak, bangs seemed too modern, so she allowed them to grow out, pulling them back off her face. Even inside the house, she wore the traditional scarf over her head and face, as did all of the women. The one exception was her mother-in-law, who didn't bother with the tradition. She wore a small silk square over her head.

One day early on in their stay, Maiwand came down with a fever and an uncontrollable nosebleed. The one local clinic was at the village security station, but only men were allowed to visit it. Abdullah's nephew offered to take Maiwand, but at four years old, Maiwand didn't want to leave his mother's side. There was one alternative to a visit to the clinic, however. At a particular location in the village that was considered holy, people reported being healed from various ailments.

"Let's take Maiwand there," Abdullah's sister suggested.

Lailoma had worn open-toed shoes to Wardak, which wouldn't do for a trip to the holy site, so Abdullah's sister gave her a pair of plain shoes that didn't show her toes and a longer, more modest burqa to wear. Appropriately attired, the little caravan walked to the holy place. When they arrived, Abdullah's sister placed dust from the ground on Maiwand's face. Success! His nose stopped bleeding, and by the time they returned home, his fever had broken.

Later on, Lailoma's mother-in-law came down with flu-like symptoms and as she was prohibited from going to the clinic herself, Lailoma wrote down the name of a syrup her family had used in Kabul for Abdullah to get at the clinic.

"Oh, you have a doctor in the house," the clinic's manager said after hearing the request. "I'd love to meet him!"

"No, we don't have a doctor," Abdullah answered him. He wasn't interested in exposing Lailoma to the outside world, so he said nothing about how he knew of the syrup.

"Then who wrote this prescription? We don't have that syrup, but here is something similar."

"What did you write?" Abdullah asked Lailoma when he returned home with the medicine. "The pharmacist was shocked that you knew about that medicine. But he gave me this to give you," he said, handing her a book about simple remedies.

With plenty of time to kill and with her interest in medicine, Lailoma read the book quickly. Shortly afterward, one of the distant relatives suffered a miscarriage when she was four or five months pregnant. When she didn't stop bleeding, her husband went to the clinic for a remedy. The pharmacist sent him home with four vials of medicine, a syringe, and instructions to give his wife two injections daily. But who would give the injections?

"You can do it!" the family told Lailoma. She had proven her skills with a needle and thread on fabric; now they urged her to apply her dexterity with a needle in another way.

Really? she thought. She had never given an injection.

She gathered alcohol, the syringe, and the medicine and went into the woman's room. She remembered from her reading that it was of utmost importance that no air get into the syringe. She made certain of that! On her first injection, she wasted about a fourth of the medicine as she pushed it through the syringe to avoid air bubbles. Nevertheless, she bravely pulled down the subject's leggings and inserted the needle.

Evidently, she was pretty good at it. "I didn't feel a thing," her patient said.

After that, anyone who needed an injection came to Lailoma. Abdullah was so proud of her and from here on she became known not as Lailoma, but as "Abdullah's daughter-in-law."

I am good at this, she told herself. *If I really studied, I could be a good doctor.*

Her self-training was a little bit trial and error. When one of Abdullah's nieces broke her leg, she needed to have an injection of pain medicine. This time, the needle had to hit the vein. When Lailoma came close to her with the needle, the frightened niece screamed and yelled uncontrollably. Lailoma tied her arm with a soft, improvised tourniquet, told her how to pump her fist, and got lucky. Blood spurted out the minute she inserted the needle. Her mistake, though, was that she forgot to remove the tourniquet so the medication pooled in that one spot. Lesson learned. The niece stayed for another six days, and Lailoma didn't forget again to remove the tourniquet.

In spite of her temporary and sporadic role as doctor, Lailoma was both bored and homesick. Sometimes on a sunny afternoon, she and Abdullah took their food outside and sat on the patio to eat. But to Lailoma, who had grown up in the relatively open social world of Kabul, this wasn't enough. Her perceptive father-in-law sensed this.

✳ ✳ ✳

News travels in a small rural community. When Lailoma's uncles—Qurisha's brothers—learned she was in the area, they were anxious to make contact with Abdullah to see if Lailoma could visit them. Had Abdullah lived in the village, they would have met with him at the mosque outside the village walls, as it wouldn't have been proper for nonrelatives to enter the home. But because Abdullah lived out in the country, he had built a small guesthouse outside the walls around the house. There he could receive guests.

When her uncles unexpectedly arrived one morning, Lailoma—and this was slightly bending the rules—was allowed to meet with them (in the company of Abdullah) in the guesthouse.

"Lailoma, come out and see who's here!" Abdullah called to her, knowing she would be excited to see them.

And there they were: Mama Khalid, Mama Naeem, and Mama Rahim. Nothing could have made her happier!

"Come back with us," her uncles urged. "We want you and Maiwand to visit. Your aunts want to see you too!"

"Oh, please, may I go?" Lailoma asked Abdullah. She so wanted to leave the stifling house filled with all of his relatives.

"Yes, you can go! It will be good for you. Stay two days and enjoy your family," Abdullah told her.

The uncles had rented a two-bench pickup truck, and with Abdullah's permission, she and Maiwand joined them for the hour-and-a-half trip over the snowy, unpaved road to the village.

She had such a good time with her relatives. The aunts and cousins cooked every kind of special food she remembered, and all of them fussed non-stop over Maiwand. The two days flew by!

Her mini-vacation was over so quickly. She rose the third morning and began packing for the journey back. But when her uncles came home from prayers, they brought bad news. She knew it had snowed heavily during the night, but she didn't realize that would stop them from driving on the roads. Of course it would stop them. There certainly were no snowplows coming through this remote farm area.

"We can't go today," her uncles told her. "The roads are impassable. And today, the snow is too soft to walk in. We'll leave tomorrow morning before daylight. By then the snow will have crusted over and we will be able to go on foot."

This was alarming news, not because she wouldn't relish an additional day with her relatives, but because Abdullah had specifically said she could stay two days. Lailoma ran up to the roof to look at the snowfall. The surrounding mountains and villages had disappeared in the flurries of snow. Her stomach twisted into knots. She didn't want to be disrespectful to Abdullah by not returning when he said to, but she didn't know how she would be able to get there. *Don't worry,* she told herself. *He will understand. It will be fine. He's not going to kill you.*

Well, he probably wouldn't kill her, but she still wanted to honor his wishes.

Her aunts and uncles were so pleased she had come to visit, and they wanted her to be happy, so early the next morning, her aging uncles put the saddle on their donkey. "Ride on the donkey," they told her. "We will walk."

"No, I'm not riding while you walk," she told them.

But Lailoma wasn't dressed to walk. A city girl, she hadn't thought about the treachery of walking in rural areas, let alone in the snow. She had worn those open-toed high heels on her trip with Abdullah to Wardak, and they were the only shoes she had with her.

Fortunately, Mama Rahim's wife wore the same size and gave her fleece-lined shoes to wear. She donned her lined, almost knee-length jean jacket, tied her white scarf around her head, and put on the sunglasses Mama Rahim insisted she wear to cut down the glare on the snow when the sun rose.

"When anyone sees you, they will think we took our daughter to the village, not a niece," Mama Rahim said, aware that even traveling with her uncles was an impropriety for Lailoma.

"I'm not sitting on the donkey," Lailoma said again. "I've never been on one."

"You need to sit on the donkey and hold Maiwand. You will never be able to walk that far."

"No, I'm not riding the donkey while you walk," she repeated, stubbornly.

Her two uncles and she took off walking before sunrise, immediately after prayers. They hoped to reach Abdullah's house before the melting snow made the walking more difficult. Part of the way, Mama Naeem rode on the donkey with Maiwand on his lap. At one point, even the donkey lost his footing, stumbled, and fell. Luckily no one was hurt.

"Are we almost there yet?" Lailoma asked repeatedly.

"Almost!" was always the reply.

Her endurance surprised her uncles. She kept pace with them pretty well, at least for the first part of the trip. About midway through their journey, Lailoma began to feel dizzy and wanted to stop for a while. "Keep walking," one of her uncles insisted. "We can't stop. Stay in my footprints."

Finally, after six or seven hours of walking, Abdullah's house came into sight. They had reached their destination. Abdullah's sister warmed a glass of milk for her, enriching it with butter. "This is good for you," she said, handing it to Lailoma. "It will help take away your dizziness." Lailoma took one look at it and knew she would get sick if she drank it.

While her uncles had lunch in the guesthouse with the men of the family, Lailoma lay down and passed out from exhaustion, not waking up until after sunset. By then, her hardy uncles had already left to return home.

The winter in Wardak was harsh. One morning after a heavy snowfall, Lailoma looked out the window and could barely see because of the fog. Her mother-in-law Rahima, with whom she got along but wasn't close, was baking naan, and the delicious smell was wafting throughout the house, but Lailoma sat thinking about Mussa, her family in Kabul, and the rockets that had fallen. Her only contact with the outside world was one small radio, and it didn't always have good reception.

She was jolted out of her thoughts by Abdullah.

"Mamo, the snow has melted. Make yourself ready! We're going to Kabul tomorrow morning!" Abdullah burst into the room, calling her the pet name he had used for her since Maiwand's birth.

The conditions were as good as they were going to get. Bus service was available in the area only twice weekly, and Abdullah knew the bus driver, whom he trusted to avoid the jihadi.

Her eyes welled with tears as she reached for his hand and kissed it.

"You can't go now," his sister told Abdullah. "You can't travel in this weather. It's too cold! Maiwand will get sick and die!" But Abdullah had made up his mind.

The news of their departure traveled throughout the village. That afternoon, all of the people Lailoma had helped during her stay showed up with gifts—butter, baked cookies, boiled eggs, bread dough, dried apricot seeds threaded on a necklace, and what seemed like a thousand uncooked eggs packed carefully in straw. There would be some for Mussa, Maiwand, and her, and some for her parents and their household. Such an outpouring of love was unexpected.

What they discovered upon their arrival in Kabul wasn't as heartwarming. Mussa was out of the city with his assignment in the army. In his absence, their apartment had been hit by a rocket, destroying the balcony and one bedroom, rendering it unlivable. Abdullah took Lailoma to her parents' home, and there Qurisha and Lailoma tried to put the pieces of her life back together. They sewed new mattresses and new drapes. They replaced some of the blue flowered dishes that had been broken.

While Lailoma and her mother worked on restoring the inside of the apartment, Ahmadwali obtained a contractor to repair the balcony and bedroom. Once again, Abdullah stepped up, loaning the money for the repairs. Mussa reimbursed his father when he returned about three months later.

Including the time Lailoma and Maiwand had been in Wardak, the family of three had been apart for nearly seven months. Their reunion was joyous, but there was also an element of concern. Mussa knew that while Lailoma and Maiwand had been in Wardak, they'd been relatively safe. He also knew that when he was called away the next time, they would be unprotected in the apartment. Yes, they had family nearby, but that wouldn't give them immediate access to help if they needed it.

As he anticipated, about a month later, he was called on assignment out of the city, this time for two or three months. After this assignment, he requested his duties be confined to Kabul, and the request was granted. The bombing continued, but they lived for a period of time in relative safety—until the Taliban took over Kabul.

CHAPTER 7

AHMADWALI, 1996

It was beginning to look as if the Taliban, a group that had emerged from a cohort of students studying at a fundamentalist Islamic school, was gaining ground over other mujahideen groups. In 1996, the Taliban captured Kabul. After what residents had experienced first under the Soviets and then the fighting mujahideen factions, many people welcomed the change. But the enthusiasm was short-lived. The Taliban instituted strict Islamic laws that affected all aspects of life. Their rules were especially hard on women, but also on political opponents and anyone who didn't adhere to their strict interpretation of Islamic law.

In his midtwenties, Ahmadwali became a target of their ideologies. He had set up a money-exchange store in the Kabul stock exchange building. There was a significant demand for this service, and his certainly wasn't the only exchange store in the area. Anyone who wanted to convert money from one currency to another went to one of these businesses to do so. By 1996, Ahmadwali was making a decent income and was able to employ his younger brother Naim in his business.

The September night when the Taliban took over Kabul, every business in the exchange building was robbed, presumably by the Taliban. Most of the businesses were wiped out and Ahmadwali, who kept almost all of his assets at the business, lost about eight hundred thousand Afghani that one night, leaving him with just a small amount of cash in other currencies.

A few days later, Taliban insurgents again stormed into his business. Ahmadwali's stash of money had made them suspicious. Not acknowledging that they had been there previously, they indicated Ahmadwali's accumulation of foreign currency and demanded of him, "How did you get this money?"

When they didn't like his answer, they seized him by his arms and forced him from the building.

As soon as they left, Naim dashed home as quickly as he could.

"They've taken Ahmadwali!" he breathlessly told his family.

"Who took him?" family members asked.

It was hard to ever really know, but Naim answered with what he felt in his heart to be true: the Taliban. Common thieves wouldn't have taken Ahmadwali, only his money. His family assumed he had been taken to jail to be shown the error of his ways, and as it turned out, that's exactly what happened.

Ahmadwali's arrest came just after sundown during Ramadan. During Ramadan, Muslims fast from sunup to sundown for thirty days. It is a time to make peace with each other and increase compassion for others through giving to the poor. The Taliban pointed out to Ahmadwali that he wasn't fulfilling his religious obligations.

"You shouldn't be keeping so much money for yourself," they said. "You should be giving it to the poor."

After throwing him into jail, they went on their way to prayers. From his jail cell, Ahmadwali observed other prisoners as they began their prayers in their cells. Something seemed off to him, some detail in the scene that he couldn't put his finger on. Only slowly did he realize what he was seeing: All of the exposed legs he saw under the prisoners' robes were black.

"Why are their legs black? Surely they would have washed their faces, hands, and feet to be clean for prayer," he commented to his cellmate. "Are they wearing black socks?"

"No, those are their legs," his cellmate answered. "You're right. They are black—it's from bruises, from being beaten. Look at my legs." He pulled up his robe to reveal his own swollen black-and-blue legs.

"My night was last night. Tonight will be your night."

Ahmadwali's presence made his cellmate safe. That night was indeed Ahmadwali's turn. When the guards returned from prayers, they called Ahmadwali's name.

"You call yourself Muslim. You're not Muslim!" they screamed.

Among the new, strictly enforced decrees was one regarding men's hair. Men were to wear their hair long, but it should be above the shoulders. Ahmadwali's hair was slightly below his shoulders. The jailers solved that: they took out a razor and on the spot shaved his head—dry.

Then they taunted him, demanding, "Why do you wear pants?"

The Taliban had publicly declared that men must wear Islamic clothing. Wearing pants was seen as a surly defiance. So, brandishing their knives, they cut his off his pant legs at the knees. Then they threw him onto the floor, with two Taliban on each side of him.

"We're going to give you a massage," they joked, beating him head to toe with branches until he passed out.

While Ahmadwali was unconscious, the Taliban hanged him from a wooden pole on the roof, tying just his hands and legs to the pole, like a lamb for barbecue. As he hung there, they whipped him. He woke up back inside the jail on the floor of the hallway.

It was almost morning. There was not another person in sight. *I can make a run for it*, he thought, trying to pull himself up. But his numb feet and legs wouldn't support him.

Eventually someone dragged him back into the cell with the other prisoner, who put ice and cold water on his legs. The cellmate obtained some herbs from the tiny, cramped commissary inside the jail and heated them with water over a small gas burner a prisoner's family had brought in for cooking. He gave the concoction to Ahmadwali to drink in an attempt to ease his pain.

That morning, Shahwali, Abdullah, and Naim went to the jail to see if they could find out why Ahmadwali had been arrested. When they asked Taliban representatives about Ahmadwali, they pointed again to his money. Their explanation for jailing Ahmadwali was that he didn't pay *zakat*—holy charity—to feed the poor, a requirement during Ramadan.

"Where did he get all of that cash? Why isn't he giving it to the poor?" they demanded.

"I want to see my son," Shahwali bit back.

The Taliban obliged. Two men held Ahmadwali under his arms and dragged him into the room. When Ahmadwali, bruised, covered with blood, unable to stand, and with his head shaved, was dragged in, all three men—Shahwali, Abdullah, and Naim—broke into tears.

"We will release him," the Taliban official said, "for Pakistani rupees." The amount they named was the equivalent of about five hundred thousand Afghani.

The three men left to try to pull together the money. Shahwali took whatever money Ahmadwali had left from the store, some of it in English pounds and some in German marks, but it wasn't enough, so he went to his brother Zaher to see if he would allow Shahwali to sell the part of the property in which Shahwali's family lived. This was the house that had been built on the hill behind the original structure where Zaher's family lived. That home was higher on the side of the mountain and from its balcony, the rooms in Zaher's house below were entirely visible. Apparently Zaher didn't want his family to lose their privacy, so he refused to allow Shahwali to sell his half.

Even though Kaka Zaher had been such a close uncle to Qurisha and Shahwali's children, he was looking out for his immediate family. "This is Ahmadwali's problem, not ours, not mine. Whatever he did, he has to answer for himself," was his answer.

Shahwali returned to his own home discouraged and despairing.

Abdullah pursued another path. He went to Lailoma in the Macroyan, whom he had entrusted with control of his money. "How much money do you have?"

Of course, the money she had was actually his.

"How much do you need?" she asked.

"Fifty thousand rupees," he said, not telling her why he needed it or that there had been an offer to release Ahmadwali for an exchange of cash.

She gave it to him without a question. He kissed her forehead and left.

Not long afterward, Roya knocked on the door of Lailoma and Mussa's home. "I think we need to go to your parents' home," she suggested.

They called a taxi and when the three arrived, Qurisha assured them, "They're going to bring Ahmadwali home."

"How?" Lailoma asked.

"Because of your father-in-law," her mother answered.

Kind, generous Abdullah loved Ahmadwali like his own son. "If you leave Ahmadwali in jail, he will die," Abdullah had told Shahwali. He made sure that didn't happen.

The family anxiously waited at the window for Abdullah and Shahwali to return with Ahmadwali. When the taxi arrived, Shahwali and Abdullah lifted Ahmadwali from the vehicle and carried him up the stairs and into the home. His legs were black-and-blue with bruises. His side and back looked as if they were made of the burgundy velvet of their mattresses from the brutal whippings. And they had used something like a cane with a sharp point screwed into the bottom to pierce his chest. Only his face was unharmed.

Qurisha grabbed a large scarf to cover her hair and partially cover her face, then she walked to the store and brought home eggs. She mixed the eggs with herbs to put on Ahmadwali's legs, chest, and back. The mixture brought him some relief from the pain, but the damage was permanent. Even years later, cold temperatures caused him to hurt all over his body. The internal wounds never healed. And like Mama Khalid after his torture at the hands of the mujahideen, at least for the time being, Ahmadwali was no longer able to work.

TALIBAN TAKES KABUL, 1996

In 1996, the year Maiwand turned five, the year the Taliban captured Kabul, and the same year Ahmadwali was arrested for "not being Muslim," the Taliban publicly lynched both President Najibullah and his brother, Shahpur Ahmadzai. Najibullah had been ousted from power in 1992, and he and Shahpur were living in the UN headquarters in Kabul. After seizing him, the Taliban paraded him through the streets of Kabul, dragging him behind a truck. Finally, they hanged both brothers from a tree at a four-way intersection. Symbolically, they stuffed money into Najibullah's nose, ears, and hair.

"You like money," they taunted. "You sold out the Afghan people to Russia."

At this point, any semblance of normal daily living had disappeared. Burqas reappeared to cover women from head to toe, just one of many strict rules the Taliban enforced. Even in Kabul, women were no longer permitted to leave their homes unless accompanied by a close male relative. But there wasn't much reason to leave anyway. A woman couldn't converse and deal with a shopkeeper. A woman couldn't be treated by a male doctor. A woman couldn't study at the schools or universities. Life in Kabul now resembled the conservative life in the villages. Maybe it was worse, because Kabul residents had known life without these restrictions.

No cosmetics. No laughing loudly. No high heels, which call attention by making noise. No riding in a taxi unless accompanied by a male relative. No playing sports or attending a sporting event or nightclub. No brightly colored clothing. No washing clothes at the river or in a public place. No music (for men or women). The list of nos continued.

But there were yeses too. Yes, paint the windows of your home so women inside can't be seen from the outside. Yes—even though an estimated 99 percent of Afghans were Muslim—change your non-Islamic name to an Islamic one.

One day at about 8 a.m., Lailoma and Mussa heard fighter planes overhead as they filled the air with rockets. From their window, they could see chaos in the streets, people running frantically for cover. Pieces of a rocket struck the bedroom of a house a couple of blocks away from Lailoma and Mussa's apartment. Some of the rocket stuck out from the window; the rest lay on the bed. The residents called Afghan soldiers, who removed it.

The only quiet time was prayer time. But inevitably after noon prayers, the all-too-familiar ugly *whooo* began again. Every day the rockets struck someone, and every day people were dismembered or died, or both. Traditional Muslim burial rituals had to be set aside. When someone died, their relatives buried him or her close to their home. They had no way to reach the cemetery, and often no way to obtain the traditional white cotton burial cloths.

Near the Macroyan, as well as near the home where Lailoma's family lived about forty-five minutes away in the Bagh-e Bala area, Lailoma recalls every fourth or fifth house being hit by a rocket. In the Macroyan, of the fifteen people who lived in one home, thirteen were killed. Only the two men who lived in the home survived, and that was by chance. They had been at work when the bomb struck the residence. A little child died in his bed, and an elderly lady who ground flour for bread was blown apart.

The grandmother in one home had her head blown off. It was later found in a neighbor's yard.

Bodies were scattered everywhere. Which parts belonged to which people was nearly impossible to tell. For the thirteen from the one home, relatives just made thirteen caskets and put parts in each one—a hand, a piece of a leg, a head. Then they sealed the coffins and put a name on each. The traditional Muslim belief that a body must return to Allah as a whole with all of its parts, unaltered by man, could not be fulfilled.

One night, when the Hazarah—one of the mujahideen groups—came to within a mile of Lailoma's parents' home, Ahmadwali called Lailoma and Mussa. "I have to move everyone because if the Hazarah come to our home, they are going to rape the women and kill our father and me. Can I bring the women to your apartment tonight? If you know of an empty apartment or house in your area, I can take them there. Or if you just give me a day or two, I can find a place for them."

"Bring them. Everyone is welcome," Mussa told Ahmadwali. "Don't worry about finding another house. Just bring them here."

That night Ahmadwali walked to a rental car location, trying to stay safely out of sight by making his way carefully from one house to the next. After successfully renting a car, he drove home and took his mother, sisters, and his new wife, Nazira, to Mussa and Lailoma's apartment. He had started walking around six in the evening, and by the time he acquired a car, picked up the women, and arrived at Lailoma and Mussa's apartment, it was 1:30 a.m. Ahmadwali didn't stay.

"Father and Naim are still at home. I want to stay with them to make sure they're safe," he told Lailoma and Mussa.

Qurisha, Mussa, and Lailoma did their best to assure him. "We will be fine. Just leave. Go now while it's dark," they told Ahmadwali. To travel by day would have been foolhardy.

To avoid detection, Ahmadwali kept his headlights off and, as much as was possible, drove through the back streets. Qurisha spent the night awake, so frightened every time she heard the cracking pop of bullets or an explosion. Not until the next morning when Ahmadwali called did the family in the Macroyan apartment know that he was safe.

Lailoma and Mussa had taken their family into their apartment with open arms, but their home in the Macroyan ultimately proved to be no protection for themselves.

NIGHT OF TERROR, 1996

Later that same year in their apartment in the Macroyan, Lailoma was preparing bolani for dinner. She rolled the dough into small, thin circles, and topped it with chives she had chopped and mixed with spices and salt. She folded one half of the dough over the other, forming a semicircle. As she was ready to drop it into the oil that was heating on the electric range, there was a knock at the door.

Before she or Mussa could reach the door, insurgents, claiming to be Taliban, kicked it open. Twenty or more—dressed in regular street clothes—stormed into their fifth-floor apartment. They shouted obscenities, cursed, and struck Mussa, throwing him to the floor. Then they tied his hands behind his back.

Lailoma grabbed Maiwand, who was crying, and held him tightly as the insurgents proceeded to rifle through each room of the apartment. They threw anything electronic—the TV, video player, radio, cameras, telephone, everything that represented "the devil's work"—out the living room window.

They flung open the kitchen cabinets and used the tip of an AK-47 to sweep the contents onto the tile floor. The crystal glassware shattered, along with the treasured baby-blue floral wedding china. With the bayonet attached to the end of the gun, they ripped apart the bedroom, slashing open the pillows and burgundy velvet mattresses. Lailoma watched as her wedding dowry and their reasonably ordered lives were decimated.

The violent search was not random. The Taliban detested the Soviets and were looking for documents that could connect Mussa to President Najibullah, whom they considered a Soviet puppet. Suspecting that he might be a target, Mussa had previously instructed Lailoma to get rid of anything that might serve as evidence of his position with Najibullah. Lailoma had burned most of the documents in their small charcoal grill. The rest she hid, mainly in her parents' home.

But Lailoma knew something Mussa didn't know. She had kept an envelope containing two documents that seemed particularly important: Mussa's commendation from President Najibullah when he had been promoted to general and his ID card. *One day Mussa might need these*, she thought. She tucked the envelope away under the clothing in Maiwand's dresser drawer.

She held her breath as the insurgents went through the drawers—afraid the Taliban would find the envelope and afraid Mussa would find out she hadn't burned everything. Miraculously, they didn't notice it. On this day, after scouring the rooms for more than an hour, they concluded there was no evidence in the home and left.

"Leave Afghanistan," Abdullah had often urged his son. "I will send your wife to you after you've left, but you must leave."

Mussa refused. Most of his cousins had left. Some were in Russia, some in Germany, some in the Netherlands, but that wasn't for Mussa. "I don't want my family to be tortured because of me, but I'm not going anywhere," he told Abdullah.

When the insurgents left, Mussa walked from room to room in a daze, not saying anything. They had escaped, but maybe Abdullah had been right. He lay down on the bed. While he rested, Lailoma took the envelope from under Maiwand's clothes and put it under their big burgundy area rug. Oddly, the Taliban hadn't looked there either. Then she turned to the kitchen and began to sweep up the mess: the bolani dough, the broken dishes, the broken treasures. That evening there was no dinner.

When Mussa called Abdullah to tell him what had happened, Abdullah again told him to leave. "You have to get out of here," Abdullah insisted.

"They didn't find anything," Mussa told his father. "There's nothing here to find. I think it's over. They won't come back."

The next morning, Lailoma and Mussa began the process of putting their lives back together. By the time Lailoma got up to take a shower, Mussa had already gone out for a walk. Along the way, he picked up *mantoo*—ground beef dumplings—that Lailoma steamed for lunch. The food made all three of them feel better. Lailoma cleaned the dastarkhan, Maiwand played with his toys, and Mussa lay down on the sofa to read a book. Lailoma and Maiwand lay down too, and eventually all three napped.

They woke up around four. After an afternoon nap, they usually would have gone to Abdullah's house for dinner. But they decided to stay home, relax, and have a cup of tea. Lailoma had just put water into the teapot when she heard a knock on the door. The door was broken from the previous afternoon, but they had managed to close it securely. Mussa went to answer the knock.

The Taliban didn't wait for him to open the door. They swung the door open, slammed the butt of a gun into Mussa's neck, and resumed the violent search they had begun the previous day. Room by room, they went through the apartment again. Lailoma had cleaned it up as well as she could, and now she would have to repeat the process. Clearly the Taliban suspected they had missed something. Again, miraculously, they didn't lift the burgundy rug, where they would have found the hidden documents.

Are they also looking for Ahmadwali? Lailoma wondered, following them from room to room while holding tightly to Maiwand.

"Stay in the kitchen," they ordered her harshly in Pashto.

Then they seized Mussa under his arms and dragged him from the home. Though she was afraid they would see her, she watched as they hanged him by a rope from the tree outside the couple's kitchen window. Maiwand clung to her as she witnessed the unthinkable: the Taliban put a gun to Mussa's head and pulled the trigger. The rope, it turned out, was just for show.

"Leave him hanging from the tree," they screamed up at Lailoma.

Using a bullhorn, the insurgents gave the same instructions to any on-lookers in the area. If anyone came to cut Mussa down, they said, that person would suffer the same consequence. Public executions had become common and served as examples for others.

Terrified beyond measure, Lailoma slumped to the floor and cried throughout the night as she sat with her arms around Maiwand, nursing him and rocking back and forth. When she dared look out into the starlit night, she could see Mussa's shadowy figure hanging from the tree.

LUNCH IN SCOTTSDALE, 2014

The Saturday Lailoma and I discussed the year 1996 started like any other, except for one thing. When I arrived and she opened the door, I was greeted by a wonderful aroma coming from the kitchen. When she happened to have Saturday off, Lailoma had invited me many times to stay for lunch, but I always had myriad reasons why that wouldn't work out. This time I knew she had prepared something special for me, and the tantalizing smell made it impossible to say no.

Before we sat down to lunch, we talked in greater detail than we had before about what had happened in 1996. As I listened, I thought back to what I was doing in 1996, fourteen years before I met Lailoma. The daughter whose wedding dress she altered in 2009 hadn't yet graduated from high school (which happened to be the same local high school from which Maiwand would eventually graduate). I was working for a local women's magazine, driving to our daughters' sports practices, volunteering at the concession stand for high school football games, and playing a little tennis. Except for what was mentioned on the nightly news or in the morning paper, I was oblivious to the events in Afghanistan.

Since that day I've also tried to establish what was going on in the rest of the world when Mussa was executed and Lailoma escaped to Pakistan with her son and only a small suitcase. I learned the first flip phone, the Motorola StarTAC, went on sale that year. *Endeavour* was launched into space for its tenth mission. NASA released the first surface photos of Pluto photographed by the Hubble Space Telescope. *Twister, Independence Day*, and *Star Trek: First Contact* premiered. Charles and Diana divorced. Roundups of major events from that year often make no mention of September 27, when the Taliban took over Kabul. I can't help thinking how odd it is that as you're going about your life, someone else can be experiencing such unbelievable trauma you know nothing about.

How she told the story so calmly, not just of the Taliban entering Kabul, but of their treatment of Ahmadwali and the torture and execution of Mussa, was remarkable. We spoke in English, of course, and I realized it was good that Qurisha didn't understand us. She had much more difficulty maintaining her composure than Lailoma did when talking about what had happened. When I had as much information as Lailoma could recall, we turned to enjoy our lunch. Just like that.

The smell that had greeted me at the door was *bamya* (okra stew). Lailoma and Qurisha had sauteed chopped okra and onion in oil, and then added tomato sauce, salt and pepper, and a Persian spice that Qurisha had ground with a mortar and pestle. They served the stew atop white rice and finished the dish with a dollop of Qurisha's homemade yogurt. Bamya was a treat, to say the least, and I could see they were pleased to share it.

AN ESCAPE PLAN, 1996

An eerie quiet came over the neighborhood after the Taliban left in the night. Everyone, Lailoma assumed, was afraid to come out of their apartments. But at around 3:30 a.m. from her window she saw two figures walk around her husband's body. She heard a knock, but she didn't open the door, afraid the Taliban had returned. Then she recognized her father's voice quietly calling to her. Her father-in-law was standing by his son's dead body. Her father and Abdullah had arrived to remove Mussa's body. They hugged her and told her they would come back for her.

That didn't happen.

Lailoma never saw her father again, though she learned later he had survived the night and apparently his actions had not been seen. She never saw her father-in-law again either, and never learned his fate. This man, who had loved her and whom she had loved so much, simply disappeared from her life. How the two men had known what happened that night, she never learned. Word travels.

In hindsight Lailoma realized that neither she nor Mussa had been surprised when the Taliban stormed their way into the apartment that fateful night. The inevitability had been unspoken, but certain; the only uncertainty had been when.

She recalled Mussa's somber statements the morning after Maiwand was born: "If I am not alive, leave the country. For his studies. For both of your safety."

Their serious conversation on the morning of Maiwand's birth had ended abruptly when Roya entered the hospital room. "Why are you so serious? What are you talking about?" she had demanded.

"Mussa thinks he will die," Lailoma had told her sister-in-law.

"Why do you say that?" his sister had shouted at her brother. "Don't say that!"

"Nobody knows the future," Mussa had told her.

As it turned out, Mussa lived for five years after Maiwand was born. During those years, though often disrupted by civil unrest, their lives were happy.

Lailoma never did become a morning person. Every morning, Mussa got up, made breakfast for himself, and left for work. Around nine thirty he called from the office to wake up Lailoma. She would get up, take a shower, and give Maiwand a shower and breakfast. The routine was comfortable and simple. Sometimes she made dinner in the evening, or occasionally they would go out for dinner, either to a restaurant or to Abdullah's house, where there were always good things to eat and family to enjoy time with. Even when the mujahideen took over and Mussa got fired, Abdullah had money and they lived comfortably.

Theirs was a happy, reasonably normal life. But then, the terror. On the first day of their ordeal, Taliban insurgents decimated their home. On the second day they returned to kill Mussa. And two days later, the Taliban returned once again. This time, they threatened to take Maiwand and put him in a Muslim school. If that happened, Lailoma knew she wouldn't see him again until he was eighteen.

She clutched the five-year-old tightly and screamed, "No! Kill me. Kill him. I won't give my son to you."

In response they beat her on the shoulder with a gun. But after, they left.

Allah is on my side, Lailoma thought when the insurgents left.

In spite of the pain in her shoulder, she held Maiwand tightly in her arms. For now she had saved her son. But what should she do next?

What could she do? She had no car, and realistically, she had nowhere in the city to go where Maiwand and she could hide safely. To whom could she turn? If she went to her parents' home, she would put the rest of her family in danger. Even if a car had been available, she couldn't drive. And anyway, if she had been caught on the streets alone her punishment would be swift and public. Then what would happen to Maiwand?

Islam prohibits a Muslim widow to remarry. Pashtun people, which both Mussa's and Lailoma's families were, particularly frown on second marriages for women. Some families force a widow to marry someone else in the family. Some families say, "No, she is a widow, and she must remain a widow."

Mussa had no allegiance to these conventions. That day in the hospital, he had told Lailoma, "If I die and you have a little boy with you, you can get married to anyone you want. Don't stay a widow. Protect your son. My father and your father are old-fashioned. Don't listen to them. If you want to leave the country, you don't have to ask them. You are a smart woman. You will survive. You can find your own way."

Lailoma never got a chance to consult either her father or her father-in-law. She knew she needed an escape plan to protect her son, and it came that very evening in the form of Magid, a neighbor who was a friend and coworker of Mussa, and whose family was among the people Mussa and Lailoma had supported with food or money when times were hard. He came to return the kindness.

"We're leaving tonight," he said quietly. "I'm taking my wife and two children to Pakistan. I think you and your son should come with us. Maybe tomorrow night it will be my turn, I will be their target, and they will kill me. If you want to save your son, you are welcome to go with us."

Lailoma knew what she needed to do. Mussa's words on the morning after Maiwand's birth came back to her, giving her confidence. "Afghanistan will no longer be a good, safe place to live. There will always be a war that robs our country of its young people. If I am not alive, leave the country."

She didn't hesitate. Time was limited, and she feared for the rest of her family. If she called them or went to see them, would she be risking their lives? Would she be helping the Taliban find Ahmadwali? No, there could be no phone call to her family or to Abdullah.

With just fifteen minutes to pack, she gathered three sets of clothing for herself and for Maiwand and put them into one small suitcase. Lately she had been wearing traditional attire—the same close-fitting cotton dress with leggings beneath it that her mother wore. Before the arrival of the Taliban, she just covered her head with a scarf that hung loosely around her neck. Now she knew she needed a burqa, and she didn't own one. Thinking quickly, she remembered that the shabby dark-green burqa she had worn in the minibus on the journey to Wardak was still in the apartment. There was a hole in it by the eye and it was too short for Lailoma, but it was all she had. It would have to do.

Then came a quiet knock at the door. She threw the burqa over her head, took Maiwand's hand, closed the still-broken door, and joined Magid and his family in a minivan he had procured. The departure was arranged so quickly that she had no time to retrieve any of the beautiful jewelry she had received at her engagement party or to even think about money. Or food.

* * *

The day she was fitting my daughter's wedding gown, Lailoma had shared with me the bare bones of these events. The images swirling in our heads when we arrived were of ivory satin and sparkling crystals, white flowers, and celebratory dancing. What Lailoma revealed was swirling in her head were images of broken china and worse—a noose dangling from a tree.

The juxtaposition of such violence against the purity of a bridal gown was jarring. The picture of evil and destruction on the one hand; the image of new life and celebration on the other. I realized that as we go about our lives in good times and bad, someone else, somewhere else, is experiencing the exact opposite. Should we temper our joy? I've come to understand that the best we can do is appreciate the joy we have in the moment and treasure it afterward.

THE CLIMB

The darkness was quiet and ominous as Magid drove the rented van east toward Torkham, the mountainous desert border between Afghanistan and Pakistan. The safety of Pakistan was just on the other side of the border, but they would need documentation to drive through the checkpoint and none of them had it. Instead, Magid's plan was to reach Shamshad Ghar, which, at nearly a mile above sea level, was the highest mountain at the border, and climb over Shamshad Ghar on foot. While he was able to contract a driver on the other side of the mountain, he had not found someone willing to risk driving them through the checkpoint.

When they passed Mahipar, about fifty miles outside Kabul, they were stopped by Taliban security, but because the women were covered by their burqas they weren't questioned. This was the first and only time either Lailoma or Magid's wife, Shrifa, was ever grateful for the burqa.

"Where are you going?" the guards asked Magid.

"Surobi," Magid answered, referring to an Afghan city in the same direction they were traveling, a logical destination.

The guards let them pass without incident. Had they known Magid was a member of the army, they most certainly would have killed him. If Magid was frightened, he had to appear not to be. He turned to Lailoma and Shrifa, letting out his breath, and said, "Thank Allah."

When they arrived in Jalalabad, they stopped for food and water at a tiny mud hut along the street. They were thankful for the filthy bathroom, and for the owners, who cooked kebabs for them to take with them.

They drove straight on to Torkham without any further stops. They had driven all night and into the next day. It was now late afternoon. Magid found the rental car company where he was to return the van, pulled in, and parked. They unloaded the very few items they had brought and could carry with them and started walking through the dry desert terrain, keeping their eyes on their goal, Shamshad Ghar. When on several occasions they saw a lookout with a security person scouring the area with binoculars, they ducked for cover in the shadow of the mountain or under whatever vegetation they could find.

It was a warm summer evening and with only limited ventilation around their eyes, Lailoma and Shrifa's burqas kept their hot breath contained, making breathing difficult. Neither complained as they walked for three or four hours through the dusty desert to Shamshad Ghar. For the first hour and a half they walked easily. But after that, Lailoma's knees became weak and began to burn. Occasionally, she or Shrifa would fall behind, and Magid went back and forth, shepherding the children through the difficult spots and walking back to help Lailoma and Shrifa.

They reached Shamshad Ghar at about 6 p.m. For a fee, Magid had arranged for Pakistani men with camels to carry the climbers' belongings, going around the mountain instead of over it for cover. Lailoma had only packed the small suitcase and a shoulder bag in which she had stowed some extra clothes for herself. She had no money, so Magid paid the Pakistanis to take the suitcase for her. Had she known how hard the climb was going to be, she would have sent the shoulder bag with the camel as well.

When Magid had knocked on her door the previous evening, she hadn't questioned how they were getting to Pakistan. She was so upset about leaving her family behind that she never thought to ask. She imagined that maybe Magid knew a way to drive the entire distance or that a camel might take them part way. That wasn't the case. They climbed and climbed—concentrating on their efforts and in silence, afraid to make noise. Were there jihadi on the mountain? Pakistani security?

Their feet slipped on loose gravel. The children stubbed their toes on protruding rocks. About halfway up, Lailoma knew she couldn't go any farther. Her legs were shaky, her thighs aching, and her calves tingling. Her heart thumped in her chest as the altitude challenged her. Magid looked back and saw that she was struggling, and once again he doubled back to help her, silently encouraging her. This was mountain climbing. No ropes, just hand holds revealed by the multitude of stars in the summer sky.

To make the climb easier, Lailoma and Shrifa tied the voluminous burqas around their waists to keep them out of their way. Five-year-old Maiwand was able to walk much of the way, especially when they occasionally had a short stretch of level ground, but when they'd start to climb again, Lailoma carried him or Magid would pick him up. He would carry his own two children one at a time to the next plain and then return for Maiwand. Lailoma couldn't look down for fear she would fall.

Around them, wolves howled, but they had to suppress their fear and ignore them to concentrate on not slipping on loose stones, using the moonlight and stars to guide their way. "Try to keep up," Magid quietly urged. "We have to reach Pakistan before sunrise. If Pakistani security sees you in your burqas, they will shoot you."

He was likely right. It was well known that Pakistan didn't want illegal immigrants entering the country.

The little group comprised just six people, three adults and three children. For each of them, this was uncharted territory.

When they reached the top, they shared a piece of naan about the size of a large pita bread and drank some water. The children were tired, hot, and hungry, but they seemed to sense the danger they were in. They quietly complained a little, but they didn't cry.

"Hurry," Magid continued to urge. "We have to reach the bottom before sunrise."

The descent was easier, but still treacherous, more so because of their shaky knees and unsteady legs. Each step offered the perilous opportunity to slip and fall. Now more than ever was the time for caution. The climbers weren't the only ones at risk. The men who were guiding the camel carrying their suitcases had told them what time to be there to retrieve their belongings. These men were also at risk of being caught, and they had made it clear they weren't interested in standing around waiting for the climbers if they were late.

Miraculously, they connected with the camel drivers at the bottom of the mountain at the predetermined location. They retrieved their belongings, and Magid inquired where he could find a car and driver.

"That way," the camel drivers said, pointing and explaining the exact path to follow so they wouldn't be seen. The trek to where they could hire someone to drive them across the border was another mile and a half walk, but at least the terrain was more level. At this point they were just putting one foot ahead of the other, almost numb to further pain.

Magid spoke Farsi, but he could communicate in Pashto enough to locate a driver who would take them the remaining few miles to Peshawar, Pakistan. For now, they could sit. The long, treacherous walk was over. They rode with the windows down for air, and the breeze felt so good. In a spirit of triumph, Lailoma took off her burqa and flung it out the window.

Magid's eyes grew wide in surprise. "What are you doing?" he asked with more than a hint of worry in his voice.

"I won't be wearing it again," Lailoma declared.

In Peshawar, no one questioned them. They took a city bus to Arbab Road, where Magid had a friend who had invited them to stay the night. Shrifa still had some naan left, and the friend's wife generously offered them more food and tea. The others ate gratefully, but Lailoma had no appetite. The magnitude of what she had just done was beginning to sink in, and left her in shock—physically, mentally, and emotionally. She was too upset and too tired to eat. Her feet were blistered and her body ached. The pressure of the enormous undertaking came crashing down on her, and she began to shake uncontrollably.

When they had left Kabul, Lailoma hadn't thought to ask how they would reach Pakistan. She hadn't thought about the possibility that the most dangerous part of the journey would be on foot. She had been wearing sandals when Magid knocked on her door, and he hadn't noticed or he would have cautioned her to put on more sensible shoes. She had athletic shoes in her closet at home, but that didn't help her during the climb. When her sandal straps broke on the mountain, she had taken them off and left them behind. She entered Pakistan on bare, bleeding feet.

CHAPTER 8

SAFETY IN PAKISTAN

The band of three adults and three children had passed the border illegally. They had no passports or other documentation identifying themselves as Afghans. At twenty-five, Lailoma, newly widowed and without shoes or money, was acutely aware of how precarious her situation was. Thoughts swirled around in her head: *What is my life going to be now? Are the Taliban going to come after me and my son? What will I do with no husband? How will I raise a small child by myself? If I work to support us, what will I do with Maiwand while I'm working? What kind of work can I do? How am I going to live in the same house as Magid, a man who isn't even a relative? What will Shrifa think?*

The next day, Magid located and rented a small place with just one bedroom, a small bathroom, and a tiny pantry area. "This room is for you and Maiwand," he told Lailoma, pointing to the pantry, "and you can share the bathroom with us. We will share everything we have with you."

Unfortunately, they didn't have much to share. They had no pillows. No blankets. No mattresses. The cement floor on which Lailoma and Maiwand were to sleep had a very old—and not so clean—Persian carpet on top of it. It would have to do.

"I don't care as long as my son and I are safe," Lailoma answered.

"Tomorrow I will get some supplies," Magid promised. "Everybody is going to have food and a blanket."

Still overcome by the events of the past several days, Lailoma sobbed, the tears streaming down her cheeks. Shrifa put her arms around her. "Why are you crying?" she asked. "We made it! You are safe. I know you worry about your family. I know you worry about how you will survive without your husband and without your family, but Magid and I are your brother and sister now. We will share everything we have with you. If we have money, we will share it. If we have food, we will share it. I promise we won't abandon you. Please don't worry."

But Lailoma was used to being the person who had enough to share. She was used to giving, not receiving. Accepting help from somebody she would have been able to help just a few days earlier was hard. She and Mussa hadn't always needed his pay from the army. Sometimes that was just extra money for them. All their food had come from Abdullah—first from his earnings from Doostiee and then from his pharmaceutical business. In the spring, she had supplies that would last all summer. In the fall, their pantry was bursting with enough food to carry them through the winter. At the holidays, when she bought something for Maiwand, she also had bought something for Magid's children.

My life was so good, she realized. *And now it's gone.*

In an instant, her reasonably comfortable existence had turned into a nightmare in which she didn't know how to survive. Her predicament went beyond the need for food and shelter: not only was she uncomfortable accepting help from someone she had previously helped, she also had no experience living among people who weren't her family. Even living with Abdullah's family in Wardak had made her uncomfortable. No matter how generous and good to her Magid and Shrifa were, she would never completely adjust to living in a home with a man who wasn't her relative—even with Shrifa there. Despite their good intentions, the reality was they were not her brother and sister.

Magid was true to his word, and the next day everyone in the small adobe house had a pillow and a blanket. They were used, so, working together, Shrifa and Lailoma washed them and then pressed them with a very hot iron to kill any germs—hopefully. Though Shrifa and Lailoma had been neighbors in Kabul, they didn't really know each other well. Theirs had been a somewhat formal relationship. Shrifa did her best under these circumstances to make Lailoma comfortable, but still, when she turned out the light each night, Lailoma lay down and just cried.

Sometimes, hearing her, Maiwand woke up. "Mamo, why are you crying?" he asked. "When are we going home?"

There was no simple answer to give the five-year-old. Was she crying for Mussa? Yes. Was she crying because she had left her family? Yes. Was she crying because she was worried? Yes.

"It's a lot of things," she tried to explain. "I cry at everything. We are homeless. We don't have any money. I don't know where to go from here."

Sometimes in the morning, Magid and Shrifa realized she had been crying. "If you feel bad that you have free food and are staying with us," Magid said, "consider that you are helping Shrifa with the housekeeping, the cleaning, and the laundry. If you do that, you will feel better. You will be earning food and a place to stay. This isn't charity."

And Lailoma did contribute. When Shrifa brought the groceries in, Lailoma busied herself cleaning their bedroom for them, and she cleaned the kitchen. She knew they didn't have a lot of money either, but she didn't know what else to do. Fortunately, Magid and Shrifa had family in Canada. When they contacted them, their Canadian relatives immediately began to send small amounts of money.

The three adults and three children stayed in these tight accommodations for three months. The children played danda together in the little backyard with a homemade bat and ball, just as Lailoma had played it with her cousins all those years ago. Sometimes they played inside the house with marbles the landlady had saved from her now-grown children. Lailoma and Shrifa worked together, gradually getting to know each other. When Lailoma washed the clothing, Shrifa helped hang it to dry. When one peeled the potatoes, the other cooked them.

Shrifa empathized with Lailoma's loneliness, often telling her, "I'm lucky. I have my family with me."

Then Magid was able to rent an apartment in a house in Islamabad. This apartment had two small bedrooms and a bathroom in addition to a small living area. The bigger space made life easier for all of them, and they fell into a reasonably comfortable routine.

One day Magid surprised the children with books. "Keep reading," he told his children. "You need to be ready to start school again when I find a way to enroll you. Read stories to Maiwand too. It will soon be time for him to start school."

Still out of touch with her family, Lailoma worried about them constantly. Since Ahmadwali had been Mussa's bodyguard, it occurred to her that if the Taliban found Ahmadwali, they might have killed him as well. What if he had gone to the Macroyan to look for her? What about her father? Had the Taliban discovered that her father had helped remove Mussa's body from the tree? What had been Abdullah's fate? And then there was the rest of her family—her mother, Naim, and her sisters. Were they alive or dead? Every day a million scenarios went through her head.

On the day she lost Mussa, Lailoma lost her family, and she also lost his family. She lost Abdullah and Roya, and she lost her extended family in Wardak.

ISLAMABAD, PAKISTAN, 1999

The landlord of the three-story home lived downstairs, and even though more than three years had passed, he and his wife weren't aware that more than one family was living in the upstairs apartment. The potential impropriety of a single woman—not related to Magid and Shrifa—living with them would not have been lost on the landlord and his wife had they known. But they did suspect something wasn't quite what it appeared to be. One day in 1999, the landlord's wife came upstairs and asked Lailoma if she was Magid's wife. She knew Shrifa was Magid's wife, but maybe he had a second wife. Lailoma smiled, but she didn't answer—she didn't know how. It was best to pretend not to understand the question.

Shrifa came to her rescue. "No, she's my sister," she explained quickly. "Her husband was killed. We brought her and her son with us to Pakistan because we didn't want to leave her behind."

The landlady returned on another day and asked again about Lailoma and Maiwand. Shrifa's explanation didn't ring quite true with her, and this time, she had a suggestion.

"If you go to the United Nations office, they can help you," she told Lailoma. "A lot of Afghan people have been able to leave Pakistan with the help of the United Nations. I've seen it! People have left this very house for America, for Canada."

Lailoma didn't believe this was possible. "I have nothing," she said. "Maybe those other people had money. I don't have money. I don't have anything. I don't have any identification. I don't have a passport. How can I go to America or Canada?"

She didn't pursue the idea—at first. She knew one thing, however: she didn't want to stay in Pakistan. The reasons were many: it wasn't home to her, she was living with a family that wasn't her own, and she needed to keep Maiwand safe. Pakistan was too close to Afghanistan. Could the Taliban find them there? Would someone in Pakistan inform the Taliban of their presence? She also knew she couldn't, and wouldn't, go back to Afghanistan. But go to America or Canada? How? And what would she do there if she did go? How would she support herself and Maiwand? The scenario seemed impossible.

A week or two later, the landlady offered help. "Tell us your story. My husband can write down what happened to you. He knows English and will be able to tell your story. You can take what he writes to the UN office and maybe they can help you leave. Maybe your sister and her husband might want to go too."

Lailoma was skeptical. She didn't believe complete strangers would be willing to do so much for her. *What's in it for them?* she thought incredulously.

Then early one morning, the landlord called on her. In his hand were a pen and paper. "Tell me what happened," he encouraged her.

Silent for so long, her words now came spilling out. She told him about Mussa's job as a general in Najibullah's army. She told him how Mussa had a premonition he might die, and how he told her to get rid of any papers that might tie him to Najibullah. She told him about the two-day ordeal when the

Taliban stormed their home, tore it apart, and then killed Mussa. And then she told him about leaving with Magid and Shrifa.

"Do you have any documentation for your husband—a picture or work ID? Something? Anything?" he asked.

Lailoma did have something, and she was the only one who knew about it.

She had the envelope she had hidden in Maiwand's dresser drawer, the one she had later put under the burgundy area rug. It contained two documents: the first was the commendation President Najibullah had given to Mussa, recognizing him for his achievements, a document he had earned by graduating from his training in Russia. The second was his ID card. Even Magid didn't know she had these papers.

When she had hastily thrown together clothes for herself and Maiwand, she had pulled the envelope out from under the burgundy carpet and put it in the shoulder bag she carried across the mountain. How the Taliban had missed this, since they ripped apart the entire apartment, she didn't know. She hadn't thought of money, jewelry, or food, but she had had the presence of mind to grab these documents.

Thank Allah, the Taliban didn't find them when they opened the drawer. Thank Allah, they didn't pull up the carpet, she thought.

She handed the papers to the landlord.

"This is good. Let's make a copy of these," he said. "I'll have my driver take you to the UN office, and you can give them the letter I wrote along with copies of these documents."

He gave her money and directed his driver to take her to a small shop nearby where she could make the copies and then to take her to the UN office.

When she returned home after dropping off the documents, the landlords, Magid, and Shrifa were eager to hear her experience.

"They kept the documents and said they would call me," she shared.

She was worried about having let even copies of the documents out of her control and hated to get her hopes up, but everyone else saw this as a good sign.

"You're going to America or Canada!" they said. "You're going to get to leave. You're going to have a good life. When that happens, don't forget us!"

To Lailoma, the possibility of going to America or Canada was still so unbelievable. "I don't know about all of that," she said. "I just want us to be safe. I don't even care about food. I don't care about money. I don't care about anything for myself."

A month or two passed during which she tried to stay busy and not think about the possibility of leaving. She occupied herself with sewing for the landlord's wife or Shrifa. She didn't think to charge; she didn't know she could have made money from it. Had she thought of it, she wouldn't have charged anyway. They had been too good to her.

One afternoon the postman asked for Lailoma by name. Her stomach flipped over. *Oh, no,* she panicked, her mind going quickly to the worst-case scenario. *They've found me.*

The landlady calmed her down. "Don't be afraid," she said. "He's not Taliban. He's just a Pakistani postman. Maybe something came from the United Nations office. Go see what he has."

As Lailoma held the letter in her shaking hands, she only understood one word: "interview." Since she could read nothing else, she ran downstairs to the landlord, who read the letter.

"They have scheduled an interview for you," he said, smiling.

At the prescribed day and time, she took a taxi to the UN office. The official handling her case asked her to repeat her story: How had her husband been killed? How had she come to Pakistan? She told them the harrowing story of Mussa's death and of the journey. She also admitted she and her son were in Pakistan illegally. This fact didn't seem to bother the caseworker. He told her to go home and await further notice. She returned to the rented apartment and waited.

One afternoon about a month later, Maiwand came into the room rubbing his eyes. "Mamo, my eyes itch," he told her, as he started to cry.

When she looked at his red, dripping eyes, she knew she had to take him to a doctor. So she set off with him to walk the several blocks to the doctor's office. They were gone for a good part of the afternoon, and when they returned home, she learned that unfortunately, that was the day a second registered letter had arrived for her. Without her there to sign for it, the postman had no choice but to leave with it.

Her heart sank. *I've lost my chance*, she thought to herself. *Oh well, if Allah is on my side, he will help me.* In her mind, her chance of leaving Pakistan had just diminished.

"I told the postman that you live with me," the landlady assured her. "I also told him you had taken your son to the doctor because of his allergies. He will return."

Two days later, a man and woman from the UN office came to the house and asked for Lailoma. She took them into her small room, which was bare except for the two pillows and blankets.

"You sleep here?" they asked.

"This is my room," she answered in an even tone. "This is my whole life."

If the caseworkers were shocked, they didn't show it. Probably they weren't. They had likely seen similar—and worse—situations. Their questions might have had more to do with how Lailoma was surviving at all.

"How do you afford the rent? How do you buy food for yourself and your son?" they quizzed her.

She explained how she helped Magid and Shrifa in exchange for food and living space.

A second and third interview followed within the next few weeks. During the third interview, the UN representative told her, "We have completed everything we can at our office. After this interview, we'll send your documents to the IOM [International Organization for Migration] office."

At the IOM office, an American woman conducted another interview, this time with the help of a Pakistani translator. After Lailoma had repeated her story one more time, the lady patted Maiwand on the head and just looked at Lailoma for what seemed like several minutes, then allowed them to leave. "We will be in touch," she said.

Finally a second invitation to the IOM office arrived. This time, when Lailoma arrived with Maiwand, the reception room was crowded with Afghan

162

families. The mother and son waited as one family after another was called into the office. Lailoma's stomach was in knots. The hot, stuffy room and the nerve-racking wait made her feel as if she was going to be sick.

"Lailoma?" Her name was called.

In the interview room the American interviewer asked her, "Why do you want to go to America?"

"Because I don't have anybody here," she replied. "My husband was killed. I don't know where my family is—they could have been killed too, for all I know. I want to save my son."

In Lailoma's presence, the interviewer questioned Maiwand too, apparently trying to establish the truth of her story. "When your father comes home at night and it's hot outside, does he bring you watermelon or some other fruit to eat?"

Maiwand started to cry. "I don't have a father. They killed my father."

That was enough for the IOM representative. She put her arms around Maiwand and kissed him. "Don't worry. You're going to have fresh fruit and a lot of other food. You're going to have a safe, beautiful home. We're going to help you. Please don't cry. You have me. You have her," she said, pointing to the translator. "You're going to a safe country, and you're going to grow big like your father."

With that, she marked the file with a red pen. "Don't worry," she told Lailoma. "We're going to call you soon."

"I trust you," Lailoma told the lady. "I don't trust Pakistani people. I don't know if they are Taliban or if they will tell the Taliban I am here. But I trust you."

It's true, she thought. *I'm going somewhere.*

Lailoma took eight-year-old Maiwand's hand and left the office, relieved, happy, and hopeful. She did not fully understand the logistics at the time, but she would not be immigrating to the United States. Rather, she would be entering as a refugee, which is an entirely different status. The detailed vetting process to qualify for asylum would be repeated when they entered America.

The next step at the IOM was a medical exam. After both she and Maiwand had been cleared medically, she needed only to wait to learn what to do next. As she waited, she felt relatively secure that she and Maiwand were safe for now at least, but also anxious not knowing how things stood for the rest of her family. Her basic instincts had told her to save herself and her son, and when in danger, she hadn't thought about the rest of her family. Now, with time to breathe, she wondered where her mother and father were, her sisters and Naim. Most of all, she worried about Ahmadwali. He was the one most closely connected with Mussa, and therefore the one most at risk.

Within a few days, she received a letter detailing their departure. It included instructions describing what she and Maiwand could take with them and how much the baggage could weigh. These instructions were relatively insignificant to her: she and Maiwand didn't have much more than what they had arrived in Pakistan with more than three years earlier. She was given a date—just a couple of days later—to be at the IOM office. "Be there at 10 a.m. sharp," the instructions stated.

When she and Maiwand arrived on the prescribed day, the institutional-looking waiting room was already filled with Afghan families, some seated on the assembled chairs, some standing and bouncing babies to quiet them, and children running everywhere. Almost immediately the IOM officials entered the room to begin orienting the families.

A television ran a video that explained to them what the refugees could expect in America. American supermarkets would offer a multitude—and later, Lailoma learned, a dizzying array—of fresh fruits and vegetables. But, they were told, many of the flavors that were so ingrained in the Afghan culture would be difficult to obtain. To buy ground lamb or naan, the future American residents were told they might have to locate a local Afghan market.

They also learned that the apartment where they would live no doubt would include an indoor kitchen, equipped with built-in cabinets, an electric or gas refrigerator, a stove, and, most likely, a microwave. The bathrooms would include, at a minimum, a tub-shower combination. Plus, there would be cars everywhere—Americans heavily relied on personal cars for transportation. In some cities, public transportation would be highly available and efficient. In others, wide-ranging public transportation wouldn't be a given.

An overwhelming amount of information was given to them quickly, and several languages were heard in the room, seemingly all at once. The presentation was in English, translated into Urdu—the principal language of Pakistan—and Farsi. To the extent they could, the families in the room helped each other understand the details, but much was lost, as Lailoma learned later.

"You must learn to speak English," the IOM representatives told the families. "You have to know what the school bus looks like. You have to know how to buy food. You need to learn how to get a job. You need to learn how to drive. You have to know how to dial 911."

The possibilities were exciting—and daunting. Lailoma had studied English in high school, but was not sure she could survive in an English-speaking country. As any traveler with a "book knowledge" of another country's language will attest, this wasn't going to be easy. Fortunately, they were told someone would greet them when they arrived at their destination, and that person would help them transition into American life.

But how will I know who that is? Lailoma wondered.

Every person and family in the room had been approved to leave. Each was shown his or her visa. "We will let you know when your flight is," the IOM representatives assured them.

This time, when she arrived back at the rented home in Pakistan, everyone in the house celebrated. "You're going! You're going!" they screamed excitedly, putting their arms around her.

I'll believe it when we're on the plane, Lailoma thought.

TIME TO TRAVEL, 2000

"If you are going to America," Shrifa announced one afternoon in August 2000, "you have to have a better hairstyle. You have to look more modern."

Maybe she's right, Lailoma thought as she looked in the mirror at her waist-length hair. For a moment, her mind went back to the day of her engagement party when the hairdresser had suggested she should cut her hair. Roya had said no, and Lailoma had known for certain that her mother would have said no. Now the decision was hers, and hers alone.

In one way, she had always wanted shorter hair. When she washed her long, thick hair, it took hours to dry. If she didn't braid it or pull it into a bun, it hung heavily on her shoulders. It slowed her down. Plus, it represented some of what she was leaving behind—the lack of control over her own destiny. But cut it? That was a big plunge.

She took a deep breath. "Cut it."

Shrifa had no training as a hairstylist. In fact, she had never cut hair before that very day. But she had scissors—for cutting fabric—and a can-do, take-charge attitude. Slowly she combed through Lailoma's long, thick mane and began to cut, albeit with shaking hands. The more she cut, the more confident she became, even producing some thick, choppy layers. A mound of hair piled up on the floor.

"We need to bury your hair somewhere," Shrifa said, giggling as she began to sweep it into a pile. "This is a lot of hair. We can't just put it in the garbage."

But that's what they did—a little bit at a time so the garbage man wouldn't notice.

Lailoma looked at her reflection in the mirror. *Not bad,* she thought.

Shrifa beamed, quite proud of her work—and their plan to get rid of the hair.

And then, as if in slow motion, but suddenly too, the big day arrived—September 5, 2000. A letter received the day before instructed Lailoma to arrive at the IOM office by ten the next morning. She had no idea they would be leaving that very day, that she and Maiwand would board an airplane and fly out of Pakistan.

At the IOM office, Lailoma turned to a woman smiling beside her. She remembered the woman from the orientation event. "You look so happy," Lailoma said, and then she asked, "Why?"

"We're all going to America!" the woman replied.

"How?" Lailoma asked her.

"You will see."

Lailoma later learned that many of the people in the room had families already in America. Maybe their families had explained how this worked to them, Lailoma thought.

She had arrived at the office in a surreal daze, and now she went through the motions, accepting the name tags handed to her for the suitcase she would share with Maiwand, the very suitcase she had sent by camel around Shamshad Ghar three and a half years earlier. She also signed every paper shoved in front of her, whether or not she understood its contents.

The destination listed on one of the papers, a Lutheran church office on the west side of Phoenix, Arizona, was meaningless to her. She was too nervous to ask where Arizona was.

"The Lutheran church is sponsoring you and has bought your plane ticket," the immigration official told her. "When you start working in America, you will need to pay them back."

She just signed.

By noon, all of the paperwork had been completed. "Be at the airport by one thirty," they instructed her.

Lailoma's heart pounded as she hailed a taxi to take Maiwand and her back to the apartment that had been their home for almost four years. But she had no money for the fare. When they arrived home, she ran into the house and Shrifa gave her money to pay the cab driver.

"What happened? What happened?" Shrifa, Magid, the landlord, and his wife wanted to know.

"I have to hurry," Lailoma answered. "We have to be at the airport by one thirty."

A scurry of activity ensued, with everyone pitching in to help. Shrifa took Maiwand by the hand and led him to the bathroom, where she gave him a shower. Lailoma had no time for a shower, but quickly threw their belongings into the little suitcase. Shrifa had lunch ready by the time Maiwand was dressed and Lailoma was packed. Lailoma was too anxious to eat, but Shrifa and Magid pressed a small meat patty with bread into Maiwand's hand for him to eat on the way to the airport—in a taxi driven by the landlord's driver.

Finally, Lailoma sank into the taxi seat, rested her head back, and let tears quietly roll down her cheeks.

She was twenty-eight and leaving behind everything familiar to her and everyone she had ever known and loved. She had no idea where she was going. She thought she could trust the immigration officials, but there was no certainty. And maybe that was the scariest part. She was fleeing with her nine-year-old son into an unknown.

A million thoughts raced through her head. Everybody told her, "Don't worry. You're going to be safe. You're going to have a good life." But how did they know? None of them had ever left everyone and everything they had ever known for a completely new world—a new country, a new language, a completely different culture.

By the time she and Maiwand reached the airport, it was a little after one thirty in the afternoon. All of the families she had seen earlier at the IOM office were there and already in line. She quickly took her place at the end of the line.

One by one the families' names were called, and each returned with a thick white plastic bag imprinted with the big blue letters *IOM*, identifying them as refugees. Each was instructed not to open the bag until they reached New York City.

"Goodbye!" the airline attendants called to the refugees around six that evening as they were called to the gate to board the plane. "Have a happy life! Have a comfortable life. Now it's time to go through that gate to a new world. Your flight is ready."

Lailoma sank into the seat beside Maiwand. In near shock she thought, *I left Afghanistan. I left my family. I am leaving Pakistan. I am going to a safe country.*

"Where are we going, Mamo?" Maiwand asked.

"We're going to America."

"Who is going to be with us in America? Who will look out for us?"

168

"It will be just you and me. I'm going to work, and you're going to go to school."

The thought of going to school was exciting for Maiwand, who at nine years old had yet to attend school. In spite of the fact that Magid had intended to enroll his children and Maiwand in a Pakistani school, he wasn't able to, mainly because of money. They would have had to pay tuition and buy uniforms and supplies. Plus, there was Lailoma's additional concern that being at a school would make Maiwand more visible and vulnerable to the Taliban.

Lailoma tried to seem assured in her responses to Maiwand, but the truth was that the process was mysterious to the refugees and, though Lailoma didn't know it at the time, it was unfamiliar to some officials as well. Later she was told these refugees were the first group who stopped in Dubai after departing Pakistan, and Dubai customs officials weren't quite certain of the process. Wondering why none of the refugees had passports, they took all of the white plastic bags the IOM office had given them along with their visas and contacted Pakistan to confirm that they were legally leaving the country. Two hours later, they returned the documents to their owners.

In the confusion, Maiwand's picture became separated from the immigration visa and accidentally was attached to another family's document. That family's child's photo was attached to Lailoma's document. She wasn't confident of her English and she spoke no Arabic, so she spoke in Farsi to the officials. "This is not my son," she said, pointing to the picture while trying to fight down the hysteria. When they didn't seem to react, she repeated herself: "This is not my son!"

"It's OK," they said.

"But I need *my* son's picture to be here," she said, pointing to the other child's picture on the document. Panic was rising in her voice.

A customs official brought out a translator, and still they said she didn't need Maiwand's photo. She dug in her heels. She wasn't going to budge until Maiwand's picture was back on the document. The Dubai officials went back into their office and about twenty minutes later returned. "We've lost the photo," they told Lailoma.

At that moment, another woman's scream could be heard. "That's not my son!" she cried, pointing to the picture on her document. Her scream demanded attention.

Finally the officials realized what had happened and switched the two pictures, handing the correct picture to each mother.

"No! Staple it to the paper," Lailoma insisted.

"It's OK. Take it with you," they told her.

Through the translator she made the customs officials understand that she wanted it stapled to the paper and stamped. "What if the photo gets lost?" she said through the interpreter. "This one paper is all I have. I don't want anyone in New York or some other place to take Maiwand from me."

The official took the paper, stapled Maiwand's photo to it, and signed it. "It's OK now," he said, patting her on the shoulder.

"Thank you," she said, relief in her voice.

From Dubai, the refugees flew to Amsterdam, where they had a two-hour layover at the large, bustling Airport Schiphol. Around them they heard a cacophony of languages and saw mostly Westerners scurrying with their luggage. Some were eating or sipping beverages. Lailoma was too worried about getting lost to explore the airport, so she and Maiwand sat at the gate for the two hours. Besides, she had no money for food. For the trip, they ate only the food they were served midair. After the two-hour layover, they boarded another plane bound for New York.

As the plane touched down at New York's JFK International Airport, the passengers broke into cheers. When they exited the plane, they were greeted by immigration officials, who opened everybody's white bags for them. "I'm going to Florida!" one said. "We're going to Illinois," said another.

"Aunt, where are you going?" one of the young men asked Lailoma.

She was taken aback. It hadn't occurred to her that all of the families would be going to different locations. She had assumed everyone would be going to the same place she had seen listed on her papers: Phoenix, Arizona.

All of us are in this together, she had thought. *If something happens, we're all together. We will look out for each other.*

That thought had been a comfort to her, and now it was dispelled.

"I don't know," she answered. "I have no idea where we're going. I don't know where this place is."

"Can I see your paperwork?" he asked.

She handed him the paper. "Oh, my god," he said. "You're going to Arizona. It's as hot as Pakistan. Why did you choose Arizona?"

She hadn't chosen Arizona. No one had asked her choice, and she wouldn't have known enough to make a choice if someone had asked.

"They picked it for me," was all she said. Her stomach twisted into knots.

From New York, every family left until only Lailoma and Maiwand and another widow with her son were left. The other mother and son boarded a plane bound for Florida, and Lailoma and Maiwand boarded a plane bound for Arizona, a five-and-a-half-hour flight away.

CHAPTER 9

ARIZONA, 2000

Lailoma and Maiwand arrived at Phoenix Sky Harbor International Airport at 10:30 p.m. on September 7, 2000. Clutching his hand tightly as they exited the plane, Lailoma wondered, *What do I do now? How will I know the person who is supposed to meet me?*

She didn't have to worry long. As soon as she passed through immigration, her caseworker from Lutheran Social Services—the group that had sponsored her—noted her stunned look and the white Mylar bag with the IOM symbol in her hand. "Lailoma?"

She managed a nervous "yes."

The man looked at her name and ID number on the bag and said, "Come with me."

Lailoma, still holding tightly onto her son, followed the man to the baggage area. Putting herself and her son into the hands of this stranger—a male at that—required a leap of faith. But he knew her name. He must be the right person.

"How many bags do you have?" he asked.

"I only have this one," she said, indicating the small suitcase in her hand.

"You only have this one?" he asked, as incredulously as the UN agents had asked if the rented room in the Islamabad apartment was hers.

"Yes," she said, warily.

Lailoma worried. *What am I going to do? Where is he going to take us?*

Her only previous experience with Americans was watching them in Hollywood movies. Growing up she and her siblings had watched as many

American movies as they could get access to on the VCR in their Kabul family room. Was this man like Rambo? Rocky?

As the three rode quietly in the caseworker's car to the west side of Phoenix, through the bare desert landscape that surrounded plain beige stucco buildings, disappointment settled in.

Oh, this place is ugly, Lailoma thought. *I thought America was beautiful.*

They pulled into the parking lot of a two-story apartment building devoid of landscaping. The caseworker got out of the car and knocked on one of the apartment doors. A young woman opened the door and spoke to him, and then he returned to the car and told Lailoma and Maiwand to "Come on in."

Up close, the young woman didn't look American, and her greeting told Lailoma that she probably was not. She spoke Farsi.

Oh, thank Allah, Lailoma thought. "You're from Afghanistan," she said to her, clutching her hand.

As it turned out, the young woman and her father had arrived in America only the previous day. A former teacher, she spoke fluent English and could help the caseworker communicate with Lailoma, whose halting English was limited.

The caseworker had acquired a twin bed for Lailoma as well as a sofa, and he had put food for her and Maiwand in the kitchen. One by one he took items from the refrigerator and showed them to Lailoma. "This food is yours," he said. "Tomorrow morning I will return and take all of you to the Social Security office."

When he left, Lailoma breathed a sigh of relief. *Oh, thank Allah,* she thought again. *He's not going to spend the night with me.* Her upbringing had made her fearful of any man outside her family, and now she had no male relative, or even a friend such as Magid, to look out for her.

After the caseworker left, the young woman offered Lailoma some tea and a little snack. But any appetite she might have had was gone because she was so tired. Lailoma just wanted to crawl into that twin bed and sleep. The nearly forty-eight-hour journey from Pakistan to Dubai to Amsterdam to

New York City and finally to Arizona had exhausted her. This appeared to be a place where she and Maiwand could finally sleep securely.

Sleep came easily that first night in the tiny apartment. She was utterly drained from the long flight and her four-year-long journey to safety and freedom. But in the early morning hours, multiple explosions rattled the apartment and pulled her from a deep sleep. The sound was deafening; she was certain the walls were shaking. She leaped out of bed.

"Maiwand!" she cried out, groping in the dark for the nine-year-old. She ran to the window to look out, then ran to the door, dragging Maiwand with her.

"Stay right beside me," she told Maiwand. "Hold my hand."

"What are you doing?" her new apartment mate asked, running toward the window in her nightgown.

"A rocket hit somewhere," Lailoma told her.

"Wake up," the young woman said, knowing Lailoma was disoriented. "You're not in Afghanistan. You're not in Pakistan. You're in America. There's no need to go outside. There's no rocket."

Lailoma looked around at the now quiet, peaceful place. Outside rain was pouring steadily; the explosions had only been thunder. She sat down and cried.

"Why are you crying? You should be happy now. You're safe," the young woman told her. "What has happened to you that could be so bad? Tell me your story. How did you come here alone with your son?"

"I will tell you about it sometime, but I can't talk now," Lailoma answered. "I'm going to tell you later, maybe tomorrow. Right now I'm going to give my son a shower. Then I'm going to take a shower. Don't ask me today."

As the caseworker had promised, he returned at 8 a.m. He took Lailoma, Maiwand, and the teacher to the Social Security office to help them obtain food stamps and insurance cards. He also made a medical appointment for Lailoma to get a TB shot.

"Now your life is starting," he told her kindly. "This is the beginning of your new life. You and your son can live with this young woman and her father until you start work."

"No, I can't live with them," Lailoma protested, still uncomfortable living among strangers. "I want my own place. I don't want to live with another family, even if we have two bedrooms."

"But you're a single mother," the caseworker said. "You can't afford an American apartment. The government will provide a place for you because you are a refugee, but you won't get your own apartment. To have your own apartment, you will have to start work immediately. Do you want to work right away? Can you work?"

"I can work day and night, but I want my own place," Lailoma answered, not knowing the eventual truth of the words she spoke to him. Indeed, she would work day and night for many years to come.

The caseworker recognized her determination. "I'll see what I can do," he said.

Life in America had begun.

The caseworker submitted Lailoma's request for an apartment immediately, and that very afternoon, the building manager came to the studio apartment Lailoma had shared the evening before with the teacher and her father. "I have an apartment with a bathroom and a kitchen," she told Lailoma. "If you want it, you can move there. Do you want to see it?"

Though the teacher was there to translate if she needed help, Lailoma clearly understood this offer.

"Yes, of course!" Lailoma leaped at the opportunity.

The apartment was located directly behind the complex's laundry facilities. When Lailoma opened the closet door, she could see the back of a washer and dryer and the electrical equipment.

"This is perfect!" Lailoma told the apartment manager without hesitation. "But when a bigger apartment becomes available, I want that one. I will work. I will find a way to pay for it."

The location behind the laundry room had a downside: both men and women did their laundry there, often in the evening and sometimes late into the night. The first time she heard their voices at night, she worried that there might be a way they could slip between the washing machines that backed up against her closet and into her apartment.

They could stalk me, she thought. *They could find out who lives in this apartment and push their way in through the laundry room.*

After an anxious few hours, she worked up her nerve to walk into the laundry room. She felt relieved, and a little silly, when she realized the size and weight of the washers and dryers would make it impossible to come through the laundry room into her apartment. She and Maiwand were safe.

Their stint in the laundry-room-challenged apartment was short-lived. Only a week or so later, an Afghan family vacated their apartment, leaving to be near family in Virginia. The manager brought Lailoma the good news along with a new key.

"This apartment costs six hundred dollars per month," she explained to Lailoma. "You will need to pay on the first day of every month. Will you be able to do that?"

"I will find a way."

With help from the management, Lailoma moved their new belongings—the bed, the sofa, the food—into the apartment. The manager had also found a sixteen-inch black-and-white TV that had been left behind by another family, and that provided an activity to occupy the mother and son for the next couple of weeks.

"Let's pretend we're at the movies," Lailoma said to Maiwand the first night, pulling him close to her on the sofa in their new home.

"Clifford!" the nine-year-old said with a grin, finding something famil-iar on the screen as they worked the remote. The smart young boy recognized his mother's anxiety and need to find safe ground. By now he was a little old to be excited about watching the Big Red Dog, but it was something to do. His mother wasn't interested in venturing too far from the apartment, and two weeks is a long time for a child to be confined to a small space without toys, books, or other children to play with.

The pair watched *Clifford* cartoons over and over. For diversion, they watched episodes of *Xena: Warrior Princess* or a show on PBS. Soon, Lailoma found herself mouthing the words along with the characters, having memorized every line. From the *Rambo* films she watched as a child in Afghanistan to the *Clifford* and *Xena* shows she watched in Arizona, she was gradually improving her language skills. Maiwand was a sponge, soaking up his new language seemingly as quickly as it hit his ears.

French fries made from the potatoes they were given when they arrived became a dietary mainstay for a while. Kids love fries, but even Maiwand tired of them. "Can we have something else today?" he asked his mother.

Sometimes he missed his family. "Where's Mama Ahmadwali?" he asked. "Where is Ana?" Even after four years apart, Maiwand longed for his grandmother and the security of the extended family.

"I don't know," Lailoma answered him honestly. "They're in Afghanistan, but I don't know where." She looked away from her son so he wouldn't see her eyes well with tears.

Still adjusting to her new life and learning to accept that her new home was safe, Lailoma left the apartment only in the late afternoon when she and Maiwand began to join other Afghan families on the lawn. The women visited as the children played. Sometimes the women shopped together. From them, she learned about the nearby dollar store where she could buy necessities and even some basic food.

Their conversations were pleasant but somewhat guarded. The community only knew that Lailoma was a widow and had come to Arizona as a refugee. Even here she was afraid to talk about what had happened. The other women seemed similarly reluctant to share the details of their previous lives.

When Lailoma and Maiwand had been in the United States for just over two weeks, she knew this adjustment period was nearing its end. Soon, that six-hundred-dollar rent would be due. It was time to get a job.

"I'm going to find work for you in a hotel," the caseworker had told her when he brought her home that first morning after applying for a Social Security card. "Your English isn't good enough for most jobs, but you can do housekeeping."

"No," Lailoma objected. "I like to sew. Why don't I get a job sewing?"

"But you can't speak English well enough," he answered.

"You don't need to speak English to sew," she countered.

The caseworker made a few phone calls until he found himself speaking to Louise Van Teal, the owner of a commercial workroom, the Van Teal Shirt Co. "She can sew," the caseworker told Mrs. Van Teal.

"OK," Mrs. Van Teal said. "Bring her in on Friday. Let's see what she can do."

Lailoma had been in the United States just a little more than two weeks, and now she had a job interview. This was the good news. She was nervous, but so excited. The bad news confronted her when Mrs. Van Teal escorted her to a big industrial sewing machine for her skills test. All around her, the room was buzzing—the noise of the machines, the busyness of the many workers who all seemed to be staring at her. *How am I going to pass this test?* Lailoma thought, panic arising in her throat.

This machine was a far cry from the simple crank machines on which she had always sewn. She knew the intricacies of creating a garment, but the thought of operating such a powerful machine was intimidating.

Where is the wheel to make the needle go up and down? she wondered. *Where do I thread a big machine like this? It's electric, but how do I turn it on? What happens if I can't do this?*

Despite the thoughts swirling through her head, she was determined— and a quick thinker. As her eyes swept over the machine, they locked on the red on/off button. *OK. One step at a time*, she told herself, taking a big breath.

When Mrs. Van Teal left to get a piece of fabric for the test, Lailoma welcomed the opportunity to examine the machine. As calmly as she could, she reached for the red switch and flipped it on. Looking down, she saw a pedal on the floor. *That must be what makes it go*, she thought. Slowly, she pressed it with her foot. But apparently not slowly enough. The needle started humming up and down at a frightening speed.

It's a good thing I tested that, she told herself.

Mrs. Van Teal returned with a piece of fabric on which she drew a straight line, a zigzag line, and a circle, and then she handed the fabric to

Lailoma to sew the shapes. This was the moment of truth. Lailoma carefully put the fabric under the needle and lowered it, and then, very slowly this time, she pressed the pedal. She successfully stitched on the straight line and then the zigzag line, but the circle gave her a little trouble.

Regardless, Mrs. Van Teal had seen enough. "Congratulations! You have a job! You can start work Monday morning at seven," she told Lailoma, who was beaming—and visibly relieved.

"Congratulations!" the caseworker said, repeating Mrs. Van Teal's sentiment when she got into his car to return to the apartment that afternoon. "I'm going to bring you taxi tickets. I will have a taxi pick you up Monday morning. Give one ticket to the driver in the morning when he drops you off at the factory, and give him one when he drops you off at home in the evening."

True to his word, Sunday evening he came by with the tickets.

When the doorbell rang at six Monday morning, Lailoma was frightened to open the door, not realizing the cab would come so early. She had no experience getting off to work in the morning, and she hadn't realized how early she'd need to leave.

"Taxi!" the man called out.

She quickly washed her face, gave Maiwand milk for breakfast, and said, "Wait here at home for the school bus."

Maiwand had been going to school for two weeks, but he also was still adjusting to the schedule. Like his mother, he wasn't particularly a morning person.

"Don't go back to sleep," she warned him. "And don't watch TV. You can't miss the bus."

That day, the school bus came at 8 a.m., and the nine-year-old managed to get on it by himself. The next weekend, Lailoma found a better arrangement for him. As she sat on the lawn chatting with other mothers, she met Zakera, an Afghan woman who had arrived from Moscow with her husband and three children. They would be taking the same bus as Maiwand to school, and one of the children was Maiwand's age and in his same classroom.

"Don't worry about him," Zakera told Lailoma. "He can go to school with our children, and in the afternoon he can come here after school and stay with us until you come home from work."

Every morning Lailoma walked Maiwand to Zakera's apartment before the taxi arrived for work. Zakera fed him breakfast and hustled all four children out the door to school together. When Maiwand got off the bus in the afternoon, he went home with the family's children and spent the rest of the afternoon with them until Lailoma arrived home. Just to be sure he had a place to go, Lailoma also gave Maiwand a key to their apartment, which he used occasionally in the afternoon to let himself in.

The diet of French fries continued, but now Lailoma was able to add eggs that she bought at the dollar store to the menu.

One afternoon Maiwand came home from school with big news. "Mamo, we had pizza for lunch!" he said excitedly. "It tasted so good! Please buy us pizza, please buy us pizza," he pressed her as only a nine-year-old can.

Lailoma had no idea what pizza even looked like. But one day in the store, she saw a ready-made pizza wrapped up. *Who's going to eat something that looks like this?* she thought.

"Have you eaten pizza?" she asked an Afghan lady who lived in the same complex one afternoon.

"Yes, and we all like it," the lady told her. "Try it! I have a coupon for a Domino's pizza. I'll give it to you so you can try one!"

Trying pizza for the first time was a bold, new experience; so was placing the order over the phone. When the pizza arrived, it smelled good to Lailoma, but she couldn't quite bring herself to try it. The white cheese that strung out when Maiwand took a bite looked strange to her, and she wasn't sure she wanted any part of it. Maiwand thought it was the best food he had eaten in America.

A few years later, Lailoma's younger Afghan friend, Samira, would take her to a New York–style pizza place and convince her to try it. "The pizza here is really good, but no pressure. Just try it. If you don't like it," Samira told her, "don't eat it."

The experience was shocking, but provided confirmation: pizza tastes as good as it smells.

NAVIGATING THE STREETS, 2000

The neighborhood where Lailoma and Maiwand had been placed was home to many ethnicities, including a sizeable population of Afghans. That little bit of familiarity made assimilating into the American culture somewhat easier for all of the refugees. The dollar store, where she had learned to shop, happened to be owned by Afghans.

The plethora of offerings at the dollar store was mysterious to Lailoma. *I wonder what these are,* she thought to herself, picking up a package of tortillas one day as she was shopping.

She had no idea how to serve the tortillas, so she warmed them in the microwave and she and Maiwand ate them plain. Nothing about the food she found at the dollar store appealed to her. The fruit didn't seem sweet and juicy like the freshly picked fruit she had enjoyed in Afghanistan, and she saw loaves of bread in wrappers, but had no idea which kind to buy. She wasn't complaining, but where was the freshly baked bread she was used to? Only the bananas tasted good to her.

With a smattering of all sorts of supplies, the establishment was a place Lailoma could buy items to meet their basic needs, and for several months it was the only place she shopped. Thankfully, however, the owner observed her purchases and realized she might want to have a wider selection, so he gave her directions to Food City, a locally owned grocery known for its reasonable prices. There, he told her, the offerings would be more extensive. Instead of taking a bus to the grocery, Lailoma decided she and Maiwand could walk the seven blocks to Food City.

"Food City is on this same street," the dollar store owner told her, handing her a piece of paper on which he had spelled out FOOD CITY. "Don't turn off this street. When you see that sign," he said, pointing to the words he had written, "you are there."

With her food stamps and some cash in her handbag, Lailoma set off with Maiwand to locate the store. By this time in mid-spring, afternoon temperatures in Phoenix could easily climb to the upper eighties or nineties, and with the heat wearing on them, the blocks seemed to get longer.

"Mamo, are we almost there?" Maiwand asked. He didn't whine, but he was getting tired. Lailoma hadn't yet learned the first rule of the desert: never leave home without water.

Finally, she looked up and saw the large sign above the doors of the store: FOOD CITY. The blast of cold as they entered the air-conditioned store was a relief, but where was its source? Lailoma had never experienced air-conditioning. In Afghanistan, cooling systems—if buildings had them—were more on the order of swamp coolers, which utilize air blowing over water. This air wasn't cool, it was freezing!

The first thing they saw inside Food City was the amazing display of colorful fruits and vegetables. Lailoma put potatoes, apples, and bananas, along with two gallons of juice and a gallon of milk, into her cart. It was hard to restrain herself, but she only had so many food stamps and a limited amount of cash. Now the dilemma was how to get her purchases home. Maiwand, at nine, could carry a small bag, but the liquids in particular were going to get heavy on the long walk home.

When Lailoma wheeled the cart out of the store into the parking lot, she hoped the people in the store would assume she was pushing it toward her car. But, of course, there was no car. She knew she was going to push the cart all the way to the apartment complex. She also knew this probably wasn't the right thing to do.

About halfway home, Maiwand turned to her. "Mamo, it's getting dark," he said.

It was early in the afternoon and the sun was still beaming. One glance at him told her something was wrong. His face had been red from the heat, but now it was stark white with a little red around the perimeter. He was getting sun stroke.

"Let's sit over here for a while," she said, pushing the cart under a tree and having Maiwand sit on the grass. She poured a little juice into his mouth and then pressed the cool juice carton against his forehead. She looked around for help, but no one was in sight. By now, Maiwand's lips had turned white and he wasn't responsive. After about twenty minutes, when he seemed to feel a little better, she loaded him into the cart on top of the groceries and pushed him the rest of the way home and into their cool apartment.

Even on a ninety-plus-degree day like this one, the apartment always seemed to be cold, uncomfortably so. Lailoma just assumed that was natural. At night, despite the fact that the temperatures were getting down only into the seventies, she and Maiwand covered themselves with blankets. There was a dial on the wall, but she didn't know until later what to do with it. So they just dealt with the cold.

By the time they needed to replenish their food supply a few days later, Lailoma had learned from neighbors that there was a Fry's grocery store even closer than the Food City. Fry's was just a few blocks away. Again underestimating the blistering spring sun, she set off with Maiwand on foot.

They started their journey around 2 p.m., and it was hot. By the time they arrived at the store and bought their groceries, the air was sizzling. This time Lailoma realized they should take the bus home instead of walking, and fortunately there was a bus stop nearby, so with a bag of groceries in each hand, she crossed the street with Maiwand to wait. But she had gone to the wrong side of the street to travel in the direction of their apartment.

"Mamo, I see it! The bus is coming from the other way! Let's run!" Maiwand alerted her shortly.

"OK," she said. "Let's hurry!"

Anxious to get into the air-conditioned bus, Maiwand darted across the street, directly into the path of a car. The driver had no chance to stop: Maiwand hit the bumper, flew into the air, and landed on the street. This time it was Lailoma for whom everything went dark as the shock of what she had seen caused her to faint. When she woke up, emergency vehicles had arrived and the street seemed to be swirling with people. An EMT had put ice on

Maiwand's head. Frantic and dazed, the only word Lailoma could understand was "hospital."

In Afghanistan, only the injured person was taken to the hospital in an ambulance. She couldn't, and wouldn't, let Maiwand out of her sight.

"No, no hospital. No ambulance," was all she knew to say.

Even when the EMT shoved a paper in front of her to sign, she said "no." She wasn't going to sign anything that would allow someone to drive off with her son.

An empathetic older woman who witnessed the accident tried to talk her through the situation, but Lailoma was so distraught she couldn't concentrate on her English long enough to understand. Finally, she just signed the paper anyway.

On the paper the paramedic had written "911" and "24H."

What does that mean? Lailoma wondered.

After what seemed an eternity, the passengers, including Lailoma and Maiwand, reboarded the bus. Lailoma sank into her seat and broke into tears. As others passed her, many put a hand on her shoulder and said a few sympathetic words. She had no idea what they were saying, but felt and appreciated their kindness.

The bus ride home passed in a fog. Somehow when they arrived at the stop closest to her apartment, the bus driver knew to tell her to get off. When she stood up, Maiwand just crumpled to the floor, so she picked him up and carried him down the steps and up the street to their apartment. She wanted to thank the people around her who had been so kind, but she was so shaken up she couldn't muster the correct words. The paramedic had put a bag of ice on Maiwand's head; when she arrived home, she added more ice and held it to his forehead.

That afternoon, the women and children who had gathered outside to play and socialize noticed Lailoma and Maiwand were missing.

"Is anything wrong?" asked one of the women, who knocked on their door.

As well as she could, Lailoma explained the accident to her.

"I don't know what to do," she said. "I don't have medication for him, and I don't know if he needs any. I'm just using ice as they did."

"Just watch him," the other mother said. "He's probably OK. If he were in danger, they would have made him go to the hospital."

Lailoma sat up through the night, keeping Maiwand under constant watch. Not sensing any danger, when morning arrived, she knew they needed to go about their regular routine. She went to work, and Maiwand took the bus to school.

At the factory, Mrs. Van Teal could tell that something was wrong.

"Lailoma," she said, putting her hand on her back. "What's wrong? Has something happened?"

Lailoma couldn't find the words to describe what happened. Picking up a pencil and a piece of paper, she drew a picture of a car and a child lying in the street in front of it. She had drawn the child with a large head to indicate it was swollen. Immediately, her boss understood the child was Lailoma's.

"Oh, my god!" Mrs. Van Teal cried. "Do you need help?"

On the paper, Lailoma wrote "911" and "24H." *Maybe she will know what this means*, she thought.

"Go home," her boss said.

Lailoma's heart sank. She had lost her first job. Now what would she do? 911 and 24H must be very bad things. Even though the IOM representative had explained 911 during the brief orientation in Pakistan, there had been just too many things to absorb that day. It didn't look like a bill. It didn't look like a phone number. Was it a location?

"No, don't worry," her boss quickly assured her when she saw Lailoma's alarm.

She walked Lailoma over to the phone, and explained that in an emergency, she could dial 911.

Oh, that's good, Lailoma thought to herself. *I think I understand 911, but what about 24H?* Mrs. Van Teal had said nothing about 24H.

About a month later when she was checking in at the Lutheran Social Services office, she showed the translator the 24H. Finally, she got an explanation. The EMT had meant for her to call the doctor in twenty-four hours.

Fortunately, though she hadn't called the doctor, Maiwand recovered nicely.

The refugee community was welcoming to them, and others were as well. Just a few months later, Lailoma and Maiwand experienced their first American Christmas—in fact, their first Christmas ever.

"I will never forget it," she told me one Saturday morning. "I don't even know what church it was, but they gave us the best evening."

The church, which was located on the opposite side of the Valley in Scottsdale, sent minivans to the west-side apartment complex to pick up several families, including Lailoma and Maiwand as well as the teacher and her father with whom they had stayed that first evening. When they arrived at the church, a delicious dinner awaited them. There was so much food spread out on the banquet table that they didn't know where to start. Actually, they were a little hesitant at first because, not knowing what the food was, they didn't want to accidentally take something they shouldn't eat. Since most were Muslim, the main food they wanted to avoid was pork.

All of their hosts were so friendly and the refugees didn't want to offend them, but they hesitated before the array of food.

"Don't worry," one of the ladies said, sensing their hesitation. "We know you are Muslim, and we haven't served anything that has pork in it."

Then the families ate with relish! The foods were unfamiliar, but good, and there was so much! Pasta, all-beef hot dogs, salad, casseroles, bread, French fries, and pizza (without pepperoni, which their hosts pointed out). The happiness Lailoma felt that evening stayed with her, even years later in recalling it.

And there was more: around the room were numerous plastic bins, marked with the family names of the guests. And there were wrapped and unwrapped gifts displayed as well.

"Everyone, please go select gifts!" they were told. Lailoma held back at first, not sure what to do.

"Please, go help yourself," one of the hosts urged her.

Finally she selected some things for her kitchen and found the bin marked "Shahwali." When she lifted the lid to put the kitchenware in, she found it contained other wrapped gifts as well, some for her and some for Maiwand. The bins contained at least one package for every single person in each family!

After the dinner, the families enjoyed listening to the choir singing Christmas music and watching a drama of the nativity. The sanctuary was filled with red flowers, which Lailoma later learned were poinsettias, and she had never seen such elegant choir robes. *They look like angels,* she thought. To be at such a festive occasion was so appreciated by the families.

As evening settled in, the hosts helped the families carry the bins to the bus. Maiwand and Lailoma didn't open their bin until they arrived home, but oh, the surprises inside. Because of her limited income, Lailoma had acquired very little for their apartment. Inside the plastic bin, in addition to what she had selected, there were more hot pads, towels, and other things for her kitchen. These items were new, not something donated from someone's kitchen. She used her new supplies at first, because she needed them, but later, after she had acquired others with her own money, she put these gifts aside as very special mementos of the wonderful evening and generous people. She showed them to me on the Saturday morning she told me about the Christmas celebration, and she still has them today. One thing in the bin made Maiwand clap his hands and jump up and down excitedly. A scooter! He had wanted one so badly but knew they couldn't afford it. He danced around the small apartment with glee.

DRIVING SCHOOL, 2001

"Mamo, where are you going?" Maiwand asked one Saturday as Lailoma was dressing to leave the apartment.

"To driving school. I'm going to learn to drive!" she told him.

Imagine that! she thought, suppressing a giggle.

One of the ladies in the apartment complex had introduced Lailoma to a Bosnian man who operated a driving school. It was a crash course—

figuratively. For $250, he gave her eighteen hours of instruction. She needed every one of them.

For the first lesson, she showed up in flip-flops. "No, no, no," he said, "you can't learn to drive in flip-flops. I'll let you wear them today, but next time you have to wear sneakers."

That was a challenge in itself. Where do you buy sneakers? She went to the dollar store, but there were no sneakers. Once again the owner came to her rescue. When she explained what she needed, he told her to try Walmart or Payless. She didn't know how to reach either of these two stores. By bus, he told her, and then walked her across the street to a bus stop. He told her where to get off the bus, and she executed the journey perfectly. She was so excited to have made the trip by herself. When it was time to return, she showed the bus driver her address, and he let her know when they had arrived at her stop.

I did it! she thought. It was another step toward independence. *I made it to Walmart, bought sneakers, and got home without a problem.*

But sneakers? she thought, much preferring to wear more fashionable footwear, even if it were just flip-flops. *Is this a law? Will I always have to wear sneakers when I drive?* she wondered.

With the eighteen hours of instruction, she learned how to drive well enough to pass the test the driving instructor gave for a driving permit. Then he drove her, along with her test score, to the DMV for her permit.

Five months later, she drove to the DMV with her Bosnian driving school instructor for her driver's license. She passed the written test with flying colors. There was just one glitch: she hadn't conquered the fine art of parallel parking. When it came time to demonstrate her driving skills, she confessed to the officer, "I can't parallel park."

"What do you mean you can't parallel park? You came for the test and you can't parallel park?" he asked, feigning irritation. "Well, get into the car and we'll see what you can do."

"Let's drive," he told her. As they approached an intersection, he instructed her to make a right turn and complimented her when she successfully negotiated the corner. "Bravo! You did that very well," he said enthusiastically.

"Thank you," she said. *Wait until I try to parallel park,* she thought.

"Turn left," he instructed her at the next light.

"You did just fine," he complimented her again. "Most people think making a left turn is harder than making a right turn, but you are the opposite. For you, the left turn looked easier than the right."

After the driving portion of the exam was completed, she successfully pulled straight forward into the parking space. Since she had already told him she couldn't parallel park, he didn't make her demonstrate her lack of skill. Instead, he looked at her and said, "You're single, and you need to drive, but you have to learn to parallel park. Take a number and wait in here."

Inside the amazingly large DMV building, she reached up and pulled a paper number from the roll and sat down with others to wait her turn.

Finally, she heard, "Number forty-seven?"

She approached the window and the lady behind the counter told her to stand and look into the camera for a picture. After she snapped it, she said, "You can sit back down until we call you."

Lailoma was sure she hadn't passed the test. But when her number was called again and she returned to the window, the lady handed her a shiny new card with her photo. Across the top it read: "Arizona Driver License." She had done it!

As a refugee, becoming independent in the United States is not as simple as it appears. The very programs that are intended to ease your assimilation into American life can also be obstacles in your path. The resettlement period in most circumstances is six months. Refugees are encouraged to use that time to learn English and get a job. For the school teacher, the transition was fairly easy. She was able to work with the Lutheran sponsoring organization as a translator. But some of the people in Lailoma's apartment complex had been receiving services well past the six-month timeframe. The community of refugees around them had become their circle of friends.

It is comfortable to live among people who speak your own language, and aside from the teacher, none of the women in Lailoma's community even thought about getting a job. The monthly $965 the US government allotted them at the time covered the basic living arrangements they had. While some of the men looked for part-time jobs to supplement that stipend, many did only the minimum necessary to support themselves.

Lailoma never intended to make the small apartment in the low-rent complex a permanent home. She was young, ambitious, and smart. Her plan was to use the help of Lutheran Social Services and the US government as a leg up. They had given her taxi tickets for six months, and then they extended their generosity for another six months as she was saving money. By the end of 2001, they told her, she would have saved enough money to buy a car. Her caseworker, who was still available as a resource, helped her open a savings account at SafeQ, a credit union. Each month, she deposited two hundred dollars into her account from her income at the Van Teal Shirt Co.

Her caseworker had done his math correctly, and she had stuck to her saving schedule. Within the year, she had saved two thousand dollars, at which point the social services program gave her an additional two thousand dollars and another milestone was achieved: she was ready to buy a car.

Knowing how to go about buying a car was another story.

From time to time, various church and civic groups came to the apartment complex to visit with the refugees, trying to ease their assimilation into the community. One of the women who had visited with Lailoma in her apartment had also been a refugee, and she continued to call her to see if she needed any help or had any questions.

"Well, I do have one question," Lailoma told her. "How do I buy a car?"

"My husband can help you with that," the woman answered, and handed the phone to her husband.

"How much do you think you can spend?" her husband asked.

"I have saved two thousand dollars, and with the gift from Lutheran Social Services, I have four thousand dollars. I think the credit union will loan me more," Lailoma replied.

A stunned silence followed. The man had lived in the United States for twenty years and still didn't know he could borrow money. Lailoma had investigated programs the Lutheran organization offered and learned they worked with the credit union to provide interest-free loans for a car or home. A year after making the US her home, she bought her first car, a used blue Chevy Geo Metro. It was the most beautiful vehicle she had ever seen.

GOOD NEWS FROM PAKISTAN, 2005

When Lailoma and Maiwand left Pakistan in 2000, she kept Magid's phone number. *Maybe I can help them,* she thought. Magid and Shrifa's plan had always been to go to Canada, where they had relatives, but if something happened and that didn't work out, she thought maybe she could help them get to the United States. She had begun calling every month or so for status updates.

One morning, around the same time she bought her car, Lailoma's cell phone rang as she was pulling herself out of bed for work. The voice on the other end was familiar: Magid. It was always good to hear his voice, and this time he sounded excited.

"I've found your brother," he told Lailoma. "I've found Ahmadwali!"

Lailoma was stunned. She hadn't heard any news of her family in five years.

"Where is he?"

"Islamabad. I found him in the bazaar."

"Is my family alive?" she asked, still so worried about her mother, father, sisters, and Naim.

"Yes, I learned they are all alive, and they are in Pakistan as well. But I don't think Ahmadwali knows they are alive."

"Oh, my god," Lailoma said. "Can I talk to him?"

Magid promised to arrange a phone call for them the very next day at his house.

At the predetermined time, Lailoma placed the phone call to Magid. The voice at the other end was Ahmadwali's. For several minutes, neither spoke. Both just cried. Knowing he was a target after Mussa had been killed, Ahmadwali had fled Afghanistan shortly after Lailoma left. Like Lailoma, he hadn't called or visited his family because he was afraid for their safety. He hadn't even taken his wife, Nazira, with him.

Ahmadwali had been able to leave the country by car. When he entered Pakistan, he was searched, but fortunately he had some cash in his pocket, which he slipped to the guard, who waved him through. From there, he had gone to Peshawar, where his former business partner had opened a store. For a while he was able to work with him, but thinking he wasn't very safe in Peshawar because it was so close to the border, he moved to Islamabad, and that's where Magid had run into him.

Every night for three months, Lailoma called him. Lailoma always placed the phone calls. Their conversations were simple, and short.

"Do you need money?" she asked every time.

"No, I have enough," he told her.

"Where do you live?" she asked.

For both of their protection, this was a question he never answered.

"How are you doing in Arizona?" he asked, after learning where she lived in the United States.

"I'm OK. I have a job! I'm sewing—you wouldn't believe the sewing machines where I work. And guess what? I've learned to drive. I have my driver's license, and I bought a car!"

"Are you sure you know enough to drive? You know you need to be careful about braking too fast. Also, if you use the emergency brake, make sure you release it before you start up again."

His advice and questions had come as quickly as he had learned about this new development in her life.

"Do you know how to take care of a car? There's a lot of maintenance—the coolants, the window wipers. What kind of car did you buy?"

By then she was chuckling. "A Chevy Geo Metro."

Late one evening about a week after their first phone conversation, Lailoma received another call from Pakistan. Ahmadwali had seen their mother in a market shopping for groceries, he told Lailoma. For a while, unable to believe it was really her, he followed her, pretending he was also shopping.

When she was finished, he followed her to the register, where he spoke to the shopkeeper. Qurisha recognized his voice.

The happy reunion in the store caused all of the people around them to cry. Finally, most of the family was together again. The rest of the family, Lailoma learned from Ahmadwali, had also left Afghanistan for Pakistan in 2000.

Ahmadwali was able to reunite Lailoma with the family via telephone. They were anxious to hear about her life in the United States—her job, how she learned to drive, where she and Maiwand lived. She wanted assurance they were well in Pakistan. At first, they kept their phone calls brief. Lailoma bought phone cards to pay for the charges—five dollars and ten dollars at a time. If they didn't have a lot to say, they saved their cards for the next time. Sometimes they called just for a quick check-in. Later, as Lailoma in Arizona and her family in Pakistan were able to download Skype, they conversed through the Internet, which meant they could talk for extended periods of time.

The fact that the rest of the family had been reunited relieved Lailoma. But she still worried. She knew they were relatively safe, but there was no work for them. In the beginning, Ahmadwali explained, he and Naim had set up a small shop, but it never became a good source of income. Thirteen family members: Ahmadwali, his wife, Nazira—who had eventually joined him— and their three children; Naim and his wife; plus Qurisha, Shahwali, Shaima (whose fiancé had never returned to her from Russia), and the three youngest daughters, Sonita, Sitara, and Susan, lived together in a three-room house. Laila still lived in Afghanistan with her husband.

Lailoma knew she needed to help.

MAKING A MOVE, 2005

Now that Lailoma was mobile, she began to think about looking for other job opportunities. The Van Teals had decided to close the factory, and though Mrs. Van Teal offered to have Lailoma work for her personally in her home, Lailoma didn't think that was the best situation. While it would have been easy to stay within the comfort zone of continuing to work for Mrs. Van Teal and living in the refugee community, she felt it was a dead-end situation. She didn't want to just live in America. She wanted to thrive. She wanted Maiwand to thrive. Her friend Samira had attended school and lived on the east side of metro Phoenix, where she felt the education opportunities would be better for Maiwand and the housing was more desirable.

By now Lailoma's English skills had improved to the point where she felt she could successfully interview, and she had more than conquered the fast commercial sewing machines. Two opportunities in Scottsdale presented themselves, both at high-end department stores, and she had the luxury of choosing Neiman Marcus, the higher-paying job with the better benefits.

Another opportunity came her way because of her position at Neiman Marcus. One of her fellow employees had previously worked part-time at a bridal store. Now the bridal store owner wanted to know if there was anyone else at Neiman Marcus who wanted to make a little money on the side doing alterations at her store. Of course Lailoma wanted to! With a full-time job and a part-time job, she knew she could help her family.

The time had come to move. Samira did some legwork and learned about a program for low-income housing in Scottsdale. There were two empty apartments for Lailoma to check out, she told her, and gave her directions to meet her there. One was on the first floor, and one was on the second. Lailoma chose the second-floor apartment. The complex had a pool, and she feared the water. What if Maiwand or she accidentally fell into the pool?

She signed the papers and made plans to move by the end of the month. On moving day, Samira came over and helped her pack. Lailoma, Maiwand,

and Samira managed the entire move by themselves. They loaded a rental truck with their few possessions and took off. With Samira at the wheel, they drove across town, arrived at the new apartment, and unloaded their belongings, carrying everything to the second floor.

Lailoma always remembered that first quiet evening—no running, screaming children as there had been in the complex where the new refugees were housed. Just peace and quiet.

CHAPTER 10

TO PAKISTAN AND BACK, 2001 TO 2005

The extended family lived in Pakistan in relative peace for a few years. But even though Lailoma had added the part-time job at the bridal boutique so she could increase what she was sending, they needed an income beyond that. Ahmadwali and Naim were eking out what living they could from their small shop.

In 2005 the Taliban approached Naim in Pakistan to come and work for them in opposition to the Afghan government, tapping into his insider knowledge of the presidential palace. When he resisted, they gave him one month to think about it. After one month of thinking about it, he still refused.

The Taliban came to the store, yanked his hands behind his back and tied them, blindfolded him, and attempted to drag him away. Ahmadwali fought back as they tried to force Naim into the back of a truck. The street was bustling with people and they couldn't drive away quickly, so the Taliban shot him. Naim, bleeding from the gunshot wound, dashed into the crowd and managed to evade capture. Before leaving, the Taliban hassled Ahmadwali and took his watch, his wedding ring, and whatever seemed of value from the store.

Naim found his way back to the store. Though he was injured and bleeding, the Pakistani police wouldn't let him go to the hospital without first questioning him. Fortunately, the Taliban hadn't taken things that seemed unimportant from the store, and the family was able to use fabric from the shop to stem the flow of blood. From 11 a.m. to 1:30 in the afternoon, Naim lay on the street, his blood soaking the fabric.

After the police took all the information they could, they released him. Ahmadwali quickly got him to the hospital, but now, because the police had been involved, the hospital didn't want to treat him. There was also the suggestion that the hospital's services were for Pakistanis, not Afghans. Ahmadwali knew of a private clinic, and he took Naim there. The clinic doctors didn't want to treat him because they determined he had internal bleeding, a situation beyond what they could handle. His face was swollen and his entire body was starting to turn purple from the internal bleeding.

"He's going to die," the emergency doctor told Ahmadwali. "We need to get him to the hospital. We can't perform the surgery he needs here."

Ahmadwali refused to accept that answer. He tracked down one of the clinic doctors he knew and said, "Do the surgery. If he dies, he dies, but we will have tried."

The second doctor took an X-ray, which revealed that Naim's liver and kidneys were undamaged, so he operated, removing the blood from his stomach. Naim remained in a coma for four days, and after he awoke the clinic personnel insisted he leave. "If the Taliban return, we don't want the clinic to be at risk," they told the brothers.

Ahmadwali secured a place for Naim to stay at a friend's house where the Taliban wouldn't know to look for him. Meanwhile, Lailoma sent money from Arizona so the doctor could make twice-a-day visits to clean the incision.

The stress was too much for Shahwali. When he learned that Naim had been shot, he was certain he had died. Shahwali's blood pressure, which was already high, skyrocketed. Sixteen days later, Shahwali passed away.

After Ahmadwali called about their father's death, the next phone call from him brought more bad news: their mother was in the hospital. By now, Lailoma could wait on the other side of the world no longer while her family was in such distress. So she made the bold move of returning to Pakistan with Maiwand. Her plan was to stay for one week. For safety's sake Ahmadwali recommended that she and Maiwand stay in a hotel, which seemed a good plan to Lailoma. There was no reason to jeopardize her freedom by associating herself with her brother, who had already been a Taliban target.

Lailoma burst into tears when she saw Ahmadwali, who was waiting at the airport when their flight arrived. Five years had passed since they had fled Afghanistan.

"You don't want to come to my house," Ahmadwali told her again. "It's not safe."

He took Lailoma and Maiwand straight to a hotel in Islamabad, where they welcomed the comfort of a nice room and a good night's sleep.

The following morning Ahmadwali returned to take them to the hospital to see Qurisha. Lailoma had assumed that Qurisha had suffered one of the panic attacks she experienced whenever she was distressed about something, but that wasn't the case this time. Her mother had had a stroke. Lailoma sat beside her throughout the day. Because the hospital limited the number of visitors, she hadn't seen the rest of her family. Toward evening, when Qurisha appeared to be sleeping comfortably, Ahmadwali drove Lailoma to the family's house for a brief visit.

Everybody was there—Shaima, her younger sisters except for Laila, Naim and his wife, and Ahmadwali's wife—and they welcomed her with open arms. There were also cousins for Maiwand to meet. Having lived together for five years, the cousins were a rambunctious group. Growing up with a mother who was always concerned, Maiwand was a little more reserved. But that disconnect ended as they played in the backyard. When the running started, Maiwand just joined in the fun.

After an hour or so, Lailoma was tired, and she knew Maiwand had to be as well. She called a taxi and returned to their hotel.

"Your brothers were just here," the receptionist informed Lailoma as she approached the front desk of the hotel. "They asked for your room number, and I gave it to them," she said. "I hope that was OK."

Lailoma froze. Immediately she knew something wasn't right. She and Maiwand were in danger. Her brothers had been back and forth between the hospital and home throughout the day, but they had had no time and no reason to go to her hotel room.

"I'm not going in there," she told the receptionist. "Those could not have been my brothers."

The receptionist sent security to the room. There they found no intruders, but her suitcase was open. Lailoma suspected they had taken her green card. When she was finally able to enter the room, that's exactly what she found. Nothing was missing or harmed except for her wallet, which had contained about fifteen hundred dollars, her American bank cards, her Arizona driver's license, and both her and Maiwand's green cards.

She felt the panic rise. *How am I going to go back to the United States?* she thought.

"Why didn't you tell me not to come here?" she screamed at Ahmadwali over the phone. "It's not safe."

Lailoma was not an American citizen. Instinctively, though, she knew her only possible help would be at the American embassy. She found her way there and explained her situation. At the embassy, the employees, who were all Pakistani, gave her an application for a new green card. But she needed proof of her US residency—an electric bill, her son's registration in school, anything that would prove she lived in the United States.

How can I do this? she worried. *I don't have anyone in America who can help me.*

Her coworkers at Neiman Marcus didn't even know where she lived. But then she remembered she had left the key to her apartment with Samira. Her friend might be able to find something and send it to her.

"Here's what I need," Lailoma told Samira. "I keep my bills in a basket on my desk. Please fax a phone bill, an electric bill, my rent bill, and Maiwand's school information."

Within the hour, Samira faxed all of the documents to Lailoma at the hotel. The following day, Lailoma took the documents to the embassy, where she was told they would determine their legitimacy.

"We have to check these out," the embassy staff told her. "We have to check your background, but we will get back to you. Call this number," they told her, handing her a slip of paper. "If your friend is an American, you can talk with the ambassador."

By now, Lailoma realized she wouldn't be returning to Arizona within the week, so she called her manager at Neiman Marcus to explain the situation. "Take your time," her manager said. "Don't worry. Your job is secure."

Then she made a second phone call to the bridal shop where she moonlighted in the evenings. "Take care of yourself," the owner said.

By chance, Samira was planning to attend a cousin's wedding in Islamabad a few weeks later. She flew to Pakistan early to help Lailoma.

"They only want to talk with an American," she told Lailoma. "It's better for me to talk with them in person rather than over the phone."

When Samira arrived, the pair met with the ambassador and a representative from Homeland Security. Lailoma broke into tears.

"Why are you crying?" they asked.

"I'm stuck here. I have a job in America. My son goes to school in America. We have to be able to go back," she replied as the tears kept rolling down her cheeks.

"If you're so anxious to return to America, why are you only coming in today to get your green card back?" they asked.

"No, I came in right away when it happened! Go get the file. It's all in there."

"Who did you give the information to?"

"I don't know the person's name. It was whoever was working here and told me the information I needed to provide."

The file validated to the ambassador and the Homeland Security representative that she, indeed, had done as she said.

"Please bring your son here," they said. "We'd like to talk with him."

Samira took a cab to the apartment where Maiwand had spent the day with his cousins and brought him to the embassy. The US officials took him to a separate room for questioning. He was dressed in his jeans and a T-shirt, while Lailoma, fearing she would stand out in American clothes, had worn

Pakistani clothing for the occasion. The first thing the embassy officials did was to show Maiwand, now fourteen, the picture from Lailoma's original application to the United Nations.

"Do you recognize this photo?" they asked.

"Yes," he told them. "That's when we left Pakistan for America."

"How far is Hawaii from Arizona?" they asked Maiwand, testing his knowledge of the United States.

"I don't know," he answered honestly, "but I do know you have to fly there."

Maiwand had put the school ID Samira had brought for him in his pocket and showed it to the official.

"Did you bring your photo?" the official asked when he returned to question Lailoma.

"No. Nobody told me to bring a picture," she said.

"Come back tomorrow and bring a photo with you," he said. "We're going to let you go back."

"As long as you tell me I can go back, that's all I care about," she replied.

When they returned the next day with the two photos, Samira couldn't resist pointing out to the Homeland Security representative that he looked like Kevin Costner. "I'm going to call you Kevin Costner!" she told him. Samira no doubt had made his day.

"Kevin Costner" brought out two sealed envelopes. "Don't open these," he said. "One is for the airline ticket agency and contains two copies of green card numbers for both you and Maiwand. The ticket agency will keep one copy, and you will keep the other. The second envelope will be opened by immigration in New York City."

Ahmadwali picked Lailoma and Maiwand up in a taxi to go to the airport. On the way he stopped by the home for both to say goodbye to the rest of the family. Many tears were shed because they would be parted again, but everyone understood she needed to leave.

By the time she reached customs and immigration in New York City, she was so stressed, fearful they would make her return to Pakistan. She kept letting other people go in front of her in line at customs, delaying when she would have to talk with the officials. By the time she worked up her nerve to present her documents, she had missed her plane.

"We see this all the time," the official told her. "Sit here."

After about ten minutes, he returned and said, "You're good to go on to Arizona!"

"Don't worry. I will never go back to either Pakistan or Afghanistan," she assured the customs official.

Having missed their flight, Lailoma and Maiwand prepared to spend the night at the airport. But how to get back to Arizona?

"Fly standby," the ticket agent recommended. "If you're lucky, you'll get seats."

They have my twelve hundred dollars. They have my ticket. They have Maiwand's ticket, she worried.

At some point, you have to trust someone, and the ticket agent seemed trustworthy. Lailoma put herself and Maiwand in her hands. The agent called a hotel and booked a room for them. She told them where to board the hotel shuttle. So off they went onto the cold March streets of New York City, Maiwand and Lailoma both in their summer clothing. Pakistan wasn't cold. Arizona wasn't cold. But it was snowing in New York City.

"Let's go see the Statue of Liberty!" Maiwand suggested.

"No. We're going to the hotel and nowhere else. We'll eat a donut and have a glass of tea. That's all."

Lailoma and Maiwand weren't the only ones stranded in New York. The spring snowstorm delayed flight after flight. One night in the hotel stretched into a second. Then a third. On the third morning, the ticket agent called. "We have a flight to Chicago, and then one from Chicago to Arizona."

Lailoma didn't hesitate. "Yes! We'll take them!"

They arrived in Phoenix at 8 p.m. and took a taxi home. When they reached their apartment, Maiwand was as relieved as Lailoma. "Home sweet home," he said as she unlocked the door.

The following day, it was business as usual: Maiwand went to school, and Lailoma went back to work at Neiman Marcus. Her homecoming was celebrated as her coworkers hugged her and cried. Coincidentally, the retailer's national operations manager was visiting the Scottsdale store from Dallas. After the excitement of her return had died down and everyone had returned to their jobs, he came to her, put out his hand, and introduced himself.

"Why is everybody crying and hugging you?" he asked. Her manager explained to him the precarious situation Lailoma had been in.

"She was stuck. She lost her documents, and she almost didn't get to come home. Before that, she lost her husband. She's been through so many difficulties."

The operations manager put his arm around her shoulders. "Don't worry," he assured her. "You are safe here."

The bridal store owner wasn't quite as magnanimous. In fact, not at all. Lailoma had called her from both New York and Chicago, telling her she would be there in two days.

"Are you coming to work the day you get home?" she asked.

"No, I am scheduled to work at Neiman Marcus that day," she answered.

The bridal store owner was extremely upset. "You left during the bridal season. Now I'm losing money because of it. I have a gown the other alterations lady has fixed poorly, and now you have to do it over."

Lailoma fixed the wedding gown, but the bridal shop owner only paid her half, giving the other half to the lady who had not altered it correctly.

Some people are just like that, Lailoma realized, and took it in stride.

Her greater concern was that while she had been able to give her siblings a final hug goodbye, she had never properly said goodbye to her mother. Qurisha still lay in the hospital recovering from her stroke when it was time for Lailoma and Maiwand to depart. Now, Lailoma resolved to make every effort to bring her mother to the United States.

AFGHANISTAN TO PAKISTAN
TO RUSSIA, 2000 TO 2012

Shaima's life had been on hold since 1988 when her parents committed her to Ghlamwali. In 2000 she had fled with her family to Pakistan. By 2001 the marriage had still not taken place. And in 2005 she continued to wait.

As Ghlamwali's sister had indicated when she first introduced herself to Qurisha and Shahwali in 1988, Ghlamwali had finished two years of his education in Kabul and then, after the engagement, went to Russia to study. The first year or two, he returned to Kabul for vacations and spent time with Shaima. They seemed happy. But things changed. Perhaps it was because two years from the time of their engagement the mujahideen entered Kabul. Perhaps it was because Ghlamwali hadn't really wanted to marry. Perhaps he found life, or someone, in Russia more interesting. When the mujahideen took over Kabul, he sent a letter to Qurisha and Shahwali to say he couldn't come back to Kabul because the mujahideen would kill anyone who came from Russia. In fairness, he may have had a point.

Following Shaima's engagement, Ahmadwali became engaged to Ojeie. Lailoma became engaged to Mussa. Ahmadwali and Ojeie married. Lailoma and Mussa married. After Ojeie's death, Ahmadwali married Nazira. Both siblings had children while Shaima waited and waited. By the time Lailoma gave birth to Maiwand in 1992, Ghlamwali had been absent for such a long time that the family truly thought he must have died. In fact, rumors circulated that he was dead. But there was no closure. They couldn't hold a memorial for him because there wasn't a witness to his death, and without proof of his death, Shaima couldn't move forward in her life. She remained engaged to Ghlamwali.

So she kept doing what she always had done. She cooked. She cleaned. She sewed. She had no house but her parents' home. She was a housewife without ever having been a wife. When her family fled to Pakistan in 2000, she went with them. Unlike Lailoma, Shaima undramatically passed the border in a bus filled with both men and women. Security guards questioned the men, but not the women, whose faces were covered.

In 2007, while Shaima and the rest of the family were in Pakistan, the long-absent Ghlamwali was discovered to be back in Helmand. In a round-about way, he and Shaima eventually connected—but through no effort on Ghlamwali's part. One of Qurisha's sisters lived in Helmand Province, and through one of his contacts in the village, her husband learned a little more of the fiancé's whereabouts. Discovered, Ghlamwali finally contacted Ahmadwali in Pakistan. With Shahwali deceased, he asked Ahmadwali and Qurisha if he and Shaima could marry. As the family suspected, the grape-vine confirmed that he had married someone in Russia with whom he ran a business, but she had abandoned him, taking with her all of the business assets. Now, he was ready to marry Shaima, deciding it was time to settle down in Afghanistan and have children.

Shaima was past forty. She had waited so long. And she had no other prospects in her life. This was not only her best option; she perceived it as her only option. Maybe it was.

In 2008 they married. For Shaima, there was no elaborate wedding, no emerald-green dress, no fairy-princess white gown, no gifts of beautiful jewelry. Her new husband took her to Helmand to live in his brother's primitive farmhouse. Eventually, Ghlamwali built a guesthouse for them with a separate bathroom, but from the beginning the change was dramatic for Shaima. The children her new husband wanted were never conceived. She was past child-bearing age.

To his own family, Ghlamwali had been something of a prodigal son. When he thought he could make money in Russia, he had left Helmand. When that didn't work out as he'd planned, he returned to Helmand and expected to become part of the family's farming operation. None of this sat well with his father. And it certainly didn't sit well with his half brothers and half sisters.

As it turned out, yes, the family did have sizeable farmland. But the catch was this: Ghlamwali had been born to his father's first wife. He had one full brother and one full sister—the woman who had encouraged the engagement with Shaima. His father's second wife and second set of children—four sons and four daughters—were the favored ones. That could only spell trouble down the road.

Hateful of Ghlamwali, his half brothers and father plotted to kill him. When his full brother learned of their plans, he warned Ghlamwali about the coming danger. "If our father comes to the door tonight," Ghlamwali's brother told Shaima one day, "don't open it. They're going to take my brother out and kill him."

His own family's grievances with Ghlamwali were many: "He's not religious," they said. "He doesn't always go to the mosque for prayers. He doesn't fast. He didn't stay with us to fight the jihadis. When the mujahideen came to Helmand, he was in Kabul, studying. Then he was in Russia, trying to make himself wealthy. We were defending our land and families against the mujahideen. He was only looking out for himself."

The family also still resented Shaima for something that had happened years earlier, during a surprise trip her future mother-in-law had made to Kabul one winter to visit her. Her prospective mother-in-law held onto the hope that Shaima and Ghlamwali would eventually marry, and she wanted to spend time with Shaima. She knew her husband wouldn't allow her to make the trip, so she told him she was going to Kandahar to visit a doctor. But she didn't go to Kandahar; she took the bus to Kabul.

While she was visiting Shaima in Kabul, her mother-in-law was kind to her, bringing her traditional clothes she had made before leaving home and giving her a small gift of jewelry. This might have been the happiest time of Shaima's adult life. She felt valued and hopeful the marriage would actually happen. Unfortunately, while the mother-in-law-to-be was in Kabul, the weather, which had been sunny, though cold, took a turn. Snow had fallen and there was a heavy fog that delayed her return to Helmand by two weeks, causing her tremendous stress because she knew she would be in great trouble with her husband when she returned. She was.

Just three or four months later, when she died, the family told people her appendix had burst and they weren't able to save her. But no one knew for sure that was what happened. Rumors circulated that her husband had killed her. The guilt of that thought plagued Shaima for the remaining years of her life.

Throughout Afghanistan, people from the small villages had never trusted people who lived in Kabul. For the most part, villagers spoke Pashto. In the city, Farsi was more common. The villages were under jihadi power, and when they thought "Kabul," they thought "government," making those living in Kabul the enemy. That made Qurisha and Shahwali's family suspect. It made Ghlamwali suspect. And it made Ghlamwali's full sister suspect because she had moved to Kabul after her husband was killed in the war.

The information Ghlamwali's full brother gave him regarding the plot to kill him turned out to be true. One evening there was knock on Shaima and Ghlamwali's door. "Who is there?" Shaima asked.

"It's me," her father-in-law answered. "Where is Ghlamwali?"

"He's out with a friend," she told her father-in-law, as she had been instructed. Hearing their quiet conversation, she knew her husband's half brothers were with him. They stayed outside the door for several minutes, then eventually left.

The next morning, Ghlamwali's full brother stopped by and drove him to Kandahar. From there they went to Kabul and finally on into Pakistan. Just a year after they married, Ghlamwali left Pakistan to go back to Russia, feeling out of the reach of his plotting family. His provisions for Shaima? None. He left Shaima behind in Helmand to fend for herself.

"They live like animals," Shaima later told Lailoma and her parents of Ghlamwali's family.

Though reputed to be prosperous, her husband's family lived as if they had nothing. There was no carpet for the hard, mud-packed floors. When they spread out their mattresses to sleep, they placed them directly on the bare dirt. The home had no indoor plumbing. The women had to carry water from the river on their shoulders as they had done when Qurisha was young. Sometimes there was no electricity—but of course, much of Afghanistan was accustomed to spotty electric service. They had no kitchen, cooking only over an open fire built in a hole in the ground. When they sat outside, they had only a plastic sheet to pull over the ground. Everyone walked barefoot. To Shaima, they lived primitively.

To provide some of the comforts of home, Ahmadwali and Qurisha sent a television for Shaima from Pakistan. The area in Helmand where Ghlamwali's husband's family lived was remote, but in the late afternoon there was often electricity and she could watch TV broadcasts from Kabul. Qurisha and Ahmadwali also bought a carpet to make her room more livable, to make it more like their home in Kabul.

Shaima continued to live in Helmand for a year after Ghlamwali left. In 2010 Mama Khalid and Mama Naeem, Qurisha's brothers, took matters into their own hands and went to Helmand to extricate her from her horrendous living conditions and take her back to Kabul. From Kabul, they sent her to rejoin the rest of the family in Pakistan.

For Shaima, one bad circumstance led to another. In 2011 she discovered a hard, immovable lump under her arm. For a long time, she was embarrassed and her modesty kept her from mentioning it to her family. When it became more and more uncomfortable, she finally told Sonita, who told their mother, who, with Ahmadwali's help, took Shaima to a doctor. As was customary, the doctor discussed the situation with Ahmadwali, not Shaima.

The lump, he said, was sizeable. A biopsy revealed breast cancer, and it appeared they had discovered it too late.

"Do something," Ahmadwali said to the doctor. "If you do nothing, she will die. I want her to have hope. I want her to fight this." His words echoed what he had spoken to the clinic doctor when Naim had been shot.

Surgery revealed the cancer had spread to Shaima's lymph nodes. "If she lives five years," the doctor told Ahmadwali, "her prognosis is good." His recommendation was standard: surgery, chemotherapy, and radiation followed by a daily dose of Tamoxifen for five years.

Shaima reached out to Ghlamwali, who was still in Russia. "Please send money so I can take these treatments," she begged of him.

He had sent five hundred dollars for her surgery, but now he balked at sending more money. "Don't ask again," he told his wife. "I have no more money." Ahmadwali paid for the treatments with some of the money Lailoma continued to send on a monthly basis.

After the surgery, chemotherapy, and radiation were completed, Ghlamwali urged Ahmadwali and Shaima to join him in Russia. As it turned out, he was more interested in Ahmadwali joining him than in his wife joining him. Nevertheless, he spoke to Shaima as if he intended to help her. "I can take better care of you in Russia," he said.

To Ahmadwali, he said, "I'm going to start a new business in Russia. It's going to be very successful, and I want you to be my business partner. We will make a lot of money together."

The opportunistic Ghlamwali thought Ahmadwali still had access to the considerable sum of money he once had.

Ahmadwali, on the other hand, now had no job. Maybe he should take a chance on Ghlamwali, he thought. Lailoma had sent an additional one thousand dollars for Shaima's care, including the Tamoxifen, and Ahmadwali used some of it to buy a three-month supply before they left for Russia. He also took her medical records with them so that after she had finished that supply, she could visit a Russian doctor and obtain a new prescription. The expectation was that Ghlamwali actually would fill the new prescription.

Nothing worked out as Ahmadwali anticipated. When Ahmadwali and Shaima arrived in Russia, they found that the big "business opportunity" was only a little flea market-type store. That wasn't all. Ghlamwali often left the shop at noon, returning only when it was time to close up for the evening—never bothering to account for his time. While he was out, Ahmadwali minded the store. Then the two would go home to a meal Shaima had prepared, a meal Ghlamwali resentfully shared with Ahmadwali.

Learning that Ahmadwali had no money to invest with him angered Ghlamwali, and life in their rented apartment quickly spiraled downward.

Eventually Ahmadwali moved out and shared a rented room with another man. Finally, he came to terms with the fact that the business venture wasn't going to work, and he made plans to return to Pakistan.

"Come back to Pakistan with me," Ahmadwali urged Shaima. "You're going to starve here. Your husband is self-centered and selfish. He's not going to make sure you have good food to eat, and he certainly isn't going to take care of your health. Come back with me."

"No, I'm going to get better medical treatment in Russia than I could in Pakistan," was Shaima's answer.

Maybe she had a point. But the quality of the medical care she received only mattered if, in fact, she received the care. And now, she was totally at the mercy of Ghlamwali to buy her Tamoxifen and continue with her checkups.

After Ahmadwali left for Pakistan, Shaima didn't dare ask her husband for the medicine. When she finished a month's supply, she silently placed the empty container on the breakfast table. Sometimes Ghlamwali refilled the prescription, and sometimes he didn't. Sometimes he just bought an over-the-counter painkiller for her.

"These are the same drugs," he told Shaima. "These will make you better. I've talked with the doctor here," he said. "This is what you should take."

Did he show a doctor her records? Did something lose itself in the translation from Pashto to Russian? Those questions were never answered. Shaima couldn't read the writing on the containers. Even if the words had been written in her own language, Shaima couldn't read.

Within a few months, Shaima noticed another lump between her breasts, close to the site of the original surgery. "Stop whining. You're fine!" Ghlamwali yelled at her. It had been more than a year since her follow-up with the physician in Pakistan. She had not seen a doctor since.

CHAPTER 11

ARIZONA, 2008

"How can I become a US citizen?" Lailoma had asked Sheila, a coworker, one day in 2002, shortly after she started her employment at Neiman Marcus. She knew Sheila had also been a refugee and was already a citizen.

"Well, you've only been here for two years, but it's not too early to start the process. First, you need to fill out an application. You can do that online, but if you go to the immigration office in downtown Phoenix, they will be able to tell you what happens next, and about how long it will take."

So in 2002, prior to her harried trip to Pakistan, Lailoma had begun the application process to become a US citizen. While five years living in the United States is required for citizenship (or three if you marry a US citizen), Lailoma, who had lived in the US only since 2000, knew that some people wait for years and years before being granted citizenship, and wanted to gain hers as quickly as she could. In her mind, she never felt completely safe living in America without it. What if they made her return to Pakistan? The experience of having her green card stolen while she was in Pakistan had led to two realizations: she didn't want to travel to that part of the world again, and she for sure didn't want to have only her green card for identification. She wanted a US passport.

When she arrived home from the nightmarish trip to Pakistan in 2005, she busied herself studying for the test required for all naturalization candidates. Preparing for the exam felt good, reminding her of her high school days when she and her friends had studied together. Now, all she could do was wait to receive her interview letter.

Her interview wouldn't be scheduled until early 2008. When she met with the naturalization officer for her interview, he quizzed her about her eight years in America, her job, her trip to Pakistan, and why she wanted to become an American citizen.

The test itself included ten questions on civics and American history, only six of which she needed to answer correctly. *When is Independence Day? How many stripes and how many stars are on the US flag? What do the stars represent? Name the thirteen original colonies. What are the three branches of government? Who is the current president of the United States?* Since she knew the answers to the first six questions he asked, he didn't bother to continue with that portion. She was relieved, but the A-plus student in her wished he had asked all ten questions. She knew she would have known the answers. The next section of the test evaluated her understanding of both reading and writing in English. She had three chances to correctly read a sentence in English. She passed on the first sentence. Then he read aloud a sentence to her, which she was to write correctly on the exam paper. Again, she passed on the first attempt.

"Congratulations!" the immigration officer said. "You have passed both sections!"

"What happens next?" she asked.

"The next step is a background check," the official told her, "and sometimes that can take a while. We have your fingerprints from your green card, so we won't have to fingerprint you again."

On March 7, 2008, Lailoma, Maiwand, now seventeen, and Sheila, the coworker who had coached Lailoma through the naturalization process, arrived at the US District Court for the District of Arizona in downtown Phoenix for Lailoma's swearing-in ceremony. The federal judge presiding over the proceedings spoke briefly about the benefits and responsibilities of being an American citizen. When he announced it was time to take the oath of citizenship, Lailoma's eyes welled up with tears.

"I know how you're feeling," Sheila whispered, putting her arm around Lailoma's shoulders. "I was emotional too. You're crying because you're happy."

"Yes, I'm happy," Lailoma said, "but that's not why I'm crying. I'm crying because I don't have any of my family here. My husband's family is big. My family is big. I should have a lot of people here to watch me become an American citizen. And none of them are here."

Through her tears she raised her right hand and swore allegiance to the United States of America. Even when the certificate was securely in her hands, she worried.

"What if this isn't real because I lost my green card?" she said to Sheila anxiously.

"They invited you here," Sheila assured her. "You've taken the oath. It's real. You're in. You are an American."

Just eight years after arriving in America, twelve years after fleeing Afghanistan in the middle of the night, Lailoma had become an American.

Following the oath, a celebration was held on the lawn in front of the courthouse. The judge who administered the oath asked if any of the new Americans wanted to share their story. One woman told a moving story of crossing the harsh Arizona desert from Mexico. An Iranian man spoke about how the government had tortured his family, and the United Nations had enabled them to come to America. One woman whom Lailoma knew from Neiman Marcus had brought her sister to the United States and now, twenty years later, that sister had become a US citizen. In times past, Lailoma might have felt too timid to speak out, but on this day, encouraged by the others' stories, she volunteered.

"I am from Afghanistan," she told those assembled. "My name is Lailoma Shahwali. I left Afghanistan because the Taliban killed my husband. I left Pakistan because there was no future for us there."

As she related the story of Mussa's death, her flight from Afghanistan, her struggle to leave Pakistan, her long journey to the United States and then getting a job, learning to drive, and buying a car, the assembled crowd became quiet. Many people had tears in their eyes. Those who didn't were choking them back.

"Who is with you?" the judge asked.

"This is my son, Maiwand Mussa. He has gone through all of this with me. We came to America because a generous church organization sponsored us. I don't want to ever go back to Pakistan or Afghanistan. I want to be an American. Maiwand wants to be an American."

The year Lailoma became a citizen, she realized another aspect of the American dream. The same programs that seven years earlier had helped her buy her used Chevy Geo Metro now enabled her to purchase her own condo in a quiet complex near downtown Scottsdale. There, Maiwand was close to an excellent high school within walking distance.

THE FAMILY IN AFGHANISTAN, EARLY 2000S

While life looked up for Lailoma and Maiwand in the United States, those who stayed in the Middle East didn't fare as well. Ever since the tragic loss of Ojeie, a pall had come over the entire family. Such promise, such loss, was hard to bear. In the years that followed, the loss of young people continued.

Mama Khalid, Qurisha's older brother who had been present on the night of Ojeie's death, remained in Kabul for a time, but eventually he returned to Wardak and his family. Years earlier, he had met his future bride in their walled village, and he actually had a hand in selecting her. Most of the houses in Wardak surrounded a plaza-like center with towers on each of the four corners. The homes were connected to the four towers, and villagers could walk around the entire settlement on the conjoining roofs. Both men and women went in and out of their homes within eyesight of everyone.

One young woman walking from roof to roof caught Mama Khalid's eye, and he pointed her out to his father, Baba Amin. Amin went to see her family, and they agreed to allow their daughter to marry Khalid. Unfortunately, family members who lived in Kabul couldn't travel to Wardak for the wedding because the road between the two was under constant threat of ambush by the mujahideen. A bus traveling from Kabul to Wardak likely would have been stopped, and the passengers risked being removed and possibly taken to the mountains to be shot. Accounts of such treachery were common.

So Mama Khalid and his wife married in Wardak with only some of his family present to celebrate. Within a short time, their first child, a son, was born. Then a second child arrived, a daughter. Then a third, a son. The fourth was a daughter, followed by two more children. In all, he had three sons and three daughters.

Mama Khalid wasn't a prosperous man, and his health was still frail from the torture he had endured when the mujahideen held him captive. Eventually he became almost totally disabled, unable to work. The villagers, who were like family, helped him grow wheat and vegetables to feed his family.

In 2002, when Tahmina, his first daughter, was nineteen, she became very sick and weak. Whatever ailed her caused her stomach to swell as if she were pregnant. Mama Khalid took her to each of the several doctors in the village, but none could diagnose her illness. By this time, even though the roads were bad, travel between Wardak and Kabul had resumed, and Mama Khalid decided to move his family to Kabul to get better care for Tahmina. Once again, this time in Kabul, Mama Khalid and Tahmina made the rounds from doctor to doctor. Still no one could determine what was wrong. With Mama Khalid's limited resources, they couldn't afford the more highly trained specialists because their fees were so steep. And these doctors wanted to be paid up front.

As Mama Khalid and Tahmina left the office of one of the many doctors they visited in Kabul, still with no results, Tahmina began to vomit blood. Mama Khalid tried to hail a taxi, but not one taxi stopped for him. Finally he picked Tahmina up in his arms and carried her to the hospital. But the hospital also required payment up front. Tahmina was turned away.

Totally dejected, Mama Khalid sat down under a tree just outside the entrance to the hospital, holding Tahmina on his lap and cleaning the blood from her mouth with his handkerchief. Doctors and other medical personnel went in and out of the hospital, chatting and passing the father and daughter as if they were invisible, unmoved by their dire situation.

Mama Khalid carried Tahmina back home and could do nothing but watch her daily decline. Eventually she died. As Baba Amin had done for him when he was held in custody by the Taliban, Mama Khalid would have gone to any length to take care of his children. But sometimes those efforts could not change the outcome.

As if Tahmina's death weren't enough to break Mama Khalid's heart, in 2012, his eighteen-year-old son Hassan died of bone cancer, a condition he didn't even realize he had. There was that dull, deep ache in his bones at night, but he chalked it up to his day's activities. Even though the pain never seemed to go away, he became accustomed to it, considered it a fact of his life. So his cancer went undetected—until he fell off the roof of the house and broke his arm. The doctor who set the bone didn't mention, or didn't notice, anything unusual about the break. But after the surgery to put a metal plate in his arm, Hassan's forearm slowly started to swell. Over the course of a year, the swelling continued. The doctors in Kabul offered no diagnosis—and no treatment. Something was clearly wrong, if only some doctor would take the time to investigate. Better care must be available in Pakistan, Mama Khalid thought. Maybe there was.

On the map the journey from Kabul to Peshawar looks like a reasonably straight 140 miles or so, east and slightly south. But it isn't straight, and it has never been easy. To reach Peshawar, a traveler who chooses to drive from Kabul has to cross the "Silk Mountain" and go through Jalalabad first. The Kabul–Jalalabad Highway, which is the only way to make your way through the high mountain pass, is one of the most treacherous in the world. In 1969 the narrow two-lane road had been paved. But by the early 2000s, it had deteriorated into gravel.

The forty-mile Kabul Gorge, as the passageway through the chasm of mountains and cliffs is known, would be breathtakingly beautiful if it were not for the harrowing ride it presents. Aggressive drivers take the curves far too quickly, and adding to the danger of cars that are driven too fast for the conditions are the trucks that can't maintain speed as they climb, making car drivers even more impatient. Crashes are commonplace—several on any given day—and few live to tell about their experiences, as cars sometimes fly off the cliffs some two thousand feet above the Kabul River.

The road was dangerous, for sure, but Mama Khalid and Hassan had no choice. Hassan's shoulder had swollen so large it looked as if he had a pillow under his shirt. So they rose at two one morning to board a bus to Jalalabad. Every rut in the road caused Hassan to grimace in pain. If they hadn't been frightened out of their minds by the wild driving of the bus operator, they might have appreciated the magnificent views as they recklessly flew around the precipitous corners, dodging other drivers.

Amazingly, they successfully reached Jalalabad at about 6 p.m.

From there, they changed buses to complete the journey, first to Torkham and then on to Peshawar. From Peshawar, they proceeded to Islamabad, where other members of the extended family, including Ahmadwali and Qurisha, now lived. Over the course of two weeks, Qurisha and Mama Khalid took Hassan to doctor after doctor, just walking unannounced into any office that indicated it was a medical facility. Finally a physician sent them to Shifa International Hospital. It was a good hospital, where they learned not very good news.

Mama Khalid had found someone who was willing to make a more thorough diagnosis on Hassan's arm. It was dire: bone cancer. Hassan was bleeding internally, and sometimes bleeding externally as well.

"If we operate," the doctor told Mama Khalid, "he would never survive the surgery. The cancer has spread throughout his body."

With no hope, Mama Khalid took his son back to Kabul. Hassan knew he was dying, but he tried to stay positive for his father's sake. "I will be fine," he told Mama Khalid. "But I have some money saved, and if I die, it might help you."

His son losing hope broke Mama Khalid's heart. "Why do you say that? You will be fine. You will use that money for school," he told him. But, inside, he knew what Hassan knew. Hope was gone.

A month later, Hassan died.

On the other side of the world, Lailoma's cell phone rang just as she was getting into her car to go to work. In her arms was a long garment bag containing a wedding dress she had completed altering, and she arranged the bag carefully in the back seat before fumbling in her purse for her phone.

It was Ahmadwali, calling from Pakistan. "Hassan has died," he told Lailoma. "Mama Khalid has no money for the burial."

The ask of this phone call had become recurring. The extended family struggled to make sufficient money to take care of their most basic needs. In Pakistan, Ahmadwali and Naim were unable to find work, even odd jobs that might supplement what Lailoma sent to them.

Lailoma's sister Laila's husband had a job as a fighter pilot, earning two hundred dollars a month, but he turned each paycheck over to his father, who controlled all of his family's finances. For Mama Khalid to ask Laila for help was out of the question. In fact, Laila's father-in-law was so selfish that he eventually kicked her and her husband out of their family home. With the expense of $150 for rent, Laila and her husband didn't have enough money to heat the small apartment they hastily moved into or to buy food.

When Lailoma heard this, she sent her sister two hundred dollars immediately and then began sending one hundred dollars to her monthly.

When Tahmina died, Lailoma had sent money so she could have a proper burial. And this time, she would do the same for Hassan.

But in her mind, she knew she had to set limits. When Laila's daughter was accepted to medical school, they could not afford to pay her tuition. Could Lailoma send the six hundred dollars they needed up front for her to enroll, they asked?

No. Lailoma was at the limit of her resources.

Almost as soon as she gained her US citizenship, Lailoma had begun the nearly year-and-a-half-long process of sponsoring her mother to come to the United States. Qurisha had recovered from her stroke, and Lailoma wanted to take care of her. The feeling was mutual: Qurisha didn't want Lailoma and Maiwand to be alone in America. The rest of the family in Pakistan and Afghanistan had each other. When she arrived in 2013, Lailoma and Maiwand were thrilled to have her live with them. But one of the issues confronting them was that Qurisha had little to no understanding of money; she had never worked and never paid a bill. Now, she was quick to offer Lailoma's help to the others.

"Lailoma will send you more money," she assured them. If and when Lailoma declined to help, Qurisha became angry with her.

"You just spend your money on yourself," she screamed at her. "You just buy things you want."

When Sonita married in 2012, she lived with her husband on family property in Kabul. The couple seemed able to support themselves with the money Sonita's husband made as a driver for a business executive. But Sitara and Susan still lived with Ahmadwali in Pakistan. The money Lailoma sent to Ahmadwali supported these two sisters as well.

The evening Ahmadwali called her with the news of Hassan's death, she stopped at the Circle K after work and wired five hundred dollars to Mama Khalid. This would be enough for him to hire a bus to transport Hassan's body and the rest of the family to Wardak, a three-to-four-hour drive from Kabul on the deteriorated roads. At least the eighteen-year-old would be able to lie in peace in his home village. It was the most the family could do.

It was the most Lailoma could do.

A year passed, and another of Mama Khalid's daughters died with the same symptoms her older sister had. She was just twelve when the condition struck her. As in the case of Tahmina, Mama Khalid was unable to find help for this daughter. Lailoma sent money to help with medical expenses, but no help was found for her young cousin.

"She was so beautiful," Qurisha told Lailoma. "We were going to engage her to Maiwand. Her face was perfect."

Mama Khalid was doing his best, but he just wasn't able to support his family and their needs. He and his older son worked for a large street-construction company, and each earned about one hundred dollars per month.

With this income, they were able to rent a house and pay for food. But Mama Khalid was older by now and no longer physically strong. Unable to do the heavy construction work required, eventually he lost his job and his older son became the family's sole support.

And Mama Khalid's troubles weren't over. His third and last daughter, only seven years old, followed her sisters in death, with the same symptoms, which were never diagnosed for any of them.

"Now sometimes when I call Mama Khalid," Lailoma said to Samira, "he's just lost. He's sixty years old. In his pictures, he looks a hundred."

Mama Khalid suffered post-traumatic stress from his time in jail and his torture by the mujahideen. He became insecure financially, and his wife claimed his mind was going. Often he retreated into his room and cried, mumbling to himself.

"I wish I had had money," he told Lailoma one night over the phone. "I couldn't even get a good doctor for my children."

"I have such good memories of Mama Khalid," Lailoma told me. "When I was young and he was in the army in Kandahar, he visited us in Kabul every summer. In Kandahar they had more elaborate sewing machines that would make all the modern stitches and designs. Each time he came, he brought pretty clothes to us as gifts."

In those days, Mama Khalid had access to an army vehicle and sometimes he would load all of Qurisha and Shahwali's children into it and drive outside the city of Paghman at the base of the Hindu Kush mountain range for a picnic in the lush Paghman Gardens.

"In the two weeks he visited each summer, we had so much fun," Lailoma said. "We went to the movies or played in the park. He bought ice cream for us or boiled corn on the cob. He even let us pick and eat the 'forbidden' grapes and almonds in the park. 'Shh! Don't tell your baba,' he would say with a wink."

SPONSORING NAIM, 2008

In 2006 Naim and his wife had their first child, a baby boy. Reza was born in Pakistan and spent his first seven years in the crowded home with Ahmadwali's family, Qurisha, Sonita, Susan, and Sitara. He was a happy, bubbly baby until he was about eighteen months old, when the family began to notice he was becoming listless, lacking energy. His skin looked sallow, he had a cough. Something was wrong. A few trips to the doctor generated a frightening diagnosis: childhood leukemia.

Reza needed blood transfusions, chemotherapy, lab work, and monthly treatments for three years. Naim had no health insurance, and the hospital wouldn't admit Reza until it received payment. As she could, in addition to sending money for living expenses to Ahmadwali every month, Lailoma also sent money to help care for Reza. Qurisha (who returned to Pakistan from America for a visit during this time), Susan, and Naim's wife had the same blood type as Reza and were able to give blood for him.

Lailoma urged Naim to bring Reza to the United States for the ongoing monitoring he needed. The process would be long, but she began the paperwork for sponsoring Naim to come to the US as she had Qurisha. Reza's medical condition was the reason she put forth for their potential immigration.

"Lailoma is going to bring Sitara and Susan to America too," Qurisha told Samira one day.

Lailoma wanted to scream at her mother. She tried not to let her anger show, but sometimes it was just too much. She tried to explain to her mother the legalities of bringing her sisters to the United States, but Qurisha refused to understand.

"I can't bring my sisters here. If you worked, you could bring them here, because they're not married, but I can't bring them here. I was able to sponsor Naim because his son was sick. They aren't sick."

The family's trials were not over.

One night in 2013, Ahmadwali called Lailoma from Pakistan. "Shaima is really sick," he told her.

Lailoma called her in Russia from Arizona. "I'm coughing blood," Shaima explained. "Sometimes blood comes out of my nose. My eyes are getting purple around them."

Livid, Lailoma placed a call to Ghlamwali. "I know you don't take her to the doctor. I know you didn't give her the correct medicine. I know she's not getting good food. She needs to see a doctor!"

Her call only made things worse. That evening, Ghlamwali took his anger out on Shaima, yelling at her and kicking and slapping her.

"I'll call him again," Lailoma told her sister when she heard what happened. "I'm going to call him again."

"No," Shaima told her. "That won't help. I am so weak. If he beats me, I don't have the energy to take it."

Lailoma sent an additional two hundred dollars for Shaima to see a doctor in Russia. Interestingly, this doctor could see that Ghlamwali had neglected her and kicked him out of his office while he explained to Shaima that she needed more surgery. On the day of the scheduled operation, Ghlamwali falsified an insurance document, gave it to the doctor, and left Shaima alone to have the surgery while he went to work. As they put her on the operating table, she was cursing her husband. "God," she said, "please punish him for what he has done to me."

When she was released after the surgery to remove her remaining breast, the doctor recommended a second round of chemotherapy. Ghlamwali wouldn't drive her to her treatments, so for each, Shaima walked a few blocks to catch a bus. One day when Lailoma called, Shaima was breathing heavily.

"Why are you panting?" Lailoma asked her. The walk to the bus had sapped her strength. Each trip further depleted her energy.

Shortly after her second surgery, Ghlamwali called Shaima one afternoon from work to let her know there was laundry to be done. "Get up out of bed and get some work done, you lazy thing," he yelled into the phone. "You're using your treatments as an excuse. Quit being lazy. You still need to do your chores. When I come home from work, I'm too tired to have to do women's work."

Finally, Shaima stood up for herself. "Do the laundry yourself," she screamed back at him, slamming down the receiver.

Shaima lived her final days in Russia with a husband who didn't love her and didn't have the decency to take care of her. In the evening after work, he picked things up for his own dinner, but didn't share any of the food with her. He sat down with his bottle of vodka, ate his dinner, and went to bed. A week before her death, she dragged herself to the kitchen to boil water for rice, the only food left in the house. He didn't seem to care whether she ate or not.

Lailoma sent another hundred dollars. "Call your friend Leena," she told Shaima. "Have her call the store and set up delivery so you can have milk every morning."

"When I die, don't leave me here. Send me back to Afghanistan," Shaima begged Lailoma.

But I can't do anything from here, Lailoma thought. *Don't give me this responsibility.*

"Go back to Pakistan," Lailoma told her. "I will send you more money. I will send you a ticket. If you would like to take some gifts to our sisters, brothers, and mother, I will send you money for that too."

"You think I can shop? I can't even walk. I don't have energy to shop for gifts," Shaima told her, "but I will go to Pakistan as soon as my doctor says I can."

Bitterness crept into her voice. "My life is nothing. Our mother and father ruined my life by not sending me to school."

Lailoma recognized the truth in Shaima's words.

Shaima's spirits were lifted somewhat at the thought of rejoining her family in Pakistan, but her body was swollen and she couldn't move. Her skin was on fire from so many treatments and from lying in bed for so long. Ghlamwali told her that her doctor thought she should wait ten or fifteen days to regain some strength before making such a trip, but even then she was happy just knowing she would be surrounded by people who loved her.

Had Ghlamwali actually talked with her doctor? No one knows. She struggled to her feet and packed a small suitcase so she would be ready to leave when she was able. Five days later, she died.

Ghlamwali called Shaima's friend Leena to tell her that Shaima had passed away. He didn't have the decency to call Shaima's family to let them know. Leena picked up Shaima's cell phone and found what she thought was Lailoma's number. Instead the number belonged to Sonita.

In the early morning hours, Leena called Sonita in Pakistan. "Shaima has passed away."

Sonita called Lailoma in Arizona. "When did she pass away?"

"Just last evening," Sonita answered through her tears.

Lailoma called Leena. "Please send my sister back to Afghanistan," Lailoma urged her. "She wants to be buried in Afghanistan."

Earlier, Ahmadwali had made the same request of Ghlamwali. "I don't have money for that," Ghlamwali growled at Ahmadwali. "Dirt is dirt. All around the world, it's the same dirt. It doesn't matter if she's here or there."

Leena promised Lailoma she would do everything she could. In Russia, Leena's husband invited the Afghan community in the place he worked to help. They put their money together and they, not Ghlamwali, sent her to her resting place in Afghanistan.

"Here," a coworker at Neiman Marcus said to Lailoma, pressing a piece of paper into her hand. It was a check for five hundred dollars, enough to buy a burial plot for Shaima in Afghanistan. Her generosity brought tears to Lailoma's eyes.

She remembered what Ahmadwali had said to her when she was young: "I wish you were my brother." In a way, she realized, she had become like a brother to Ahmadwali. She had become like a brother to her entire family.

Less than a year later, Naim and Reza arrived in Phoenix on April 9, 2014. Reza had finished his treatments in Pakistan and would do his follow-up doctor visits in the United States.

Naim and Reza moved temporarily into Lailoma's condo, sharing a bedroom with Qurisha—Reza and Qurisha sleeping in the bed, and Naim sleeping on the floor.

Like any seven-year-old, Reza's favorite parts of the school day in America were recess and lunch, but he quickly made friends and polished his English skills. After school or on Saturday mornings, he could be found playing video games with his big cousin Maiwand. The family rejoiced over Reza's recovery.

Naim's status in America was not as a refugee, as Lailoma's had been. And while he didn't have the resources of a sponsoring group as Lailoma had, he had Lailoma. With her encouragement, he found employment stocking shelves at a Dollar General store. She urged him to open a bank account, to get a driver's license, to save his money, to improve his English. On many of these counts, he was reticent. Possibly because Lailoma seemed to have all the necessities—a home and a car—in place, he wasn't as willing as Lailoma had been to do whatever it takes to succeed in America.

Qurisha was thrilled to have Naim and Reza living with them. She cooked their food, washed their clothes, and walked Reza to the bus stop. She cut Reza's food for him and picked up his toys after him. She helped him use the bathroom.

Lailoma encouraged her mother to allow Reza to do some things for himself. "His teachers aren't going to do these things for him," she told Qurisha.

Within a few months, Naim made arrangements to work with a friend in Baltimore, and in the summer of 2015, he, Qurisha, and Reza left the apartment to start a new life on the East Coast. Lailoma was skeptical, but wished them well and was silently grateful to have her condo back to herself and Maiwand.

AHMADWALI, 2016

Lailoma continued to send money to Ahmadwali in Pakistan and to Susan in Kabul. She continued to sew day and night to make all of this possible.

One early evening in January 2016, as she lay on the sofa for a brief rest after work before going upstairs to begin sewing, her cell phone rang. Not recognizing the number, she didn't answer. *They can leave a message or call back*, she thought.

Within just a couple of minutes, the phone rang again. The same number. And then again. Finally, she sat up and answered. The hysterical voice on the other end was barely intelligible. "What? I can't understand you," she said.

"It's baba," cried the young man on the phone. "He's dead."

Slowly she began to absorb the most tragic news of her life.

Baba, to this young man, was her brother Ahmadwali. Her nephew was calling from Pakistan. Ahmadwali had suffered a massive heart attack in the night and died. Lailoma sobbed into the phone. Her closest ally, her friend, the one who had wished she were his brother, was gone, just three years after Shaima died. This was a loss she didn't think she could bear.

But she must. Her family leaned on her for everything. This would surely be no exception.

She knew what had to be done.

"Take him to the hospital, and have them keep him until I can get there," she told her nephew. "I'll be there as quickly as I can. Then we will have him moved to Afghanistan for burial."

Even as she booked her flight, she knew she was embarking on a journey that could spell doom. She had vowed never to return to the Middle East, but now she knew she had no choice. She called her brother Naim in Baltimore. "You need to buy tickets for yourself and our mother. You need to get to Afghanistan."

At first he didn't seem inclined to go. "The tickets are too expensive," he said. "I don't have enough money."

"You find it!" she yelled into the phone back at him. "You find the money. I can't help you this time."

She arrived in Pakistan two days later. Naim and their mother arrived shortly after. With Ahmadwali gone, the family chose to return to Afghanistan. Lailoma had arranged for the hospital to keep Ahmadwali's body in Pakistan until they arrived. Then she arranged for the transportation to Kabul—for Ahmadwali's remains, for the family, and for whatever furniture and household goods were worth taking back to Afghanistan. She paid for Ahmadwali's burial plot next to their father's plot, for the mullah, and for the food served to the guests. While she wanted to be able to just grieve, she knew the family counted on her for these details. She was the big brother.

Qurisha and the rest of the family moved back into the house in Kabul that had been vacant since they fled in 1996. They rolled out the few bare carpets that were left and placed their meager furniture. Qurisha took charge. "You will sleep there and you there," she directed. The daughters-in-law, Ahmadwali's and Naim's wives, could only follow her orders. With nieces and nephews, and Lailoma's unmarried sisters, there was little room to maneuver.

For these momentous occasions in life—whether joyous or heartbreaking—the family kept to the same ritual they had followed for decades. Two chefs cooked all day and all night in rainy weather under a tent in Kaka Zaher's backyard. After the burial, guests would come to the home and most would stay to give condolences to the family and eat lunch.

The rain continued the day of the burial, but still a large group of people went to the cemetery. Not knowing all of the guests and fearing she would be seen, Lailoma stayed in the car with Qurisha and Ahmadwali's daughters.

Afterward, at the family home, she went through the motions of mingling with the many guests who came to pay their respects and eat the elaborate meal. Not present among the guests were Abdullah and Roya, about whom no one seemed to have heard anything since the family had fled Afghanistan. After the burial day had ended, Lailoma stayed in the house for the duration of her stay. She didn't feel safe venturing out in Kabul lest she be recognized and detained. The last thing she wanted to do was to get stuck in Afghanistan. Plus, she had determined never again to wear a burqa, and once again women's faces were not to be seen in public.

She and Maiwand, who had stayed in Scottsdale, kept in constant contact via phone and email.

It was small compensation, but during her two-week stay, Naim confessed to Lailoma and the rest of the family that she had been right all along about what he needed to do to make a successful life in the United States. His move to Baltimore had not gone well, and his friend could no longer give Qurisha, Reza, and him a place to stay, let alone employ him.

"After I go back to Pakistan and get the money owed to Ahmadwali from his job, I'm coming back to Arizona," he told Lailoma. "I'll do whatever you say."

The news was not necessarily what Lailoma wanted to hear. She and Maiwand had happily returned to a simpler, quieter life without extra people in their condo. Now, it seemed, the chaos would return.

"You will only come back if you follow my rules," she told him. "You will pay for your food. You will help pay for electricity and water. You will pick up after yourself. If you don't do these things, I will kick you out of the house."

Qurisha decided she was needed more in Kabul than in Scottsdale, so she chose to stay put. Only Naim and Reza would return to America with Lailoma.

Before the requisite thirty days of mourning had been completed, Lailoma booked her return flight to Arizona. She gave Nazira, her sister-in-law and Ahmadwali's widow, what cash she had left to take care of the rest of the meals that would be needed, and she left behind a small amount of money for each of her nieces and nephews so they could have a little to spend on themselves.

"Mamo," Maiwand told her over the phone, "if Naim causes any trouble, I will beat him up myself—and throw him out."

Naim and Reza returned to Scottsdale in 2019. Naim took a job stocking shelves at Walmart, became a US citizen, and applied for his wife to come to America. To get on his feet, he and Reza lived with Lailoma and Maiwand for a time, but he understood that his wife and other children wouldn't be allowed to come into the country until he established a separate place to live.

THE THIRD-BEST DAY

Normally a speed-limit-abiding driver, Lailoma drove as fast as she could, and desperately tried to avoid having to stop at red lights. Her heart was thumping wildly in her chest.

"Mamo, slow down!" Maiwand yelled at her. "We're going to get in an accident. Then I for sure won't become a citizen."

Maiwand's path to citizenship hadn't been quite as smooth as Lailoma's. He should have automatically been granted citizenship when Lailoma became a citizen, but there was a glitch. During that fateful trip to Pakistan to check on her family, his green card had been stolen along with hers. Even though she sent all of the documentation she had received in Pakistan, immigration needed more proof, and returned the documents. Ultimately, Maiwand didn't have to take the citizenship test. When he became eighteen in 2009, he needed only to show up at the immigration office for the ceremony.

Maiwand's swearing-in was to take place in the afternoon. On the appointed day, he went to school in the morning, taking a note Lailoma had written for him to give to the school secretary saying that he should leave school at eleven thirty. Because they lived close to the school, he could easily walk home to arrive by eleven forty-five so they could drive to downtown Phoenix for the ceremony at one thirty.

But eleven forty-five came and went. No Maiwand. Then noon passed. Panicked, Lailoma drove to the school to see where he was. The office staff had thought he was to leave at twelve forty-five and hadn't sent a note to the teacher to dismiss him. The secretary hastily sent a runner to his classroom, and within minutes he showed up in the office. He and Lailoma took off. In midday traffic, the drive might easily take forty-five minutes.

They reached the immigration office at exactly one thirty. Lailoma dropped Maiwand at the door and went to park the car. No space in sight. Fortunately, she saw a security guard who, when she told him why she was there, pointed to a numbered space for her to use. "Your car will be safe," he told her, reading her concern that it would get towed if she parked where he suggested. Then, with her still wavering, he urged, "Go, go, go! You don't want to miss the ceremony."

With that, she parked and ran as fast as she could to the building. Meanwhile, Maiwand had told the inside security officer that his mother was on her way. When she opened the door, the guard recognized her from her own ceremony just a few months earlier.

Once in, Lailoma found a seat quite far from where Maiwand stood, but she had a seat. Every member of this group of new citizens was young. As it turned out, the actual ceremony wasn't until 3 p.m. All of that anxiety for nothing!

Maiwand became a duly sworn citizen of the United States of America on March 19, 2009.

"I've never forgotten how happy I was on these three days of my life," Lailoma would repeat whenever she shared her story. "One, the day I arrived on American soil from Pakistan. I was scared, but I was happy. Two, the day I became a US citizen. Three, the day my son became a US citizen."

After Maiwand's ceremony, he took the keys from his mother. "I'm driving," he told her. "You almost killed us!"

"OK," Lailoma laughed, holding out the keys. "But remember, I got you here."

EPILOGUE

Lailoma continued to sew and to enjoy her tidy, well-furnished home. It was hers. She paid the mortgage.

Interestingly enough, few of Lailoma's refugee friends ever learned the details of her past. When Lailoma first arrived in the United States, she was still leery of sharing her story. Nor does she know many of the details that brought her fellow refugees to the US. Maybe they felt the same way she did. The young teacher is still unaware of what happened in Afghanistan to force Lailoma to leave. To this day, only a few of her coworkers, Samira, and I know many of the details.

"People came from everywhere for so many different reasons," she says of those whom she first met in the United States. "We would just tell each other the broad reasons for why we were here—our husband had died, or we had come to join family. We weren't trying to hide our stories, but we didn't necessarily share too many details."

As we sat in her condo Saturday after Saturday, she recollected more and more of the details of each anecdote she shared with me. As much as she was revealing her story with me, I had the impression she was also making sense of it for herself. She was finding her truth. And now she was willing to share it.

One summer Saturday morning, Lailoma and I sat at her dining room table, enjoying a beautiful plate of sliced watermelon as she reflected on her amazing journey.

"So many people helped me along the way," she said, "and I appreciate that. The people at Lutheran Social Services helped me so much. They got me started. They gave me confidence to take the first steps—to get an apartment, a job, a driver's license, a car.

"Mrs. Van Teal gave me a job and helped me with my English. She always listened to my problems, and even after she closed the factory, she offered me a job.

"When I started at Neiman Marcus, everyone said, 'Don't worry. We'll help you.' And they did. I appreciate the refugees I know, but I also think it helped a lot to be around regular people who aren't refugees. I know my English isn't perfect, but my coworkers help me by correcting me. I want them to tell me when I've said something wrong."

As Lailoma reflected on her journey, I thought about what I had learned through my encounter with her. People are not necessarily what you see on the surface. There is a story behind every face, and asking about it can only expand our own horizons. In recent years, I have become more of a news junkie than I used to be. I find myself wanting to know how people, especially women, are faring in other parts of the world. I'm not certain whether or not that's because of my connection to Lailoma, but I do know that when I read the plight of others, whether in the United States or somewhere else in the world, I'm more empathetic. I have a changed perspective.

Growing up, I had so many opportunities and few, if any, obstacles in my path.

Lailoma had fewer opportunities and so many obstacles. Her life was altered by chance, but she found a way to tailor it to her own bespoke fit. I remember what she told me about the day when she realized the university was no longer an option: "I said to myself, 'Forget it. Just move on. It's not meant to be.'" Throughout her life, she leaned into the strengths she had always possessed—the desire to nurture, to help others, to "fix" things for others. Her life is an affirmation that our strengths are inside us. We just need to tap into them. By leaning into her strengths, she became a successful American mother who kept her son safe, lent financial and emotional support to her extended family, and created a good life for herself and her son.

"I haven't done everything right in America," she continued. "I guess no one does. One thing I'll confess: That shopping cart I took from the grocery store all those years ago when I didn't know how to get home with my

234

groceries? I never returned it. I bet it's still at the apartment complex. I tried not to think about whether or not you were supposed to take your groceries home in it.

"I just did it. Nobody stopped me either."

Apparently, no one ever could.

GLOSSARY OF PASHTO WORDS
USED BY LAILOMA'S FAMILY

Adai	Mother
Ana	Grandmother
Baba	Father (Lailoma's family used "baba" to refer to their grandfather)
Daiee	Woman who assists during childbirth
Dastarkhan	Cloth put on the floor on which to serve food
Farsi	Persian language widely used in Afghanistan
Imam	Worship leader
Kaka	Paternal uncle
Khala or maami	Maternal aunt
Mama	Maternal uncle
Mamo	Mommy
Mujahideen	Guerrilla fighters
Mullah	Spiritual leader
Naan	Leavened, oven-baked flatbread
Pashto	Native tongue of Pashtuns, the dominant ethnic group in Afghanistan
Shia	One of two main branches of Islam
Sunni	The larger of the two main branches of Islam
Tandoor	Clay, wood-burning oven
Tandoorkhana	Outdoor kitchen

ACKNOWLEDGMENTS

Many people encouraged me in the development of this book, foremost among them my late husband, Jim, who gave me my first critique. He was a prolific reader, and his eye for details greatly improved my first efforts. Laurie Nikolski, an editor and columnist for Gannett Newspapers in New York for thirty years, also read an early draft, pointing out passages that needed clarification (and improvement). My first editor, Alexis Rizzuto, gave me invaluable input in shaping the story. She also pushed—and pulled—me through the process of signing with an agent. Leticia Gomez, Savvy Literary, appreciated Lailoma's story from the get-go, and enthusiastically represented me. Much appreciation also goes to Julia Abramoff, Apollo Publishers, for recognizing the book's significance and ultimately publishing *The Alterations Lady*.

I would be remiss if I didn't mention that all three of our daughters as well as extended family and friends have listened patiently as I have shared bits and pieces of this project over the years. Their encouragement kept me moving forward, and I know they are glad the book has come to fruition.

And finally, I thank my late mother and father, who modeled for me how to work and who instilled in me the confidence to pursue and complete this endeavor.